PATTERNS OF PARLIAMENTARY BEHAVIOR

Patterns of Parliamentary Behavior

Passage of Legislation Across Western Europe

Edited by

HERBERT DÖRING

MARK HALLERBERG

Routledge
Taylor & Francis Group
LONDON AND NEW YORK

First published 2004 by Ashgate Publishing

Published 2016 by Routledge
2 Park Square, Milton Park, Abingdon, Oxon OX14 4RN
711 Third Avenue, New York, NY 10017, USA

Routledge is an imprint of the Taylor & Francis Group, an informa business

British Library Cataloguing in Publication Data
Patterns of parliamentary behavior : passage of
legislation across Western Europe
1.Parliamentary practice - Europe, Western 2.Legislation -
Europe, Western 3.Comparative government 4.Europe, Western
- Politics and government
I.Döring, Herbert II.Hallerberg, Mark
328.1'094

Library of Congress Cataloging-in-Publication Data
Patterns of parliamentary behavior : passage of legislation across Western Europe /
edited by Herbert Döring and Mark Hallerberg.
p. cm.
Includes bibliographical references and index.
ISBN 0-7546-3936-3
1. Legislation--Europe, Western. 2. Parliamentary practice--Europe, Western. 3. Law and politics. I. Title: Patterns of parliamentary behavior. II. Döring, Herbert. III. Hallerberg, Mark.

KJC5349.P38 2004
348.4'01--dc22

2003060497

ISBN 9780754639367 (hbk)

Transfered to Digital Printing in 2013

Contents

List of Figures and Tables

Figures

Tables

List of Contributors

Rolf Becker is Privatdozent and Assistant Professor (Oberassistent) at the Department of Sociology at Dresden University of Technology.

Erik Damgaard is Professor of Government at the Department of Political Science at the University of Aarhus.

Lieven De Winter is Lecturer at the Université Catholique de Louvain and the Katholieke Universiteit, Brussels.

Herbert Döring is Professor of Comparative Politics at the Department of Economics and Social Sciences at the University of Potsdam.

Mark Hallerberg is Assistant Professor of Political Science at the University of Pittsburgh.

Ingvar Mattson is Deputy Head of Secretariate to the Committee on the Constitution in the Swedish Parliament.

Thomas Saalfeld is Senior Lecturer in Politics at the University of Kent, Canterbury.

Kaare Strøm is Professor of Political Science at the University of California, San Diego.

George Tsebelis is Professor of Political Science at the University of California, Los Angeles.

Acknowledgements

The data set on which this book is based was compiled by the joint efforts of the multinational 'Parliaments and Majority Rule in Western Europe' research group. Data collection was supported by a grant from *Deutsche Forschungsgemeinschaft* to Herbert Döring under research grant number Do 204/6-1. We are also grateful to *Fritz Thyssen Stiftung* for sponsoring a research conference where draft chapters of this book were first discussed. Memorable hospitality for this project conference was provided by *Hans-Ulrich Gajewski* at *Internationale Begegnungsstätte für Jugend- und Erwachsenenbildung, Jagdschloss Glienicke.* We are also grateful to several anonymous reviewers at various stages of this book who improved the final outcome.

Country contributors collecting data from the primary sources kept in parliamentary archives and libraries for 650 sampled bills across 18 countries were for Austria: *Wolfgang Müller and Marcelo Jenny*; Belgium: *Patrick Dumont and Lieven De Winter*; Denmark: *Erik Damgaard and Asbjorn Skjæveland*; Finland: *Matti Wiberg, Tuomas Alaterä and Katri Pölkki*; France: *Yves Surel*; Germany: *Herbert Döring, Robert Kösling and Bertram Welker*; Greece: *Nicos Alivizatos*; Iceland: *Ragnar Kristjánson and Baldur Thorhallsson*; Ireland: *Thomas Saalfeld and Craig Beaumont*; Italy: *Pier Francesco Lotito*; Luxembourg: *Lieven De Winter and Patrick Dumont*; Netherlands: *Lia Nijzink and Peter Bootsma*; Norway: *Bjørn Erik Rasch and Erik B. Petterson*; Portugal: *Manuel Braga da Cruz and Teresa Evaristo*; Spain: *Carlos Flores Juberías and Göran Rollnert Liern*; Sweden: *Ingvar Mattson*; Switzerland: *Annina Jegher, Prisca Lanfranchi and Ruth Lüthi*; United Kingdom: *Thomas Saalfeld, Ghazi Al-Naji, Craig Beaumont.*

Most helpful in constructing a machine-readable data set ('Study of the Parliamentary Passage of Legislation' – SPPL) from these materials were *Hanno Ferdinand, Jewgenij Sven Noth and Martin Weiß* (Potsdam). We would also like to thank *Kathrin Decker*, *Silke Hans*, *Jewgenij Sven Noth* and *Sascha Walther* for producing the layout of this book and *Nils Ringe* for his assistance in compiling the index.

Introduction

Herbert Döring and Mark Hallerberg

Purpose

This book provides a comparative, and theoretically driven, study of the effects of legislative institutions on legislative outcomes in Western Europe. It consciously complements the work that appears in Döring (1995a). While the initial volume documents the many institutional variations across West European parliaments, this volume considers the effects parliamentary institutions have on the course of legislation. Using a unique data set created for this volume, ten authors consider a set of fundamental questions in legislative studies. Topics include: the link among the type of government in place, the electoral system, and the legislative rule; the effects of government declarations on law production; the length of time it takes for passage of legislation; agenda-setting control in parliament; explanations of committee organization; predictors of conflict vs. consensus in parliamentary committees; the use of restrictive rules that limit or forbid amendments to bills; and the effect of increasing veto players on law production.

Background

Comparative studies of legislative institutions are rare. One reason historically may have been a general belief during the behavioral revolution after World War II that institutional studies were misguided because institutions did not matter. Scholars brought attention back to the importance of these institutions in a movement often referred to as 'neo-institutionalism'. The dominant variant of this approach that examined legislative institutions used rational choice methodology. Initial studies focused on the American Congress. Shepsle and Weingast (1981; see also 1994) argued that Congress was organized to preserve logrolls across committees through 'structure-induced equilibria'. In contrast, Krehbiel (1991) contended that Congress was organized to provide information rather than to guarantee distributional gains. Rational choice analysis has recently progressed in the comparative study of presidential systems. Carey and Shugart's (1998) edited volume considers the use of executive decree authority outside of the US context (see also Cox and McCubbins 1993). In a study more similar to ours, Haggard and McCubbins' (2001) edited volume focuses on the effects of institutions on policy outputs, but their work is based primarily on presidential systems. Like Carey and

Shugart (1998), they include several focused case studies to their theory of the separation of power and the separation of purposes.

Rational choice analyses also examined parliamentary systems, although they did not at first focus on the functioning of parliaments. Lijphart's studies (1984; 1990; 1999) connected a series of institutional variables, such as the electoral system, the type of government, and the like, and classified them according to whether they constituted distinct models, such as the Westminster and consensual systems. Tsebelis (1990) more explicitly illustrated the uses of rational choice theory in comparative politics to explain Labor Party tactics in Britain, consociationalism, and the cohesion of French electoral coalitions. Strøm (1990) focuses on the functioning of minority governments. Laver and Schofield (1990) and Laver and Shepsle (1996) sought to explain government formation in parliamentary systems. Similarly, Strøm and Müller (2000) concentrated on the main document that emerges from coalition formation, the coalition agreement. The edited volume indicated that the agreements are becoming more common, longer, and more complex, and they focus mostly on policy issues, not on procedures or the distribution of portfolios.[1]

Recent work on legislative institutions in parliamentary democracies has illustrated the importance of legislative institutions (Damgaard 1992; Liebert and Cotta 1990; Wiberg 1994; Huber 1996). There have also been some cross-national studies of legislative rules and procedures (Olson and Mezey 1991; Shugart and Carey 1992). Yet the first book to consider legislative institutions from both a rational choice and a truly cross-national perspective was Döring (1995a). Over the course of 22 chapters the volume documented the institutional structures, procedural rules, and, in some cases, patterns of behavior of parliaments in 18 Western European countries. The main task of the first volume was a thorough documentation of the rules as they existed.

Themes

This volume begins where the first one leaves off by considering what effect the rules have on the course of legislation. To do so, authors analyze a unique dataset that codes the parliamentary life of 650 bills across 18 Western European countries during the years 1981-1991. The bills concern either the deregulation of working time and working contracts or social security benefits. Country specialists created this quantitative database according to the research design of the multinational research group on Parliaments in Western Europe as outlined in the conclusion of the first volume the group produced, Döring (1995a). The last part of this chapter

1 Rational choice studies have also considered what makes political systems differ from one another beyond the more traditional presidential-parliamentary distinction. Tsebelis (1995a, 1995b; 1999; 2002; this volume) differentiates systems according to the number of veto players. Strøm (2000) in contrast contends that the key difference between types of government is based on the method of delegation.

provides more detail about the data set, but, because of its centrality in the book, initial comments are in order. It is important to note that we define 'legislative output' in technical terms only. We are not interested in the content *per se* of each bill. Whether the United Kingdom has more deregulated working contracts than Germany is an important topic, for example, but one that is left for another set of authors. Rather, we want to explain why bills followed the paths that they did. We consider topics like why subcommittees are called for some bills and not for others and whether knowing something about the proposer of a bill can tell us something about whether that bill is more or less likely to pass. The data set includes successful as well as failed bills, so it is not necessary for a bill to pass for the authors to consider it.

Before introducing the chapters individually, it is useful to consider the themes as they develop through the text. The first chapter begins the volume with a theoretical discussion of electoral systems and government organization on parliaments. The goal is to provide a general discussion of legislative organization. The second chapter then considers the importance of government priorities on legislation as well as the timing of the passage of bills. Unlike in presidential systems, governments in parliamentary systems depend upon the legislature's confidence to remain in office. The relationship between the executive and legislative branches is therefore central to the functioning of government. The middle chapters discuss institutional features of parliament itself, and how those features affect other institutions. The focus of these chapters, therefore, is on the interconnectedness of different types of legislative rules and why sets of rules are used under certain conditions. Topics covered, such as agenda-setting power, parliamentary committees, and restrictive rules, lie at the heart of traditional studies of legislatures. The final substantive chapter then brings the different elements of the process together to consider when important laws are, or are not, passed. The Blanpain coding for important legislation that is integrated into the data set allows the author to differentiate important from non-important bills. The conclusion considers explicitly the theoretical implications of the chapters taken together. Regardless of the particular focus of each author, all chapters use theories developed in rational choice to deduce a set of testable hypotheses.

Mark Hallerberg begins Chapter 1 with an examination of how the organization of government and the electoral system affects the legislative process. The central premise is that both governments and parliaments face a central common pool resource (CPR) problem. This problem arises when decision makers focus on concentrated benefits for their constituency but pay for the benefits out of a more defuse revenue base. There are three responses that parliamentary governments may have. Single-party governments and coalition governments where parties are ideologically close can solve the CPR problem through delegation to a strong finance minister. The finance minister considers the full tax burden and solves the problem. In governments where coalition partners expect to run against each other, commitment to detailed fiscal contracts as part of the coalition agreement can serve the same purpose without empowering the finance minister. Finally, under the form of government known as 'fiefdom', governments ignore the CPR problem and fall victim to it. Parliaments similarly face the same problem, although the key variable in this case is the electoral system. The more the electoral system encourages the personal vote at the expense of the party vote, the greater the CPR problem.

His analysis of the SPPL data set indicates that the three government types translate into differences in the organization of parliament. States with strong finance ministers have weak parliaments so that MPs do not undercut the authority of the central player. States with detailed coalition agreements concerning the budget have a stronger ability to collect information, but often do not use their ability, and, when they do, usually collect information out of the public limelight where disagreements among coalition partners are less likely to be seen. States with little centralization of the budget process, in contrast, seem to have the most active parliaments. Similarly, states with an electoral system that promote the personal vote over the party vote use restrictive procedures more often on parliamentary votes. Such restrictions reduce the size of the CPR problem in practice in parliament, and are most needed where the personal vote is high.

In Chapter 2, Lieven De Winter explores the effects of government commitments on specific policies. He begins with a consideration of whether a given bill's contents regulated a policy problem that the government mentioned either in its election manifesto (if a one-party government) or in its coalition agreement (multi-party government). In practice, he is able to get this information from the declaration the government submitted to parliament at the beginning of its term of office. He then compares the performance of bills that cover an issue area mentioned in the government's declaration and those not mentioned in the declaration. Relying upon both agenda-setting and principal-agent theories, he formulates a set of hypotheses to test the impact of government declarations. He finds that mentioned bills are: longer than non-mentioned bills; more likely to face dissent and minority reports; lead to higher party discipline on votes in committee; and are more likely to lead to ministerial testimony before committees. Counter to his expectations, he also finds that mentioned bills take longer to progress from first introduction in parliament to their final promulgation.

In Chapter 3, Rolf Becker and Thomas Saalfeld combine a consideration of veto player and agenda control perspectives to evaluate the effects of legislative institutions on the time it takes for bills to work their way through parliament. They begin by describing the 'life cycle' of bills. Using event-history analysis techniques, they find that Tsebelis's veto players' theory has explanatory power for single episodes during the life of a bill, but they find only limited empirical support for the theory for the entire life cycle of a bill. Their evidence also indicates that the more agenda-setting power the government has the faster bills will work their way through parliament. A crucial issue as well is whether minorities can effectively delay the consideration of a bill even if they cannot stop the bill's passage.

Ingvar Mattson and Kaare Strøm in Chapter 4 explore the role of parliamentary committees on legislation. They evaluate committee structures based on three theoretical perspectives: the arena perspective, the universalist perspective, and the partisan perspective. According to the arena perspective, committees exist as forums where legislators can pursue strategies of self-advertisement and blame avoidance (Mayhew 1974). The universalist perspective contends that committees provide certain economies of operation. Hierarchy and delegation guarantee certain distributive rights (Shepsle and Weingast 1994) or provide information to the plenary (Krehbiel 1991). Partisan perspectives, in contrast, contend that committees are extensions of party power (Cox and McCubbins 1993).

In Chapter 5, Erik Damgaard and Ingvar Mattson consider why there is variation in the level of consensus and conflict in committees. They define conflict in committee as existing if one (or more) of the following three is present: there is not a unanimous recorded vote in the committee; there is a minority report; or there is dissent in another committee that handles the bill. They evaluate differences in the level of conflict based on two theoretical approaches. Sartori (1987) claims that committees represent the ideal forum for making decisions and resolving conflicts. Committee members make tradeoffs and form logrolls, and most decisions should be unanimous. Standard game theory, in contrast, predicts that conflict will be less common when conditions approximate a repeated game but more common when the game is not repeated.

Counter to Sartori's (1987) expectations, Damgaard and Mattson find that conflict is common and occurs in more than half of the cases in the sample, or 58 per cent. Consistent with standard game theory, conflict is more common in ad hoc committees. This situation represents a case where the game among the committee members is played over fewer rounds. They also find that important bills are more conflictual than non-important bills, and, consistent with Lieven De Winter's findings, that bills proposed by the government are more likely to be conflictual than bills not proposed by government. Conflict is also in greater evidence in 'strong' rather than 'weak' parliaments, which again does not fit Sartori's (1987) argument. Finally, there is evidence that the importance of voter identification of legislatures plays a role. There is more conflict both where hearings are open instead of closed and where voters cast their ballots for individuals instead of parties.

Herbert Döring in Chapter 6 examines the likelihood that governments invoke restrictive rules in decisive readings on bills. He evaluates hypotheses from the empirically informed rational choice literature on parliaments. In keeping with Tsebelis's veto players' theory, the most important reason for government imposition of restrictive rules turns out to be the strategic position of partisan veto players, which in parliamentary democracies is the number of and policy distance among parties in government. Consistent with this argument, minority governments of the single-party type are most likely to invoke restrictive rules. Building on seminal work by John D. Huber (1992, 1996a), who was the first to transfer the study of restrictive rules from the U.S. Congress to the Western European parliamentary democracies in his study of France, Döring furthermore confirms one of Huber's hypotheses and rejects another one. Logistic regression for Western Europe confirms that governments impose restrictions to protect dimensionally complex packages against being rolled on the floor. But there is no supporting empirical evidence for a second Huber hypothesis that argues that restrictions are rarely, if ever, invoked to speed up the passage of contentious legislation. On the contrary, as Döring (1995b) and Henning (1995) predicted from a transaction-cost approach, controversy over bills and time as a scarce resource towards the end of the legislative term increase the likelihood of government imposition of restrictive rules. If Huber's findings fit France well (the testing case of Huber's more general theory) it may be due to a country-specific rule, but the argument does not appear to have general applicability throughout Western Europe.

George Tsebelis in Chapter 7 finishes the substantive chapters with the use of veto players' theory to consider the passage of important laws. Veto players' theory requires one to determine the individuals or collective actors whose assent is necessary to change the status quo. In practice for European countries, each party in a government coalition is a veto player no matter its size because of its threat to leave the coalition and, thus, break the government. Hence, the number of parties in government signifies the number of political veto players whose assent is required for a bill to become law. The theory predicts that the greater the ideological distance among the relevant players the smaller the change from the status quo in any successful legislation (Tsebelis 1995a, 1995b, 2002). Consistent with the theory, he finds that the greater the ideological distance of the most distant veto players in government the fewer the number of important bills that passed between 1981-1991.

Our evaluation of legislative output required the creation of a unique data set. Because this data set lies at the heart of this book, it is important that we explain how we collected and processed this information, which we do in the final section of this chapter.

Data and Methodology

The research group fashioned its own specific research tool. In a collaborative effort involving many contributors from different countries an original data set concerning the 'Study of the Parliamentary Passage of Legislation (SPPL)' was built under the auspices of the present incumbent of the Chair of Comparative Politics at the University of Potsdam (Herbert Döring).

Creation of this machine-readable data set with 130 variables for 650 bills proceeded in three steps:

> (1) Taking up issues raised in the first volume, members of the research group agreed upon a theoretically inspired set of questions for each of the 650 particular bills.

This joint 'questionnaire' outlined organizational features and procedural steps in the procedure for passing legislation. This questionnaire is accessible at

Döring's homepage at http://www.uni-potsdam.de/u/ls_vergleich in the form of a codebook summarizing structural and procedural information on the parliamentary passage of altogether 650 bills from 18 countries during the 1980s. With publication of this book, the SPPL data set will also be available for download.

(2) The research group conducted a stratified random sample of 650 bills in two steps.

In a first step, a random sample of bills was chosen from the sum total of all bills, limited to two specific and narrow policy fields, in each of the 18 countries. A basis for sampling was provided by the huge, and easily online accessible, International Labor Organization's (ILO) NATLEX database (http://www.ilo.org/).

The NATLEX database contains information for each country, with abstracts in one of the three ILO languages of English, Spanish or French, which amounts to an almost exhaustive inventory of legislative instruments. With some early gaps, but with high reliability from 1981, it provides a comprehensive index of all legislative instruments in labor legislation and social security benefits across its member states.[2] In a second step, the research group also included a sub-sample of bills that failed to get legislative enactment. This additional sampling allows the researchers to avoid a bias due to looking only at successful bills. It also makes it possible to examine hypotheses using event-history analysis, where the dependent variables are (a) the success rate of a bill and (b) the number of time units the bill remains in the 'risk set'. Thus, over and above, the bills sampled for the period between 1981 and 1991 from the ILO's NATLEX database, country specialists responsible for each of the 18 Western European countries randomly selected a number of unsuccessful bills for the policy area of flexibilization of working time and working contracts from their national sources.

For reasons to be explained, we deliberately did not select bills across the total legislation of countries in specific periods. We rather limited ourselves to two policy fields during the 1980s: (a) deregulation of working time and working contracts and (b) social security benefits. The NATLEX database allowed us to target with cross-national reliability bills from these two policy fields. Three substantive reasons of policy making in the 1980s also contributed to the research group focusing on these policy areas.

First, it is imperative for cross-national analysis covering several countries to focus comparison on only one policy area at a given time. Even within a parliament of one country, patterns of parliamentary activity may widely diverge at the same time if different policy areas are taken into account. For example, Richard Rose showed the proportion of bills approved unanimously with the consent of the parliamentary opposition even in a country like Britain, the 'nominal home of adversary politics', to be very high in foreign policy matters (Rose 1980). Other policy areas were bitterly contested as usual. Such discrepancies between policy areas might become uncontrollable if many countries are included in a study such

---

2 For a detailed description of this data base see, in the research group's first volume, the contribution by Scholz and Trantas 1995.

as ours. Had we sampled bills from the sum total of all bills per country rather than concentrating on a specifically targeted policy area, such within-country variations might have severely distorted cross-national variations we wanted to discover.

Second, deregulation of working time and work contracts became a salient, and heavily contested, burning political issue from 1980 onwards (Birk 1987; OECD-report edited by Dahrendorf et al. 1986; OECD report on flexible working time, collective bargaining and government intervention 1995). Rising oil prices, stagnating or declining rates of economic growth and rising inflation combined to form the new specter of what was called 'stagflation'. An exogenous shock, the sudden trebling of oil prices, constituted a comparable challenge to quite different political systems (Scharpf 1997b). At this time, the flexibilization of working contracts became an important issue. Governments in many countries set about the task of arriving at greater flexibilization within their respective labour markets. Yet, in spite of a common effort, the results were indeed widely divergent. This is a situation that should be appealing to any comparativist.

Thus, deregulation of working time does appear to be, at least for the period we chose, a unique field for comparative analysis. However, we do not want to study material changes of policy but rather take bills sampled from this field as a means to put most general rational choice theories to an empirical test. Additionally, NATLEX provides the chance to include social benefits bills because they keep a register on that field, too. Much of the rational choice literature discusses the likelihood of the production of particularistic-benefits bills instead of general-benefits legislation (Cox/McCubbins 1993: 90-94). Such particular benefits serve a narrow clientele but are financed from the 'common pool' of total tax receipts.[3] Particular benefits are, if geared to regional or local interests, also discussed under the heading of 'pork barrel politics' (for an extention of this American research tradition into a Western European political setting, see Lancaster/Patterson 1990).

Over and above the preceding reasons for concentrating on the policy fields singled out for analysis, there is a third, more technical reason. Selecting bills from the ILO's Natlex database adds to cross-national comparability and validity in spite of different legal systems and diverging methods for legislative crafting.[4] All bills recorded in Natlex have undergone expert assessment by the ILO's staff before being registered and translated into either of the three ILO languages, English, French, or Spanish. Sampling the 'successful' bills from NATLEX, we can be reasonably certain we are not comparing apples and oranges of legislative instruments by picking them at random from disparate country sources, but rather relying on a systematic account.

A word of caution, finally, must be added. The time period selected for study is the 1980s only (precisely from 1981-1991). This decade gives a snapshot of a

3 For a theoretical discussion and empirical analysis of this 'common pool resource problem', see the chapter by Hallerberg.

4 For an overview of legal styles between nations see, in the first volume, the contribution by Trantas 1995.

still ongoing process of deregulation of labour-market legislation. The year where the sample begins is justified by the political issue having become salient right then. But the end of the period chosen, that is, 1991 is a somewhat arbitrary cutting point. In some countries important legislative enactment in the specific area of deregulating working time and working contracts did follow after 1991.[5] Hence, readers will be aware this research study does not provide an exhaustive account of changes in a policy field but takes only one decade of changes as a means for empirically putting flesh onto the bones of rational choice assumptions about the possible policy effects of legislative institutions.

There is one unavoidable pitfall of the sampling procedure to which readers and analysts must be alerted from the outset. Due to the existence of real differences in number of legislative instruments among countries (ranging from only 29 in Greece to 525 in Sweden), bills included into the SPPL data set amount for some countries to the sum total of all enactments, with no selective sampling having taken place at all, whereas in other countries a random selection had to be conducted. This particularity of selecting bills for study should be kept in mind when assessing tests of significance in subsequent chapters of this book.

(3) Supplied with both the 'questionnaire' (as from above 1) and the names of the bills to be scrutinized (as from above 2), country specialists went into the libraries and archives of the 18 Western European parliaments to fill in the questionnaires.

Contributors were requested to answer the theoretically interesting questions about the parliamentary passage of the 650 bills sampled for 18 countries. The SPPL data set was immediately made available to researchers who had devised the questionnaire in the first place. We also invited scholars who had already left their mark in a theoretically inspired neo-institutional empirical analysis of parliaments to use the data set. Deploying this novel data set, the book is able to consider the extent to which parliamentary procedures contributed to shaping legislative enactments.

A quick word or two should also be said about the use of the data set. The methodology depends naturally on the research question posed, but in practice ranges from cross tabulation to regression analysis to event-history analysis. Authors also consider possible intervening variables and investigate the robustness of their results.

5 For detailed accounts see the online accessible Natlex database at http://natlex.ilo.org/scripts/natlexcgi.exe?lang=E.

Chapter 1

Electoral Laws, Government, and Parliament

Mark Hallerberg

Introduction

The Döring (1995a) edited volume illustrates in superb detail the extent of institutional differences, and consequently of institutional power, across 18 European countries. Yet that volume concentrates on the formal rules and powers of the government, committees, and the like. The creation of the 'Study of the Parliamentary Passage of Legislation, 1981-1991' (SPPL) data set provides a rare opportunity to examine how those rules are put into practice.

This paper provides one explanation for why there are systematic differences across parliamentary democracies in how their parliaments are organized and how those rules are executed. Section 2 argues that all governments and parliaments face a central problem, known in the literature as a common pool resource (CPR) problem. Solutions to the problem in the government depend on the number of party veto players and, if there is more than one, on the ideological distance between them and the likelihood that they will run together again in future elections. In one veto player governments or in governments where veto players have similar ideologies as well as the expectation that they will run together in future elections, they can delegate strategic powers to one central player to reduce the CPR problem. In other multiple veto player cases, commitment to fiscal contracts can similarly reduce the extent of the problem. Finally, a third class of governments, which I label 'fiefdom', is unable to address the problem.

Section 3 considers how electoral rules affect the extent of the CPR problem in parliament. Based largely on the insights provided in Carey and Shugart (1995), it considers how certain attributes of the electoral system lead voters to care more about the candidate in an election than the candidate's party. This 'personal' vote encourages legislators to support particularistic bills that benefit their constituencies to the disadvantage of their party. Increases in the personal vote therefore lead to increases in the size of the CPR problem in parliament.

Section 4 considers how both government type and the size of the personal vote in parliament affect behavior in parliament in practice. It finds that *Delegation* states have extremely weak parliaments so that MPs do not undercut the authority of the central player. *Commitment* states have a stronger ability to collect information, but often do not use their ability, and, when they do, usually collect information out of the public limelight where disagreements among coalition partners are less likely to be seen. *Fiefdom* states, in contrast, seem to have the most active parliaments. Similarly, states with high levels of the personal vote are more likely to use restrictive procedures more often on parliamentary votes. Section 5 concludes.

Coordination Problems within Governments and their Implications for Parliaments[1]

The Nature of the Problem

By their very nature all governments and parliaments face a coordination issue. The problem arises because benefits to constituencies, interest groups, and political parties tend to be concentrated, while the costs to be paid for generating benefits is usually spread out more widely than the benefit. This leads to what the literature refers to as the common pool resource (CPR) problem (Ostrom 1990; Velasco 1999; Alt 2000). One can think of the problem in practice when one considers the most important action of government, the making of the budget. The common pool that budget players draw upon is state revenue. The crucial assumption is that decision makers care most about their constituencies when they make budget bids. They therefore concentrate on the benefits of additional spending and costs of additional taxes for a small subset of the general population only. Because a given constituency will enjoy the full benefits of every additional Euro in spending but have to pay only a fraction of additional taxes for the additional spending, decision makers will make budget bids that are larger than if they were to make bids that included the full tax burden.

Governments have reason to want to avoid CPR problems. The available resources in terms of taxes collected, and potential taxes that can be levied in the future, are limited. CPR problems lead to higher spending, higher budget deficits, larger political business cycles, and, over the long term, higher taxes than the decision makers themselves want (Hallerberg and von Hagen 1999; Clark and Hallerberg 2000). There are institutional solutions available to solve these problems. The shape that they take, however, depends upon the nature of the problem within the government and within parliament.

1 For a more detailed treatment, see Hallerberg and von Hagen 1999 and Hallerberg 2003.

The Common Pool Resource Problem in Governments

Functionally most ministries share common traits. Ministers receive a portfolio for which they are responsible. Ministers and their ministries execute laws and formulate specific policies as the law allows in their jurisdictions. They spend money, and they formulate plans how to spend more money in the future.

Ministers have reason to care most about the performance of their ministry and about policy in their jurisdictions. On a personal level, ministers are usually the most visible person from their ministries. If there are complaints about the state of the environment, it will be the minister for the environment who will make the rounds on the talk shows and offer herself for interviews to newspapers. Ministers also represent their ministries in private, such as during cabinet meetings or before the prime minister.

These roles place a premium on ministers who closely identify with the interests of their ministries. The public generally judges them based on the performance of their ministries. This is especially true for the subset of the public that stands to be most affected by any ministerial action. Farmers and their organizations monitor closely the actions of the agriculture minister, while unions pay close attention to the behavior of the labor minister. A minister may also represent a given wing of a political party that cares most about a given policy area, and she may have gained her position in government precisely because she had been a strong advocate of a given constituency in the past.

Ministers in such positions have little reason to care about negative externalities on the rest of government that might result from their actions, and this is the root of the coordination problem. An agriculture minister, all else equal, has little incentive to consider how increased minimum price guarantees to milk producers might hurt low income families with children. This incentive structure is most obvious when it comes to financial decisions. In ministries where a primary function of the ministry is to spend money (which is most of them), there is little reason for the minister to consider the tax burden implications of additional spending in her ministry.

There therefore exists in all cabinets a CPR problem. Spending ministers consider fully the implications of every spending decision for their ministry and for their ministries' constituencies, but they care most about the negative externalities on their constituencies.

Delegation, Commitment, and Ministerial Fiefdoms within Governments

While spending ministers represent most of the cabinet, they are not the only ones who are members. The prime minister is responsible for the welfare of the government as a whole. She has reason to care about the negative externalities any ministry might produce on the health of her government. She also has one ally in cabinet whose performance is not evaluated based on how much she spends but rather on how well the overall budget performs – the finance minister. He usually considers the full tax burden of government decisions.

In many coalition theories that consider the distribution of portfolios this minister is absent entirely from the analysis because he alone does not represent a payoff to a particular party's ministry, but he can play an important role in coordinating the activities of the government.[2] Indeed, one institutional solution to the CPR problem is to delegate strategic powers on any issue that has financial implications to one central player who considers the entire tax burden, and in governments the finance minister is ideally suited to serve this role. To be effective, the central player must have the ability to monitor the others, possess selective incentives that he can use to punish defectors and/or reward those who cooperate, and have some motivation to bear the costs of monitoring himself (Cox and McCubbins 1993).

The finance minister is ideally suited to play this role. He has the responsibility to coordinate the formation of the budget, and the overall conduct of fiscal policy, including the size of budget deficits, is the principal indicator that others use to judge his effectiveness. He often also has a trivial budget when compared with other ministers, and he cannot defect in the game being played in the cabinet. His interests therefore generally coincide with the general interests. He is also in practice the minister who can most effectively monitor the others. The finance minister has a staff trained in budgeting and accounting, and he is most likely to find 'tricks' spending ministers use to justify additional spending.

In order for the finance minister to be effective, he needs to have strategic powers at two stages of the budget – when the budget is being formulated (*ex ante*) and when the budget is executed (*ex post*). In the first stage, the minister of finance can serve as an agenda setter in the formulation of the budget. The minister of finance makes the first proposal for the budget, and he has the power to constrain any amendments that the spending ministers might submit to his proposal. This procedure is the one commonly found in France. The minister of finance, together with the prime minister, issues a framework letter for every spending ministry that indicates the level of spending that ministry should expect to receive in the next budget year (Hallerberg and von Hagen 1999).

This strengthening of the finance minister in the government is what Hallerberg and von Hagen (1999) refer to as *delegation*. The principal, who is in this case the cabinet, delegates strategic powers to its agent, the finance minister, on budget issues. Such an action, of course, requires enormous trust in the finance minister not to misuse his power in a way that privileges policies that he favors. Agency losses in terms of both omission (the finance minister fails to monitor some ministries) and commission (the finance minister takes decisions that directly hurt certain ministers and their constituencies) can have dire consequences (Strøm 2000). Governments will face future elections, and agency losses can translate into lost votes.

---

2 The Finance Minister, for example, seems to serve no important function in the formation of coalitions in Laver and Shepsle (1996).

Both the number of political parties as well as their ideological distance from one another affects the likelihood of agency losses through a strong finance minister. The agent will be most effective when his interests coincide with the principal's interest. This is most likely the case when the minister comes from the same political party as other ministers in government. *Delegation* is therefore a viable option in one-party majority governments, such as in the United Kingdom, where ideal budgets of the players are close and where all cabinet members will be on the same side in the next election. In veto player terms, one-veto player states can select delegation (Tsebelis 2002). Yet *delegation* is not limited strictly to states with one-party governments – it is also possible in some coalition governments. As parties become closer to one another ideologically, differences in spending preferences will similarly narrow, and the number of veto players will approach one (Tsebelis 2002). The German CDU and CSU, for example, are formally different parties. Yet their policy preferences are close to one another, and indeed many authors treat them in analyses as simply the CDU/CSU.

Yet there are also coalition governments where *delegation* to a strong finance minister is unlikely. Coalitions where the parties expect to run against each other in future elections are unlikely to allow such a concentration of power in one cabinet minister. Any excessive spending by one party potentially helps that party in the next election and hurts its present coalition partners. An obvious example comes from the coalition government in Greece in the early 1990's. The right-leaning New Democracy Party formed a coalition government with the Communist Party in an alliance against PASOK. These parties had no intention of working together after the next elections, however, and would have had no basis to delegate powers to the finance minister.

There is a second way to resolve the CPR problem in states where coalition partners expect to run against each other in future elections, and it is known as *commitment* to fiscal contracts (Hallerberg and von Hagen 1999; Hallerberg 2003). The future coalition partners commit themselves to a detailed coalition agreement that lays out policy and spending plans for every ministry for the life of the coalition. In this way the partners consider the effects of decisions made in individual ministries on the entire government in the course of their coalition negotiations.

The classic example of a commitment state is the Netherlands. Coalition partners generally negotiate detailed coalition agreements that include spending targets and policy goals for every ministry in government. Moreover, the partners strike such agreements on the budget and on policy *before* they distribute portfolios. This ordering of the process makes it much harder for parties to negotiate extra spending for their ministers. Of course, such negotiations do not solve the CPR problem if the parties and/or ministers can easily violate the agreement *ex post*. Once again, the agreement will be kept only if the parties can monitor each other and if they can punish each other if one of them violates the contract.

Like in the *delegation* case, the finance minister is a likely player who can monitor the actions of the members of the coalition. He continues to have an entire ministry behind him, and it is in all parties' interest to make sure that their ministries are open to the finance ministry's inspection. The finance minister might also have some strategic powers relative to the spending ministers even in commitment states, but these powers are designed to keep the coalition agreement, not to solve a common pool resource problem during the government's term in office *per se*.

The punishment mechanism clearly differentiates commitment from *delegation*. It is unlikely that a prime minister in a multi-party coalition can easily dismiss individual ministers who violate the contract if they come from a different party. The likely punishment is therefore the dissolution of the coalition government itself, but this form of brinkmanship is a blunt, and often unsuccessful, tool.

The effectiveness of such threats depends upon the ability of current coalition members to find alternative partners to replace any defectors. This requires some dynamism in party system structure (Hallerberg 2003, Chapter 3). Coalition theorists tell us about the likelihood of a new coalition forming. In particular, Laver and Shepsle (1996) argue that some parties cannot be excluded from a possible coalition because of their electoral strength combined with their position in the middle of a given country's political spectrum. Such *strong parties* in the perspective presented here cannot be punished by other coalition partners. Fiscal contracts in the presence of a strong party are unlikely to work.

Countries with a history of 'strong' parties in the Laver-Shepsle meaning of the term are likely to have the third type of government discussed here, namely *fiefdom* governments. *Fiefdom* governments exist where the distribution of cabinet portfolios is the most important decision that the government makes in terms of spending and policy. Ministers have relative autonomy over decisions in their jurisdiction; that is, ministers are essentially lords of their ministerial fiefdoms. This is little or no coordination of policy across ministries. In practice the full cabinet makes all decisions, which provides opportunities for logrolls among ministers to get their full budgets. There is a direct analogy to distributive theories (Weingast and Marshall 1988) of committee action. In Congress, committees are composed of high demanders in a given policy area, and committees have relative autonomy over their policy areas. This autonomy comes from procedures, such as closed votes, that do not allow members of Congress to change the content of the bill before them. It also comes from informal guarantees across committees to support each other on votes. If one substitutes 'ministers' for 'committees' one gets a good idea of how ministers preserve relative autonomy over their ministries.

This type of government is common where there are strong parties because of the difficulty of punishing potential defectors. Coalition partners cannot exclude a strong party from any reorganization of the coalition to punish the defector. It is possible both in one and multi-party governments. Prominent examples from the 1980s include both Greece and Belgium. Greece was characterized by one-party governments except during the brief New Democracy-Communist coalition. The finance minister was quite weak relative to other ministers. While there were bi-lateral negotiations between the finance minister and spending ministers, the full cabinet made all decisions on the budget. In practice, spending ministers set policy in their jurisdictions with little outside interference from other ministers (Hallerberg 2003, Chapter 4). Belgium, in contrast, had multi-party coalition governments where fiefdoms were the rule. The coalition agreements that emerged were general. There was little reason to expect the partners to stick to what was agreed to anyway – the Christian Democrats were a 'strong' party in the system. In a more general sense the regions of Wallonia and Flanders were 'strong' as well – each region had its own socialist, Christian Democratic, et cetera, party that in coalition looked out not only for the interests of a given political perspective but also for the interests of a region (Hallerberg 2003, Chapter 5).

Table 1.1 Government Type in 16 European Countries

Country	Government Type
Austria	Fiefdom 1981-84, Commitment 1985-1991
Belgium	Fiefdom
Denmark	Fiefdom 1981, Commitment 1982-1991
Finland	Commitment
France	Delegation
Germany	Delegation
Greece	Fiefdom
Ireland	Fiefdom 1981-1987, Commitment 1988-1991
Italy	Fiefdom
Luxembourg	Commitment
Netherlands	Fiefdom 1981-1982, Commitment 1983-1991
Norway	Commitment 1981-1986, 1990-1991; Fiefdom 1987-1989
Portugal	Fiefdom
Spain	Fiefdom
Sweden	Fiefdom
United Kingdom	Delegation

Iceland is missing from the analysis because of a lack of data on Icelandic coalition formation. Switzerland is not a parliamentary democracy, and is excluded from the analysis. The coding comes from Hallerberg (2003).

In sum, there are three types of governments that one finds in parliamentary democracies – *delegation*, *commitment*, and *fiefdom*. Two types of government deal with the coordination problem that is inherent in all governments, while one type does not. The choice of which one of these solutions one puts in place is related both to the number of party veto players and, if there are two or more veto players, whether they regularly ally with one another in elections or whether 'exit' options exist for parties to form new coalitions with parties that are in the opposition. For the purposes of this chapter, minority governments also fall in the commitment category. A strong finance minister solution to the common pool problem is difficult under minority situations. While a finance minister may be able to keep one-party minority cabinets in line, he does not have the same ability to punish recalcitrant legislators. The government's negotiations with the opposition are instead functionally equivalent to the coalition negotiations necessary under multi-party majority governments, which suggests that commitment is the feasible option.[3]

Before proceeding, it is important to categorize the countries in our sample according to the three ideal types. Table 1.1 lists the types of governments in place in the states in the SPPL data set. The coding rule is as follows. Data to categorize the SPPL countries for the time period 1981-91, as well as the coding rules, comes from Hallerberg (2003) for European Union countries, while data in Marthe Narud and Strøm (2000) was used to classify Norway.[4]

Previous Evidence for the Structure of Parliamentary Committees and Government Types

In the first Döring (1995a) volume, the article by Mattson and Strøm provided a detailed analysis of the organization and structure of parliamentary committees. They examined the extent to which committees conformed to three theoretical expectations that have arisen from the literature on the organization of the American Congress. The distributive theory argues that committees exist to guarantee deals made among legislators to distribute spending across different policy areas (Weingast and Marshall 1988). In contrast, an information approach contends that committees are designed to provide information to the legislature at large about a bill (Krehbiel 1991). Finally, they consider a party-centered theory based on Cox and McCubbins (1993).

Mattson and Strøm (1995) confirm that there is great variation in the functions that committees play in European parliamentary systems. They find that information collection is of primary importance in many legislatures, and that drafting authority and the property rights that accompany them are also relevant.

---

3 Hallerberg (2003) treats such governments as *mixed* systems because they incorporate elements of both *delegation* and *commitment.* For the purposes of discussing the impact of the form of governance on the design of parliament, there is no functional difference between *commitment* and *mixed*, and this chapter treats the two as equivalent.

4 Concerning Norway, the minority government under Prime Minister Willoch 1981-1983 had stable and pre-negotiated support from opposition parties, and for this reason the period 1981-1983 is classified as 'commitment'. There were no similar agreements negotiated during the rest of the period.

Hallerberg (2000) uses the data from Mattson and Strøm (1995) to consider whether *delegation*, *commitment*, and *fiefdom* translate into differences in committee power in both the distributive dimension and the information provision dimension. The expectation is that *delegation* states will have weak committees. Once the decision has been made at the cabinet level, there is little left for the parliament to do except to pass the legislation. Any 'interference' on the part of committees in the affairs of government could potentially undermine the authority of the finance minister.

Similarly, *fiefdom* states should have weak committees as well. Bargains and logrolls struck among ministries that assure that they have autonomy over policy decisions in their ministries are items that government ministers do not want overturned in parliament. They also do not necessarily want too much information about the details of the work that they do. *If* parliaments are designed to reinforce the functioning of the different types of government, then information provision in *fiefdom* parliaments should be low.

The only type of government that should yield stronger committees is *commitment*. For *commitment* to fiscal contracts to be effective, some sort of mechanism is needed to monitor the actions of ministers and to punish those who overstep their targets. While the finance minister can provide some information, parliamentary committees can serve as essential institutions that the coalition partners can use to monitor each other.[5] Committee structure and responsibilities that include committee jurisdictions that match the responsibilities of the different ministries, the requirement that the chairperson of the committee come from a different party than the minister, and the power to compel witnesses are all ways to strengthen the information provision abilities of committees.

Hallerberg (2000) finds that the types of governments discussed here, combined with a consideration of single or multi-party coalition governments, seems to affect committee organization. Under all three types the government does not want the parliament to rewrite government bills, so there should be little evidence for the distributive approach. Indeed, outside of Italy, Mattson and Strøm (1995, 286) confirm that no country has committees with distributive power in an American Congressional sense. The expectation is that there is a divergence in information provision with contract states more likely to have such committees, and the article finds some evidence in support of this hypothesis as well. Once again, both *fiefdom* and *delegation* states have committees with weak information provision as predicted. *Commitment* states, in contrast, have committees with stronger information-collecting capacities. The exceptions to this general rule are states that are classified as *fiefdom* but that are also multi-party coalition; all multi-party coalition governments but France have ministerial correspondence, for

5 Note, however, that the information collection function of committees differs in commitment states from that assumed by Krehbiel (1991). For Krehbiel, committees provide information about the implications of a given bill to non-specialists in Congress. In this case, the information collection is necessary to determine whether or not a given coalition partner is cheating.

example, and many have other traits as well, such as the ability to compel witnesses.

There are not enough cases to have convincing levels of statistical significance in his analysis, but Hallerberg (2000) finds some evidence in terms of the structure of committees based on Mattson and Strøm (1995) that is, at a minimum, consistent with the theory introduced here. Whether that theory holds in practice is the question that the next section investigates.

The Common Pool Resource Problem in Parliament: The Importance of Electoral Systems

The common pool resource problem also exists in parliaments. Early research on the CPR problem in politics, in fact, focused on its dynamics within parliament rather than within the government (Weingast, Shepsle, and Johnsen 1981). Yet, with the notable exception of Lancaster (1986), little has been written about how the CPR problem might vary systematically across parliament. I argue that differences across electoral systems lead to systematic differences in the level of fragmentation within parliament. In particular, the more *candidate-centered* the electoral system the higher the level of fragmentation.

The standard dichotomy one finds in the literature on electoral systems is between plurality and proportional representation systems. Under plurality (often referred to as first-past-the-post), voters cast their ballots for an individual. The winner is simply whoever receives the most votes. While an absolute majority of 50 per cent +1 guarantees victory, if more than two candidates run in a given electoral district the percentage required to win a seat can be much lower than an absolute majority. Only one candidate can win from each electoral district. This means that the district magnitude (DM) under such systems is one.

Proportional representation systems take two forms, and the difference between the two is important. Under *closed* list systems, political parties determine the order of candidates on a party list of nominees. Voters cast their ballots for parties only. The share of the vote a given party receives determines how far down the list one goes to determine who is elected. If a party nominates candidates for all seats in a district with a district magnitude of 100, for example, and the party wins 33 per cent of the vote, the first 33 persons on the list would be elected. Under *open* list systems, the procedure is the same except that voters determine the order of the party's candidates on the list.

This seemingly small modification to the system makes a big difference in terms of the level of fragmentation within the congress. It shifts the focus of the election from political parties to individuals, and in doing so it changes the incentives that candidates face. Under an open list system, candidates must appeal directly to voters in an electoral district to get elected. Moreover, as district magnitude increases, intra-party competition for *district* voters increases as well, and candidates have an incentive to promise particularistic benefits to an ever smaller group of voters to assure (re)election. In contrast, under a closed list system, candidates must appeal to party leaders to get a high ranking on the list. The effects of district magnitude then *reverse*: as district magnitude increases, fragmentation decreases (Carey and Shugart 1995). Consider, for example, a country where district magnitude is just four. It may make sense for individuals to appeal to specific constituency interests when district magnitude is small – in a district with four seats, for example, the marginal gain in seats can jump with minor electoral gains from 25 per cent of the seats (1 of 4) to 50 per cent of the seats (2 of 4), and the candidate who appears second on the list has every incentive to make such an appeal directly to the constituency. If there are 40 seats in the district, however, candidate order on the party's list is far more important to an individual than appeals to a particular constituency within the district. Candidates therefore have an incentive to care more about the wishes of party leaders (Shugart and Haggard 2001).

Carey and Shugart (1995) create an index for the extent of the personal vote based on three classifications. First, they consider the extent of power political party leaders have over who appears on the ballot. Countries where leaders are present and where voters may not disturb the party list receive a score for *ballot* of '0', countries where leaders exist but where voters may disturb the list are scored a '1', while countries where leaders have no control over the list are scored a '2'. The logic of the ranking is based on the importance of party leaders in determining who appears on the ballot in the first place. Their second variable, *pool*, concerns how votes are pooled. Countries where pooling occurs across the party are scored a '0', countries where there is pooling at the sub-party level are scored a '1', and countries where there is no pooling at all are scored a '2'. Clearly, candidates have more incentives to care about their party's support when all pooling is at the party level. Finally, *vote* expresses the number of votes one can cast; '0' represents the case where voters can cast one vote only, '1' is the case where voters cast multiple votes, and '2' is the case where individuals cast one vote only at the sub-party level (that is, for a party faction or an individual). Using these classifications one can then rank countries from systems that provide the least incentives for the personal vote (all three variables scored a '0') to systems where the personal vote is extremely important (all three variables scored a '2').

Table 1.2 compares my coding of the electoral systems of Western Europe based on the Carey and Shugart (1995) classification scheme. It also displays a new variable, 'Personal', which is the coding of the relative incentives of a given system for the personal vote. This variable is created in the following way. First one takes the log of district magnitude.[6] Second, one adds ballot, pool, and votes together and adds '1' to them to create the variable *a*. If the electoral system has a closed list and is not plurality, we divide this number by the natural log of the district magnitude. This reflects the intuition that, as the district magnitude increases in closed list systems, the extent of the personal vote should decline. In all other cases, one adds the log of district magnitude to *a*. Increases in district

6 See Hallerberg and Marier (2003) for more justification on the use of this index.

magnitude are expected to lead to increases in the personal vote. The index also indicates that plurality electoral systems, such as the one found in the United States, encourage the personal vote less than systems like Italy's with an open list but more than systems with a closed ballot. One can see that the personal vote is least apparent in the Netherlands and most apparent in Finland.

Table 1.2 The Personal Vote in 18 European Countries

Country	Ballot	Pool	Votes	Average District Magnitude	Personal
Finland	2	0	2	13.30	7.6
Italy	1	0	1	20.00	6.0
Luxembourg	1	0	1	16.00	5.8
Ireland	1	1	1	4.00	5.4
Switzerland	0	0	0	8.00	3.1
Denmark	0	0	0	5.90	2.8
Greece	0	0	0	5.10	2.6
France	0	0	1	1.00	1.0
United Kingdom	0	0	0	1.00	1.0
Germany	0	0	0	1.00	1.0
Iceland	0	0	0	6.10	0.6
Spain	0	0	0	6.70	0.5
Belgium	0	0	0	7.10	0.5
Norway	0	0	0	8.30	0.5
Sweden	0	0	0	11.10	0.4
Portugal	0	0	0	12.00	0.4
Austria	0	0	0	20.33	0.3
Netherlands	0	0	0	150.00	0.2

Figures on district magnitude are from Taagapera and Shugart (1989, pp.136-137). Whether the ballot is effectively open or closed in proportional representation systems is coded according to Table 11-3 Gallagher, Laver, and Mair (1995, p.282). Note that Table 11-3 in Gallagher, Laver, and Mair (1995, p.282) reflects the state of affairs in 1994 and is not accurate for either Austria or Italy for the time period under study in this paper; see Gallagher, Laver, and Mair (1995, pp.285-286).

Theoretical Expectations and Behavior of Parliaments

The SPPL data set represents a novel opportunity to investigate what parliaments did in practice on a subset of bills during the time period 1981-1991. The data provided in Döring (1995a) largely examined the structures of parliaments. This comparative study filled an important gap in the literature. The SPPL data set allows one to build on Döring (1995a) to investigate the extent to which the powers accorded to some institutions are implemented in practice. For example, while Mattson and Strøm (1995) indicate that committees in a *commitment* state like Denmark and a *fiefdom* state like Portugal both had the power to compel witnesses to testify before them, it is unclear whether parliaments used their powers in practice. Did committees regularly compel witnesses? If so, are there systematic differences in a comparative framework across the three types of government?

The hypotheses to be tested are broken down into two groups. The first group is related to expectations about the distributive and informational powers of parliament based on their government type. They are summarized in Table 1.3. For *delegation* states, the expectation is that parliament will be relatively powerless in both its ability to affect legislation that comes from the government and will have little ability to collect much information on that legislation. Most important decisions will have already been made in the government. Similarly, *fiefdom* states will also have weak parliaments. The reasoning follows from Laver and Shepsle (1996) – ministers want autonomy over their ministries, and once portfolios are distributed the game is essentially over. *Fiefdom* works most effectively when parliament is weak. The expectation is that parliaments will do little in practice. The theory would lead one to expect that only *commitment* states should display some differences. There will be plenty of information collected on the bill to be sure that a given minister is not 'cheating' from the contract. Moreover, this information will reinforce any monitoring that a finance minister does in a *commitment* state to be sure that his accounting is not unduly influenced by his own political party. At the same time, parliament's ability to affect the content of the bill should be fairly limited, as it is in the other cases. Table 1.3 summarizes the hypotheses.

A second set of hypotheses relates to the role of electoral systems in encouraging the personal vote. This leads to H7; the greater the personal vote index, the more likely it is that government restrictions on parliamentarian actions will be put in place.

The empirical section also examines alternative explanations. One alternative hypothesis is that it is the dichotomy between one-party and multi-party government (or one party veto and more than one party veto player) that is driving the results. One-party governments may solve any coordination problems within

Table 1.3 Summary of Testable Hypotheses

Hypotheses Related to Government Type:

Delegation to a Strong Finance Minister

H1: There should be little evidence of distributive politics, and a weak ability to affect the content of laws.
H2: There should be little evidence of information collection.

Commitment to Fiscal Contracts

H3: There should be little evidence of distributive politics, and a weak ability to affect the content of laws.
H4: There should be strong evidence of information collection.

Fiefdom

H5: There should be little evidence of distributive politics, and a weak ability to affect the content of laws.
H6: There should be little evidence of information collection.

Hypothesis Related to the Electoral System:

H7: States where the personal vote is high should have more restrictive procedures on the actions of parliamentarians than states where the personal vote is low.

Alternative Hypotheses:

A1: Parliaments reflect the one-party/multi-party cleavage rather than differences in government type.
A2: Parliaments reflect the difference between minority and majority governments.

the party, and they would want parliament to have as little say as possible on bills. In contrast, coalition governments cannot solve such coordination problems, and they are the only ones that need to have monitoring powers in parliament. This leads to A1. Note that there are *fiefdom* cases with one-party and multi-party governments, and there are also two multi-party governments (France and

Germany) that qualify as *delegation* states, so there is variation to examine whether this alternative is more robust than the argument made here. Another possibility is that minority governments have distinctive traits (Strøm 1990). A2 examines whether minority governments drive the results.

Data Analysis

This chapter takes all questions in the SPPL data set that are related either to distributive politics or to the provision of information. It begins with a consideration of whether there are systematic differences across the three types of governments based on simple chi-square analyses of the relevant answers. It then uses more advanced statistic techniques to consider whether alternative hypotheses are better predictors for the differences we observe. In general, there are statistically significant differences across the board. They do not always accord well, however, with the theoretical predictions. There are two basic findings. First, what evidence there is for distributive politics appears in the *fiefdom* states. Second, while previous work indicated that *commitment* states are most likely to have the *potential* to collect information in parliament, in practice they rarely use this ability. Rather, *fiefdom* states are the most common collectors of information.

The analysis begins with a consideration of questions that are related to distributive powers. The theoretical expectation is that no form of parliamentary government should have much experience with distributive procedures. One set of questions concerns the influence of the government in the process. The expectation is that the more control the government has, the less the opportunity for parliamentarians to play distributive politics within parliament themselves. The first question concerns who is the official initiator of the bill. The more often this actor is the government, the less room parliament has to serve as the agenda setter. The second question concerns whether there is a vote before the committee stage. Such votes occur before there is a debate, and little information is revealed about the bill. It can be seen as a show of hands in support of the government that makes it more costly for parliamentarians to vote against the bill in the future.

A second set of questions concerns the ability of parliamentarians to make deals with one another. Packages of bills allow parliamentarians to put together potentially diverse bills that satisfy different segments of parliament on different issue areas to get legislation passed. The American 'Omnibus' bills are probably the best-known examples of how packages of bills can allow parliamentarians to attach spending bills targeted to their specific constituency into one package on which most, or even all, parliamentarians can agree. Such packages are a mechanism that leads potentially to severe common pool resource problems within a body (Weingast, Shepsle, and Johnsen 1981). Their prohibition would represent less distributive politics. Similarly, votes clause-by-clause make it more difficult for logrolls negotiated within single bills to pass.

Tables 1.4a and 1.4b compare the frequencies for the questions related to the committee and plenary stages of the legislative process in the SPPL data set. One notices immediately two trends. First, the expectation that there is no difference among the three types of government is incorrect; there are statistically significant differences across the three categories across *every* category. Second, there are important patterns within the three types of government. The biggest contrast is with *delegation* and the other two cases. Consistently, *delegation* states have mechanisms in place that make it harder for parliamentarians to change the bill before them. They are more likely to have the government introduce the bill itself, have frequent open votes before a committee considers the content of the bill, invoke restrictive procedures on bills three times as often as the other categories, usually vote clause-by-clause, and almost never have votes on a package of bills. These findings, of course, are consistent with the theory introduced here – parliament represents an opportunity for spending ministers to try to add back in spending that they proposed but that the minister of finance cut in the bill. In order for *delegation* to a strong finance minister to be effective in practice, his decisions made in cabinet should not be easily overturned in parliament.

Yet the expectation that the other two government types would be equally restrictive on parliamentary behavior is not borne out. *Commitment* states do not seem overly concerned that parliamentarians would have opportunities to make changes to government bills. Unlike *delegation* states, they almost never have votes before the committee stage, they rarely invoke restrictive procedures or vote clause-by-clause, and they had occasional package votes. This evidence seems to suggest confidence that parliamentarians will not try to sabotage the existing fiscal contracts. Indeed, while one can only speculate at this stage, it is plausible that the potential damage from any defections on the part of one parliamentarian would be high indeed, including a possible end of the coalition, and that this punishment would serve as an effective deterrent. Restrictive procedures in parliament would then be superfluous.

The findings for *fiefdom* states are curious. They illustrate that parliamentarians have some ability to influence the content of bills, but that that influence is more restricted than in *commitment* states. They have fewer votes before the committee stage than *delegation* states but almost 30 per cent more than *commitment* states, the government relatively rarely imposes restrictive procedures, about half the time votes are clause-by-clause, and package votes occur about one in five times. There are two possible interpretations. One positive one is that parliaments take more initiative in these states because the common pool resource

Table 1.4a Differences in Committee Treatment of Legislation According to Form of Fiscal Governance

	Was there a vote before committee stage?		Were subcommittees involved?		Did committee arrange hearings?		Type of hearings	
	Yes	No	Yes	No	Yes	No	Public/both	Private
Fiefdom	46%	54%	25%	75%	17%	83%	13	87
Delegation	72%	28%	0%	100%	35%	65%	95	5
Commitment	8%	92%	0%	100%	10%	90%	0	100
	Pearson chi2(2) = 48 1466 Pr = 0 000		Pearson chi2(2) = 64 5894 Pr = 0 000		Pearson chi2(2) = 16 7002 Pr = 0 000		Pearson chi2(4) = 86 9519 Pr = 0 000	

Table 1.4b Differences in Plenary Votes According to Form of Fiscal Governance

	Were packages of more than one bill put to vote?		Voting clause-by-clause		Did government invoke restrictive procedures during decisive reading?		Was there a vote before committee stage?	
	Yes	No	Yes	No	Yes	No	Yes	No
Fiefdom	21%	79%	47%	53%	11%	89%	46	54
Delegation	1%	99%	75%	25%	34%	66%	72	28
Commitment	12.5%	87.5%	29%	71%	7%	93%	8	92
	Pearson chi2(2) = 23 7366 Pr = 0 000		Pearson chi2(2) = 47 9917 Pr = 0 000		Pearson chi2(2) = 40 1394 Pr = 0 000		Pearson chi2(2) = 48 1466 Pr = 0 000	

Table 1.4c Committee Staff and Committee Referrals

	Number of Staff, Committee				Number of Committees Consider Bill		
	No Staff	0.5-1 Staff	2 Staff	3+ Staff	1 Committee	2 Committees	3+ Committees
Fiefdom	16%	6%	32%	47%	81%	4%	15%
Delegation	3%	38%	59%	0%	66%	9%	26%
Commitment	11%	61%	28%	0%	78%	22%	0%

problem is not solved at the cabinet level. Parliamentary action could be beneficial in terms of the quality of legislation. A darker view is that the CPR problem is also not solved in parliament. The evidence for the use of package votes would be consistent with possible log rolling in parliament that reinforces logrolls in cabinet.

Information Provision

The second set of tests concerns the use of parliamentary devices to collect information on bills put before parliament. The potential interpretation of these variables is, for the most part, transparent. The submittal of a bill to more than one committee increases the amount of information on a bill. Presuming that committees are specialists in particular dimensions of a bill, the consideration of a bill by more than a social committee allows greater monitoring of the implications of any bill. The use of subcommittees, in contrast, probably increases the amount of specialized knowledge within one jurisdiction. Hearings allow more information to come from people outside of the committee. The general expectation is that countries that have committees with the power to compel witnesses are the ones more likely to use that power to hold hearings. Whether a hearing is public or private, however, has a bearing on what type of information is being provided. Krehbiel (1991) would expect largely public hearings to signal to other legislators the general quality of a bill. Moreover, open hearings make 'fire alarms' more likely (McCubbins and Schwartz 1984; Saalfeld 2000). Public access to voting records would similarly provide cues to other legislators about the value of a bill according to Krehbiel (1991). Finally, who testified at the hearings might provide some evidence about the specialization of the discussions. Government ministers are likely to provide broader information about the bill than a civil servant, who is presumably more specialized. At the same time, calling a minister to account may be evidence of some power on the part of the legislature vis-à-vis the government.

Once again, Tables 1.4a-1.4c provide information to consider whether there are systematic differences across government type in terms of parliament's actions to collect information. The expectation is that *delegation* and *fiefdom* states will consistently restrict information collection and there should be little evidence for it, while *commitment* states should exhibit plenty of activity so that coalition members have knowledge about what their partners are doing. Once again, the evidence for *delegation* states is perfectly consistent with this interpretation. They never used subcommittees and they had a staff person or two assigned to the committee but never more. One particularity is that they were most likely to schedule hearings. While this may be some prima facie evidence for information collection, the manner in which they were held, and who was invited, is suggestive about the use for that information. The hearings were almost always public, and, as a general rule, they did not include anyone of substance who would know something about policy – only rarely is either a government minister or civil servant invited. This suggests that the hearings themselves are not important. They could, however, be a convenient opportunity for a parliamentarian to discuss in a public forum any disagreements she has with the government. This can allow her to signal to voters in her district her unhappiness if a given bill is expected to hurt her constituency.

Unlike the results for the *delegation* states, *fiefdom* and *commitment* states exhibit behavior that is the opposite of what one would expect. *Commitment* states are as unlikely to provide information as *delegation* states; they have the smallest committee staffs, they usually recommend a bill to one committee only, they rarely have hearings, and when there are hearings they are almost always closed to the public. In fact, the nature of the hearings and committee activities illustrates some attempt to collect information on behalf of coalition members. Hearings tend to call in government ministers and civil servants in equal measure. Yet, unlike what Krehbiel (1991) would expect, the discussions as well as the votes tend to be closed. This finding is unusual when one considers the analysis of Mattson and Strøm's data in Hallerberg (2000), which indicated that *commitment* states are more likely to have the ability to compel witnesses, to have committee jurisdictions that matched ministerial jurisdictions, et cetera. The actions *commitment* states took indicate that these states often leave the power to collect information as a mere potential. When they do use that power, they prefer to keep discussions behind closed doors. One can imagine that there are fears that open disagreements among committee members from coalition partners may damage the coalition more generally, and it is better that the public and the press do not follow the discussions directly. The general absence of subcommittee use, which presumably have more specialized knowledge on the merits of a given bill, reinforces the view that parliaments in *commitment* states are not focused on providing information to the parliament as a whole, as Krehbiel (1991) would expect.

Finally, *fiefdom* states show a surprising level of activity. They have pretty elaborate staffs, they call more committees to consider a bill than the other forms of government, they use some committees and hold some hearings. Like *commitment* states the hearings tend to be private, but they often include ministerial testimony. They also exhibit fairly frequent use of subcommittees. This suggests that there is a role for parliament in the decision-making process in *fiefdom* states. Indeed, this may represent greater distrust on the part of parliament about the value of minister-sponsored bills. More broadly, it is possible that 'dysfunctional' governments allow some correction of government legislation in parliament and as well as encourage some scrutiny in an attempt to catch the worst failings of the government.

In sum, *delegation* states have parliaments that fit the theoretical expectations. They have little ability to change legislation or collect much information on it. *Commitment* parliaments tend to have the opposite of what was predicted – lax controls on the ability of legislators to change legislation and relatively low levels of information collection. Finally, *fiefdom* states are relatively active on both fronts.

Whether an explanation for these differences follows the speculation provided above cannot be proven at this point. Something that cannot be ruled out is that, exactly because of the institutional design discussed in Mattson and Strøm (1995), what one is picking up is differences in institutional efficiency. *Commitment* states could be the most efficient information collectors and have little reason to have larger staffs, more meetings, et cetera. *Fiefdom* states, in contrast, where committee jurisdictions do not overlap, committees cannot compel witnesses, et cetera, need more staff, more hearings, et cetera, to gather similar information. Even if this is the case, howėver, there are nevertheless significant differences across the types of institutions.

Table 1.5 Logistic Regression Analysis

	Are there restrictive procedures on votes?		**Are there package votes?**		**Did Committees arrange hearings?**	
	Coefficient		*Coefficient*		*Coefficient*	
Commitment	1.93**	(0.41)	2 33*	(1.07)	-1.66**	(0.52)
Fiefdom	1.38**	(0.32)	2.80**	(1.03)	-1.19**	(0.38)
Coalition Govt	-0.76*	(0.38)	-0.62	(0.38)	-0.09	(0.38)
Minority Govt	0.06	(0.48)	0.85*	(0.36)	0.50	(0.39)
Constant	1.19**	(0.35)	-4.23**	(1.02)	-0.58	(0.31)
	LR $\text{chi}^2(4)=41.49$, Prob>$\text{chi}^2=0.00$		LR $\text{chi}^2(4)=54.96$, Prob>$\text{chi}^2=0.00$		LR $\text{chi}^2(4)=18.32$, Prob>$\text{chi}^2=0.00$	

The second question to ask is whether these differences are merely a proxy for another explanation. The previous section mentioned alternative hypotheses for predicting differences across the data set. Table 1.5 provides two logistic regressions from the distributive questions and one from the information questions. It indicates that in all three cases the categories introduced here have significant effects on actions within parliaments. They also indicate that the alternative hypotheses on their own have an effect as well; minority governments, for example, are likely to have package votes. Yet the alternative explanations do not 'wash out' the consideration of the three forms of government.[7]

The Personal Vote

The second set of hypotheses considers whether the extent of the personal vote that the electoral system encourages affects action in parliament. The expectation is that restrictions on parliamentarian behavior on bills should be especially stringent in countries where the personal vote is high.

Table 1.6 compares the extent of the personal vote in the eighteen countries in the SPPL data set for three questions: the use of restrictive procedures, votes clause-by-clause, and package votes. To make the comparison tractable, it also divides the personal vote group into two – those states with a personal vote index below 1, and those with a personal vote index one or greater. The former cases correspond to PR states with closed ballots, while the latter case considers everyone else.

Table 1.6 Differences in Plenary Votes According to the Level of the Personal Vote

	Were packages of more than one bill put to a vote?		**Voting clause-by-clause**		**Did the Government invoke restrictive procedures?**	
	Yes	No	Yes	No	Yes	No
High Personal	9%	91%	64%	36%	20.5%	79.5%
Low Personal	16%	84%	37%	63%	6%	94%
	Pearson $chi^2(1)$ = 15.5293 Pr = 0.000		Pearson $chi^2(1)$ = 9.3466 Pr = 0.002		Pearson $chi^2(1)$ = 23.0178 Pr = 0.000	

The evidence is more mixed than in the cases above, but it is generally consistent with the theory. States with a high personal vote were three times more likely to impose restrictive procedures on the vote and also more likely to have

7 See Mattson and Strøm (this volume) for a systematic consideration of distributive and informational perspectives.

votes clause-by-clause that would presumably make logrolls more difficult. The possibility that legislators that have higher incentives to consider the personal vote might add additional provisions to a bill that favors their personal reelection chances does have some effect on the use of restrictive voting procedures. While package voters were relatively rare in the data set, states with high personal votes were half as likely to allow package votes as states with low personal votes. This finding again suggests that parliaments seek to prevent package votes where legislators may have particularistic electoral incentives.

Conclusion

This chapter considers how the way that parliamentary democracies deal with a common pool resource problem that is at the heart of governance affects the organization of parliament. It finds systematic differences across the three government types of *delegation*, *commitment*, and *fiefdom*, although those differences do not always accord with *a priori* expectations. *Commitment* states in particular seem to have more potential power, both in a distributive and an informative sense, than legislators use in practice. *Delegation* states, in contrast, have parliaments that have little power. The most important things parliaments do in these countries seemingly is to elect the government and then to get out of the way once the government is installed. *Fiefdom* states, in contrast, seem to fall somewhere in the middle.

Choices on the electoral system also have an effect on parliamentary organization. States with high incentives for the personal vote may lead to greater use of restrictive votes as well as more clause-by-clause votes in an effort to discourage the MP from providing particularistic goods to her constituencies.

Electoral system choice also has another consequence that has not been emphasized so far in this chapter, namely its influence on government type. As Duverger (1954) taught us decades ago, the choice of a plurality electoral system leads to the likelihood of one party veto player in government, which confines these states to either *delegation* or *fiefdom*. Plurality states will have moderate levels of the personal vote, and, combined with the imposition of *delegation*, will probably have restrictive rules in place that reinforce rules already in place to limit the personal vote. In contrast, the choice of proportional representation with high levels of district magnitude makes it more likely to have multiple veto players with a wider degree of ideological divergence, and to a possible adoption of *commitment* to fiscal contracts.[8] At the same time, whether increases in district magnitude under proportional representation lead to a larger or smaller CPR problem in parliament depends critically on whether or not there is an open or

8 As Neto and Cox (1997) persuasively argue, the exact effect of a change in electoral system depends upon the underlying cleavage structure in society.

closed ballot. The lesson is that changes in electoral systems should have profound changes in the organization of parliament. A future project could consider whether such changes to parliaments have occurred in countries that have recently changed their electoral systems, such as Italy, New Zealand, and Japan.

Chapter 2

Government Declarations and Law Production

Lieven De Winter

The Role of Government Declarations in Law Production

Government Declarations as Agendas and Contracts

Government formation research of the past four decades has mainly focused on the party composition and portfolio allocation question (Laver and Schofield 1990). The significance of the formation stage for policy formulation has received little attention (De Winter 2002). While in West-European parliamentary systems, government policy agreements constitute a central instrument in linking party policy preferences to government policy outputs, empirical and theoretical research on such policy statements remained embryonic until the 1990s (Strøm and Müller 1999, 2004). Focus has been on the impact of parties on cabinet decisions, or on implemented policies, rather than on the legislative process that transforms these governmental decisions into legally binding and implementable policies. However, from the more general literature on governmental agenda setting and principal-agent theory applied to the government formation process, one can deduct a certain number of hypotheses with regard to the impact of the announcement of the subject matter of a bill in a government policy statement on the subsequent passage of legislation.

We will use the term 'government declaration' to cover two main types of documents. In single-party governments, it concerns the governing party's legislative program presented to parliament at the beginning of its term, and reflects the party electoral manifesto. In multi-party governments, it usually concerns a written coalition policy agreement, whose content is presented by the PM in an abridged version to parliament at its investiture (or equivalent legislative kick-off session of the new government).

Agenda Setting Theories

Agenda setting theories divide the policy making process into different stages, to which certain types of agendas correspond (Rose 1973; Hogwood and Gunn 1984). In this 'stagist' approach, the inscription of a policy issue in the governmental policy declaration constitutes the stage that succeeds the stage of transforming private problems into public issues (the inscription of a problem on the 'public agenda') and the stage of transforming public issues into government issues (the inscription of a public problem on the 'governmental agenda'). It selects the issues that the government recognizes as important and that merit a public policy response in the upcoming legislative term (or in what remains of it in case of mid-term governments). The governmental policy declaration is a portfolio of commitments to action (March and Olsen 1995: p.17). Hence, government formation is an essential, if not crucial, policy-making arena (Peterson and De Ridder 1986).

The government declaration constitutes an inventory of governmental agenda issues, composed at a crucial moment of its existence, during the formation of a new government (or the reconstruction of an old government after general elections).[1] Thus, it is designed at a moment when in principal the government still has ample time left for tackling the problem, even the most complex ones, that could take several years from problem definition and selection of alternative solutions to their actual implementation.[2]

However, the government policy agenda will not necessarily overlap with the parliamentary policy agenda. There are many reasons why some policy problems treated in the legislative process may not figure in the government declaration. They may not have been recognized as a governmental or public agenda issue, and may have not existed at all at the moment of government formation and, pop up 'out of the blue' to emerge into a major issue in a short time span. The problem may have been considered too minor to be included in the declaration (that for reasons of space can not contain every single existing public policy problem and therefore will always be incomplete). Or, they may have been too contentious to find a compromise and therefore were omitted (Klingemann et al. 1994: p.33). Likewise, the government is not the only engine of legislative initiation. Even in systems in which the executive exercises strong legislative agenda control (Döring 1995c), a considerable number of bills are introduced by individual MPs or opposition parties. The latter is especially the case in minority governments.

Still, there is a high probability that bills that cover a policy problem that was mentioned in the government declaration, tackle more salient (at least to the government but probably also to the opposition and the public at large), more

1 For the centrality of the formation process in European political systems, see the chapters in the Müller and Strøm volume (2000).

2 Regarding mid-term formations, where the time left to implement a policy programme is more restricted, Strøm and Müller (2004) have shown that the shorter the time span a newly formed government has left before the constitution calls for new elections, the less coalition parties use government agreements, and if they do so, agreements will be much shorter than those written at post-electoral formations. Hence, in Western Europe, the bulk of coalition agreements are drafted after elections, when the new government has, in theory, a full legislative term to implement its policy agenda.

predictable,[3] manageable and solvable (being not too divisive) problems, than bills that cover a matter that was not mentioned. We can therefore expect that these high government saliency bills will get a different kind of treatment in the legislative process than bills covering problems not mentioned in the government declaration.

One can expect the government to be the first (and probably only) actor to take the legislative initiative to solve the problem mentioned, while in the other type of bills, other actors (like majority MPs and parliamentary groups, and even the opposition) may also act as initiators. Given the higher priority of these bills, the government and the majority MPs will invest more resources in guaranteeing their smooth and swift legislative processing, and nurse these bills well from cradle (introduction to the legislature) to maturity (promulgation and eventually, implementation).

Principal Agent Theories

The second approach conceives a government declaration as a policy contract between principals and agents, whereby the agent is the government (as a collective body as well as individual ministers). The principals can be multiple, direct and indirect (parliamentary groups and extra-parliamentary party bodies, the (party) electorate(s), et cetera).

In classic parliamentary democracy, the principal is the legislature (which itself is an agent of the electorate), or at least a majority of its MPs, that de facto delegates a large part of its power to initiate bills to the government-agent, carrying out this function in the interest, and on behalf of the principal. Delegation occurs because the government is presumed to be better equipped to draft legislative policy initiatives than the legislature or its subdivisions (parliamentary committees, party groups) (Strøm 2000).

A central problem of agent/principal relationships is 'agency loss', the fact that the agent starts serving his own interests and not those of his principal. One way of avoiding agency loss is the drawing up of ex ante contracts that stipulate the legitimate expectations of the principal vis-à-vis the agent, or at least a vision of the agent about which interests of the principal he will take in charge and how this will be done. Thus, in the government declaration, the government formateur and his ministers promise the parliament to tackle a number a policy problems, often already suggesting the type of solution that will be sought. On the basis of this contract, majority MPs and groups invest[4] a new government, or decide to abort the formation attempt by refusing to vote the investiture motion. The government

3 We may assume that the policy sectors of working time/contracts and benefits constitute a type of policy that can be rationally planned ahead, 'programmed' relatively well by governing parties. These policy sectors are probably less subject to disasters, critical opinion shocks, massive and sudden shifts in the economic environment, et cetera.

4 Explicitly in countries with positive formation rules (Bergman 1993), or implicitly, in countries where there is no formal investiture vote.

agreement also plays a central role in ex post monitoring, reporting and sanctioning, as it provides a common indisputable point of reference for settling policy disputes among ministers, and between ministers and parliamentary supporting parties (Andeweg and Timmermans 2004). Coalition agreements are ex ante contracts designed to allow parliamentary parties to delegate their decision-making authority to a specialized group of leaders, while maintaining an acceptable degree of accountability (Strøm 2000) and avoiding abdication (Lupia and McCubbins 2000: pp.1-4).

In the partisan theory of democracy (Keman 2002), the principals of the government are political parties (which themselves are agents of the electorate). In case of single-party majority cabinets, the governing party promises its support to a set of party leaders in order to implement the policy program endorsed by the party organization (defined in the wide sense, including all bodies, from ministers, party executive, parliamentary groups to the rank-and-file organizations), a program that has been legitimated by the party electorate (and often also directly or indirectly by the party rank-and-file that, through the party's campaign conference, endorse the party manifesto). Hence, manifesto agreements serve as a vertical link, from top (the party leaders delegated to the government), to bottom (party the rank-and-file and electorate).

But in coalition government, government agreements are contracts that in the first place link parties horizontally. They represent a compromise between policy solution agendas of the different coalition parties. They contain an inventory of issues which the government (or at least one of the coalition parties) considers salient (Thomson 1999), often already formulate the type of policy solution that will be sought after and sometimes even the rules and procedures of the decision making mode to be followed for this policy issue.[5] As such, they may also define the role and autonomy of different types of potential actors in the legislative process (not only of governmental and parliamentary actors but also of experts, concerned interest groups, constitutional courts, et cetera).

The coalition agreement is, thus, not only a formidable legislative agenda-setting device for the problems mentioned, but also for those that are not included. Issues on the public agenda on which the coalition parties can not find a common point of view are often omitted from the agreement, with the tacit or explicit understanding that they should not be brought up by any of the coalition parties during the legislative period, and should be neglected when brought up by the opposition and the media (Strøm and Müller 2004).[6] In several countries, the coalition agreements tacitly include such agreements not to address any issues not mentioned in the agreement without prior consent of each of the coalition parties in the cabinet and/or parliamentary arena (Müller and Strøm 2000). Another strategy is to openly acknowledge that, on certain issues, no consensus could be found

5 For an analysis of the procedural contents of coalition agreements, see Strøm and Müller (2004).

6 Or in the latter case, that at least a new attempt at formulating a compromise should be made before every party resumes its freedom of maneuver on that issue.

(agreeing to disagree) and that therefore the issue should be removed from the government's legislative agenda. Sometimes agreements to disagree will refer the solution of the problem to actors and arenas outside the cabinet/parliament nexus, like party summits, round-table conferences, expert committees, et cetera (Andeweg and Timmermans 2004).

Coalition agreements also help to regulate several agency loss problems regarding the delegation of power from the collective government to individual ministers (Andeweg 2000). They prevent individual ministers from becoming policy dictators in their field of competence, essential for the survival of coalitions (Strøm 1998).[7] When coalition agreements are detailed and comprehensive, individual ministers get a complete script for the initiatives to be launched in their policy sector, a script they are supposed to carry out to the letter, independent of their personal policy views and expertise. These departmental scripts allow the prime minister, but also the other ministers and their supporting parties, to monitor the behavior of each individual minister, and if necessary – in the case of deviant policy initiatives and declarations – offer a legitimate basis to correct and punish the deviant minister and his supporting party (given the norm of *pacta sunt servanda*).

Coalition agreements not only provide for a contract between parties and their ministers on the horizontal plane, but also on the vertical plane within each supporting party. In fact, these agreements are usually endorsed by the parties' main decisional body (for example the party congress, parliamentary party or party executive), and as such, this endorsement statutorily and legitimately binds all other sections of the party, from the rank-and-file members, constituency party organizations, individual MPs and ministers, the party executive, and even the party leader. This party investiture is therefore a crucial moment for making agreements stick, not only between parties, but more importantly, also within parties (De Winter, Timmermans, Dumont 2000).

Thus, coalition agreements (and electoral manifestos in single-party governments), play a crucial role in reducing agency loss between the government, the individual ministers, and the party/parties in power (and all their intraparty bodies). They constitute the core of the common denominator of different policy views between and within parties, the main field of government activity on which the new government will try to reach policy success. As such, they are also a prime target for criticism by the opposition parties and MPs and other government opponents in the political system, criticism that is often voiced during the investiture debates themselves. In this sense, coalition agreements also become relevant to the agenda setting of non-governing parties and non-parliamentary actors.

To conclude, coalition agreements are one of the main institutions that make accountable coalition government possible. They are one of the major tools in the 'black box' of the policy-making process (Easton 1965: p.110) in which societal

7 For an opposite view, see Laver and Shepsle (1994, 1996).

and party demands are converted into policy outputs, a process in which the passage of legislation constitutes a vital phase.

The Empirical Occurrence and Content of Government Agreements in Western Europe

Two contrasting views exist on the policy relevance of coalition negotiations: the 'positive' version considers the formulation of coalition agreements as a genuine opportunity for parties to influence the future government's policy agenda (Peterson et al. 1983, Peterson and De Ridder 1986). The 'sceptics' consider coalition negotiations as 'policy irrelevant', either because they are just a 'ritual' that is carried out to ease the transition from election campaign competition to interparty governmental co-operation (Luebbert 1986), or because most contentious matters are omitted (Klingemann et al. 1994: 33), or because the link is only conditionally relevant, that is only if policy proposals supported in the coalition agreement are supported by the party that receives the relevant ministerial portfolio (Laver and Shepsle: 1996: p.42).

However, recent empirical comparative research unquestionably reveals that, in most countries, policy bargaining is the main subject of the formation bargaining process. This can be inferred from the numerous indicators:

- there is a growing tendency in West-European coalition governments to draft a government policy agreement[8] from 33 per cent in the 1940s to 81 per cent in the 1990s (Strøm and Müller 1999);
- these documents tend to grow in length and detail;[9]
- most of their content consists of agreements on substantive policies, not on procedures or distribution of competencies (Strøm and Müller 1999);
- coalition agreements contain issues that are salient to the member parties and for which they have formulated policy pledges, even when they disagree on the solution of such issues. Hence, they do not just focus on only non-divisive issues. On the contrary, during the negotiations the pledges most salient to each party tend to receive explicit support (Thomson 1999);
- in most countries, the policy formulation phase of the bargaining consumes most time, often weeks or months, while the allocation of portfolios is settled in one or a few days (De Winter 2002);
- in all countries (apart from Italy) portfolio allocation seems to be the concluding stage, after a general agreement on policy is drafted (and the parties that subscribe to the new policy have been identified) (Budge and Laver 1992: p.415);

8 An agreement should be distinguished from the government declaration the incoming PM or cabinet makes when he presents himself to parliament for the first time, which is shorter, less detailed and focusing on the politically or technically easier topics.

9 Müller and Strøm (2000, different country chapters). The record is held by the 1988 Martens VIII agreement in Belgium, with 43,600 words (De Winter, Timmermans and Dumont 2000).

- coalition bargaining attempts break down mostly on policy, not on the allocation of portfolios;
- by now, in all countries (apart from Luxembourg, Ireland and Italy) these agreements are widely available to the general public, which expands their utility for ex post monitoring of government performance by agents (parliamentary party, party executive, national congress), and for 'third party' monitoring, for instance by the media, interest groups, and retrospective voters.
- a variety of mechanisms and rules have been set up in coalition cabinets in order to facilitate the smooth implementation of these agreements, to solve conflicts over the way they should be interpreted, to solve issues that are not anticipated by, or included in the agreement, and to alter these agreements without jeopardizing the coalition's survival (Andeweg and Timmermans 2004).

Thus, empirical research suggests that coalition agreements are central instruments for coalition policy making, but their significance varies considerably over time, space and probably policy sectors. Depending on structural and contextual characteristics (fragmentation of party system, internal cabinet operational rules, et cetera) and features specific to each bargaining situation (number of negotiating parties and their preference diversity, size of parliamentary support, length of remaining term, conditions of termination of previous government), coalition agreements vary in terms of their occurrence, their formal or informal shape, their length, their comprehensiveness and completeness, their degree of specificity, the inclusion of (different types of) enforceability instruments, the moment and speed of their conclusion (Strøm and Müller 2004).

Conceiving coalition agreements as central instruments facilitating the conclusion of coalition governments from a principal/agent perspective also enhances our understanding of the process of governing by coalition once a cabinet has been formed, not only in the executive but also in the parliamentary decision arena. Coalition agreements are vital devices that make coalition government possible and help tackle some of the severe and complex bargaining problems and inherent weaknesses of coalitions (Lupia and Strøm 2004), such as limited and asymmetric (circulation of) information (Burch 1993), lack of enforceability of contracts (Shepsle 1996: pp.229-231), non-simultaneity of exchange, shifting resources and cyclical voting (Weingast and Marshall 1988); hidden action, shirking and sabotage (Strøm 2000: p.10); multilevel bargaining (Scharpf 1988; Downs 1998) and repeated games (Shepsle and Bonchek 1997: pp.207-210), ministers' and committees' discretion over departmental policy agendas, problems of interdepartmental dependency, shared competencies, and co-ordination; problems of collective principals and collective agents (Kiewiet and McCubbins 1991: pp.26-27). They reduce vulnerability to contextual changes (external shocks) (Saalfeld 2004), and to the increasing volatility of the political agenda (Strøm 2000).

Bills Announced by Government Declarations

Of all bills included in the data set, a surprisingly large proportion of bills (35.7 per cent) regulated a policy problem that was mentioned in the declaration submitted to parliament at the beginning of the cabinet's term[10] (versus 56.3 per cent for those that did not, with 8 per cent missing cases). This is a rather remarkable finding in light of the fact that, in several countries, government programs, and especially declarations to parliament[11] tend to be vague and short (Müller and Strøm 2000). Taking a closer look at the evidence, only in a quarter of the cases (26 per cent) was the matter actually mentioned in precise and detailed terms, the rest in rather vague terms (74 per cent). Even in the cases of comprehensive and detailed programs, some policy problems regulated by the bills included in this research project might not have been salient (or might not even have existed) at the moment a new government was invested by parliament. As the sector of working time/contract may traditionally be more subject to corporatist bi- and tripartite decision making, a government may prefer to await results to be achieved in this arena, rather than making premature policy engagements toward parliament.

In 36.8 per cent of the cases, the government declaration mentioned not only the policy problem to be tackled, but also a solution to it. The government declaration devoted a full chapter to the problem matter (and its eventual solution) regulated by the bill in 5.2 per cent of the cases, a section (several paragraphs) in 19 per cent of the cases, a paragraph in 47 per cent and only in 28.8 per cent just one sentence or a part of a composite-sentence. Thus one can say that, generally, in about seven out of ten cases, a reasonable amount of space was dedicated to the policy problem regulated by the bill, which, in theory, should suffice to produce a policy commitment.

Finally, in 71.1 per cent of those cases where a solution was actually formulated, the bill proposed a solution in a way quite similar to the solution mentioned in the declaration (and thus agency loss was minimal). In 20.3 per cent of the cases, certain parts were formulated in a similar way, and only in 8.6 per cent of the cases was there no or very little similarity between the two approaches

10 Countries in which half or more of the coalition governments concluded a government agreement in the post-war period are: Austria, Belgium, Finland, Iceland, Ireland, Luxembourg, the Netherlands, Norway, Portugal and Sweden. When no coalition agreement was drafted, the government's declaration when it presents itself to parliament for the first time was regarded as the main policy contract. In case of one-party governments, the government's declaration is usually heavily inspired by the party's electoral manifesto, and therefore equally constitute a contract with committing power between ministers, supporting party and the electorate.

11 In all countries, a new government will, when it confronts parliament for the first time, present a declaration regarding the government policy intentions. In countries, in which alongside this document a separate agreement concluded between coalition parties also exists, the parliamentary declaration tends to be shorter (as to be orally presented by the PM), less detailed, and flattered (in the sense that the benefits for parties and their clienteles are underlined, rather than the costs of the new programme).

to solving the problem. Thus, occasions of strong agency loss or 'sabotage' remain comparatively ráre.

Hypotheses and Operationalization

Drawing from this vision of the role of the government declaration, the general hypothesis regarding the passage of legislation is, that, for bills referring to matters encapsulated in this contract, the contracting parties (government supporting parties, parliamentary groups and individual MPs, the government and individual ministers) will invest more resources in guaranteeing a smooth and swift legislative process than for those that are less central to the core of the government contract. Not only that, opposition parties, MPs, and other non-governmental actors in the political system will equally tend to focus their resources on these bills. These bills are central to the government's policy success and, as such, they will trying to block them, delay them, amend their content, by adapting various tactical means at their disposal. Sowing dissension amongst the majority, denouncing bills in the parliamentary arena and the media, fighting them in court, or appealing to the Head of State not to promulgate them are just a few examples of the tactics that can be deployed.

Thus, we expect that a bill that has been mentioned in the government declaration/agreement, will display the following features (in comparison to those that have not):

- be more comprehensive in terms of size and scope. Given the fact that the matter was mentioned in the coalition agreement, the problem will tend to be more salient and important than those bills that regulate matters that did not make it into the government agreement (their omission would, in part, be due to lack of salience on the public agenda);
- less conflictual within the government camp (and its supporting parties) in their treatment (in terms of voting patterns and introduction of amendments by government MPs) as they form part of the core of common policy positions. Shirking or any other deviation from this core program may jeopardize the overall understanding of coalition parties and therefore the stability and performance of the government;
- yet less consensual in terms of the legislative support received from the opposition. While on other bills the opposition may offer support depending on the bill's inherent merits, they will tend to use all means to block, delay, amend and denounce government declaration bills at different stages of the legislative and post-legislative process, not only because it opposes the bills' content, but also as a strategy to harass the government, and eventually bring it down;
- wherever institutionally possible, avoiding more the non-compulsory stages of the legislative process, like plenary debates and votes before the committee stage. In order to reduce the number of veto players, the government will want to restrict as much as possible the number of legislative stages, limiting

opportunities for opposition or rebel majority MPs to fight and torpedo the bill;

- therefore be also more closed in terms of the number and variety of legislative decision-making participants, through limiting the use of participatory instruments such as hearings or minority reports, for example;
- be less left in the care of rapporteurs or committee chairman or committees that are not (or not as well) controlled by the majority;
- receive a faster treatment (from introduction to promulgation);
- more often display voting patterns at different stages of the legislative process, that will correspond to a simple confrontational pattern of majority vs. opposition, with minimal dissent on either side;
- be more contested in constitutional and other courts, as this contestation will constitute an instrument of last resort or appeal of interests that are 'hurt but not heard' (opposition parties, interest groups, regional governments, for example).

In order to test these hypotheses, we will restrict the analyses to successful bills only (that is those in the sector of working time/contract and benefits that have been promulgated), as unsuccessful bills tend to have many missing data points for the stages following their formal introduction. The reason for this is that these bills will have been torpedoed or stalled at one time or another in the legislative decision-making process, and from that moment on, all values for those bills would have to be coded 'missing'. It would be of no great benefit to draw conclusions that are based on the full data set in the earlier stages of the legislative process but refer to a gradually shrinking population at the later stages.

In the Summary Table to the bivariate analysis, we report standard statistical significance measures, but as the sample of successful bills represents a large proportion of the overall population in the sector concerned (Scholz and Trantas 1995), we report three significance levels, 0.01, 0.05 as well as 0.10).

Empirical Results

Bivariate Analyses

Size and scope of bills In terms of size and scope,[12] successful bills[13] regarding problems announced in the government declaration tend to be significantly different from those not included (see Summary Table). They are twice as long in terms of pages in the official publication (14.2 to 7.0 pages, or in characters, 39,550 to 21,668), count more articles or clauses (25.1 to. 17.2), more chapters and

12 In terms of scope, expressed in the number of keywords the content of the bill is registered under in the official publication, there is however no difference at all (that is 4.1 keywords).

13 Very similar results are reached if the unsuccessful bills are also included, that is those that were not promulgated.

subheadings (7.1 to. 4.7), modify more clauses of previous bills (18.2 to 11.1), and mention more often previous bills (5.4 to 2.9).

Legislative initiation by the government We expect the legislative initiator to be more often the government (or individual ministers) than any other category of initiators. The agent may fulfill the contract with the principal better if he takes the initiative himself, rather than running the chance that the stipulations of the contract are distorted by the involvement of third players in the initiation phase, even if they belong to the government camp.

The difference is small and insignificant: 92.6 per cent of successful bills[14] mentioned in the government declaration are introduced by the government, against 90.1 per cent of those not mentioned. In the sector of working time/contract and benefits bills, the government is overwhelmingly dominant as initiator, whether or not it announced in the government program that it would take initiatives in the field.

Avoidance of plenary reading before committee stage Parliamentary rules permitting, the government and its MPs should try to avoid discussing a government bill in the plenary before sending it to the competent committee. Preliminary plenary debate opens more opportunities for opposition MPs and parties to voice criticism. In addition, it can also invite dissent among government MPs, who under public scrutiny of the media and interest groups may feel less inclined to simply rubberstamp a bill 'pre-cooked' during the government formation phase.

According to parliamentary rules (Döring 1995c: pp.233-234), the stage of a plenary debate and vote before committee stage is quasi compulsory in Ireland, Spain and the UK (and customary in Denmark), as general principles of a bill need to be discussed in the plenary before being sent to a committee. In all other countries, the rule is that the competent committee examines the bill proposal in detail first, before the plenary makes an evaluation. This being said, the data set indicates that pre-committee plenary debates in the latter group of countries also took place. Indeed, in countries like Finland (88.4 per cent), Germany (96.7 per cent) and Iceland (94.6 per cent) it was more the rule than the exception. Debates also occasionally took place in Portugal (27.3 per cent), Luxembourg (20 per cent) and Austria (2.2 per cent). Exceptions to the rule also exist in the first group of countries: 12.9 per cent of the Irish bills and 44 per cent of the Spanish bills did not pass a plenary reading before the committee phase.

Hence, we should test our hypothesis for the group of eight countries in which there is some variation in the use of pre-committee plenary reading. In none of the

14 If we include the unsuccessful bills (n=155), differences are more significant: 83.2 per cent of the bills referring to a matter mentioned in the governmental agreement were introduced by government, against 71 per cent of those that were not referred to in the declaration. In the latter group of bills, individual MPs are relatively active, having introduced 22.4 per cent of the bills, as opposed to 14.7 per cent for the first group.

eight countries, however, were the differences significant, neither for the plenary debate nor for the subsequent vote.[15] If we group the eight countries, it seems that only half of the successful bills mentioned in the government declaration are actually subjected to a plenary reading (51.1 per cent), which is significantly lower than the 72.1 per cent for bills not mentioned. From a different perspective, of those bills on which a debate was held, 89.3 per cent of bills mentioned in the government declaration are subjected to a plenary vote, against only 72.9 per cent for bills not mentioned. Thus, it seems that the majority is significantly better at managing to avoid plenary reading for government agreement bills, but should it lose this battle, the opposition more frequently seizes the chance to also have a first shot (vote) at the proposal.

For similar reasons, we would expect that bills whose policy problem was mentioned in the government declaration would be less submitted to repeated plenary readings after the committee stage. This difference is however minor and insignificant (1.56 as against 1.61 plenary readings per type of bill).

Treatment by a single committee Following the same goal of keeping the veto and amendment arenas as tidy and restricted as possible, we expect bills whose policy problem was mentioned in the government declaration to be more frequently dealt with by a single committee, rather than to be referred to several committees.

Yet, rather the opposite seems to be the case, although differences are not significant: of the bills whose policy problem was mentioned in the government declaration, 77.7 per cent were treated in only one committee against 81.8 per cent for those that were not mentioned. Correspondingly, bills whose policy problem was mentioned in the government declaration were treated in an average of 1.5 committees, against 1.4 for those not mentioned.[16]

Treatment by government MPs in committees Whenever the government has the choice, it will prefer to send bills announced in the government declaration to committees chaired by a majority MP. This seems generally to be the case (83.3 per cent of the bills whose policy problem was mentioned in the government declaration are treated by committees that are chaired by a majority MP, against 77.4 per cent that were not mentioned). However, in Greece, Iceland, Italy, Luxembourg, Switzerland and Spain, none of the bills included in this research went to a committee chaired by an opposition MP. This may be due to the fact that parliamentary rules reserve chairs to the majority MPs (as in Italy and Greece,

---

15 The lack of significant results is partially due to the low number of successful bills in each country.

16 One of the reasons for this may be the larger scope of bills mentioned in the agreement. In fact, controlling for size of the bills (larger than three pages as opposed to less than three pages), we find that the number of committees involved is significantly higher for longer bills than for shorter bills (1.60 compared to 1.29), while within these two size groups, the differences between bills mentioned or not in the declaration are not significant (1.65 to 1.54 for large bills, and 1.24 to 1.31 for small bills).

Mattson and Strom 1995), or that for the policy sector of the bills and time period selected, the relevant committee just happened to be chaired by a government MP. If we remove all countries lacking variation in committee chairing from our calculation, the difference becomes far greater and considerably more significant: 78.2 per cent compared to 69.9 per cent, as was to be expected.

Further, we expect that, whenever institutionally possible, the government would prefer to leave the responsibility of presenting committee conclusions to plenary in the hands of a rapporteur or committee chairperson belonging to the government benches. If we look at the countries that use specific rapporteur(s) for reporting to the plenary, we find that the rapporteur(s) belonged to the governing parties for 87.2 per cent of the bills whose policy problem was mentioned in the government declaration, which is slightly more than for bills that were not mentioned (82.4 per cent). If we take the countries in which the chair is usually in charge of reporting the bill (and, as above, omit those countries lacking variation in party control of chairs), the reporting chair belonged to the governing parties for 73.1 per cent of the bills whose policy problem was mentioned in the government declaration, which is clearly more than for bills not mentioned (61.5 per cent), but, given the small numbers involved, this large difference is not significant.

Degree of partisan (voting) conflict The degree of partisan conflict on a bill can be expressed in several ways:

- the submittal of a bill to a vote at different stages of the legislative process. In many countries, bills pass certain stages of the legislative process without a vote being taken. This is often due to the less conflictual content of a bill. But for important government bills, we would expect the opposition to try and exploit every voting opportunity in order to challenge the government, expose internal divisions within the majority, and use the vote for voicing or repeating criticism;
- by presenting a minority report, in which the opposition expresses its point of view and summarizes its criticism of the government's position;
- the procedural efforts made by the opposition to oppose the bill's adoption in the final plenary reading, and other forms of dissent;
- and last, but not least, in voting block patterns (government versus opposition).

As far as the submittal to a vote in the committee stage is concerned, the bills whose policy problem was mentioned in the government declaration were more frequently submitted to a committee vote than the other type (59.7 per cent as against 52.8 per cent), though the difference is not significant. Similarly, there is no significant difference with regard to the submittal to a final vote in the plenary (78.9 per cent compared to 78.3 per cent), nor in terms of introducing minority reports (30.3 per cent of the bills whose policy problem was mentioned in the government declaration contained a minority report, against 25.6 per cent of the other type of bills). There is, however, a significant difference with respect to the expression of other forms of dissent within a committee: 53.9 per cent of the bills whose policy problem was mentioned in the government declaration provoked committee dissent against only 39.9 per cent for the other type. Also, bills whose policy problem was mentioned in the government declaration faced significantly more attempts by the opposition to oppose the bill's adoption in the final plenary reading (26 per cent) than the other type (14.2 per cent). So, it seems the opposition is often readier to resort to more unconventional methods for government declaration bills than for other bills.

As far as voting patterns are concerned, the degree of voting consensus on a bill can be expressed by the proportion of MPs voting in favor of a bill in comparison to the overall sum of For and Against votes.

The first occasion to vote on a bill occurs after its plenary reading, before it is transmitted to a committee. There is a highly significant difference between the two types, confirming our hypothesis. The bills whose policy problem was mentioned in the government declaration have an approval rate of 63 per cent against 85.1 per cent of those that were not mentioned.[17]

That being said, we do not find a significant difference for final committee vote (approval rate of 78.4 per cent compared to 79.2 per cent, depending on whether bills were or were not announced in the government declaration). This overall resemblance does, however, hide different degrees of party cohesion: for bills whose policy problem was mentioned in the government declaration, we find the Ayes to have been delivered significantly by majority MPs (84.3 per cent against 77.3 per cent for the other type. Or, expressed in terms of voting rebellion (operationalized by calculating the proportion of majority MPs voting against the bill or abstaining, plus the proportion of opposition MPs voting for the bill or abstaining vis-à-vis the overall number of votes cast), for bills whose policy problem was mentioned in the government declaration, voting rebellion is only 17 per cent against 23.5 per cent for those that were not mentioned. Hence, for government declaration bills, the final vote in the committee does seem to follow more a government versus opposition pattern, a high number of government MPs voting in favor of the bill and most opposition MPs against. Thus, even when getting similar levels of absolute support, for bills whose policy problem was mentioned in the government declaration, fewer majority as well as opposition MPs are prepared to 'cross the floor'.

For the final plenary vote, approval rates, as expected, differ significantly: 77.7 per cent to 85.2 per cent. This pattern is also confirmed for the votes that were not recorded and for which we only have a rough estimate of the result. Of the bills whose policy problem was mentioned in the government declaration, 37.3 per cent of the bills were accepted (nearly) unanimously against 60 per cent for other bills.

---

17 As there were 78 cases in which the 'ayes' were registered but only 44 with the 'nays' and only 21 that registered abstentions, we presumed that the lacking values in the latter two variables are not missing values but equal to zero.

Restriction of use of hearings In order to minimize agency loss, the government should limit the number and types of outside participants in the legislative decision-making process as much as possible, for instance by restricting the use of hearings and of reports of professional agencies (Döring 1994). Such forms of ex ante policy evaluations can distort the policy compromises agreed upon in the government agreement and therefore create tension within the government camp.

The data, however, does not reveal a significant difference: for 21.1 per cent of the bills whose policy problem was mentioned in the government declaration a hearing was organized, against only 19 per cent of those that were not mentioned. But if hearings were organized, on average, twice as many hearing sessions per bill were organized for the first type of bill (2.2 as against 1.1).

The potential of hearings for the opposition to tackle the government, however, depends on both the private versus public character of these hearings and the type of persons heard. There is no significant difference between the public or private character between the two types of bills. Looking instead at the type of actors heard during these hearings, the data suggests that the government firmly controls the game in this arena. For 64.5 per cent of the bills whose policy problem was mentioned in the government declaration, government ministers were heard, against only 31.1 per cent for the other bills.[18] Thus the opposition uses hearings mainly to challenge ministers, rather than to call upon sources of non-governmental advice, such as civil servants, experts or interest group representatives, for example.

Faster legislative treatment As a bill whose policy problem was mentioned in the government declaration probably figures high on the government's agenda of priorities, it should receive faster treatment in terms of the time lap ranging from the moment of its first formal introduction of the bill to final promulgation.

However, rather the opposite seems to be the case (although statistically not significant): the time lap is longer for bills whose policy problem was mentioned in the government declaration (208.4 days) than for the problems not evoked in the agreement (192.7 days).[19] Closer inspection indicates that bills whose policy problem was mentioned in the government declaration tend to get through the committee phase, that is the lap between formal plenary introduction and end of the committee stage, far quicker (about ten days faster) than other bills (126.6 days as against 136.2 days). Yet, they take up nearly twice as much time for treatment in

18 If we only look at hearings that hear non-governmental actors (civil servants, experts, interest group representatives, et cetera) we find no significant difference between both types.

19 For those cases where we have data for the four dates concerned: introduction to the plenary, end of committee stage, vote in plenary, and promulgation.

the plenary[20] (24 compared to 13.9 days) and are treated more slowly in the post-plenary stage (59.8 compared to 42.6 days until final promulgation). However, none of these differences in speed of legislative treatment are statistically significant.

Non-Modification by second chamber Bills whose policy problem was mentioned in the government declaration should be less modified by the second chamber. The government should try to keep discipline tight in both houses, and once approved by one chamber, pressure should be put on the majority MPs in the other to rubberstamp the bill. But this disciplining can only occur if the government effectively controls an absolute majority in the other chamber. If it does not, it is not surprising that the opposition makes use of its numeric power in the other house to block, delay or amend the bill, as opportunity (legislative competencies) combines with motive (incongruent composition).

For the period under consideration, in all bicameral countries except Germany, the majority/minority situation of the government was identical in the Lower as well as Upper House. In Germany, only a quarter (six) of the bills analyzed were introduced to a *Bundesrat* controlled by majority incongruent to the one in the *Bundestag*. This low number of cases is insufficient for a reliable test of the delaying and amending potential of symmetrical and incongruent second chambers.

If we, instead, only look at the opportunity factor, it seems that, in bicameral countries,[21] bills whose policy problem was mentioned in the government declaration are slightly less easily (but not significantly) accepted by the second chamber than the other type of bills (66.4 per cent vs. 69.7 per cent). When the other chamber disagrees, the former type of bills are more frequently modified (amendments of second chamber are endorsed by the first) (85.7 per cent compared to 58.9 per cent), but – when subjected to a navette – they are shifted slightly less back and forth between chambers (2.1 as opposed to 2.8 navette rounds). The bills whose policy problem was mentioned in the government declaration are settled far more frequently in conference committees (10.7 per cent compared to 39.7 per cent). However, these committees arrive at an agreement far more often in the case of bills whose policy problem was mentioned in the government declaration than the other bills (71.4 per cent as against 31.3 per cent), for which more often than not no agreement could be reached.

Contestation in constitutional court Bills announced in the government declaration will tend to be more contested in constitutional or other courts, as this opportunity

20 Bills whose policy problem was mentioned in the government declaration also take significantly more time for the plenary decisive reading (1.4 days compared to 1.1, or 6.7 hours compared to 3) (same selection criteria as for the sample mentioned in the note above, but there are many missing data regarding the number of hours and days of the decisive debate).

21 Taken from Lijphart (1999), but dichotomizing between unicameral systems and the rest.

constitutes an instrument of last resort for the 'losers' in the legislative process (opposition parties, affected interest groups, for example). Also, for some urgent bills, the government may have 'forced' the legislative passage of the bill, even violating constitutional or legal rules regarding parliamentary procedures. For the countries allowing a certain degree of judicial review of parliamentary legislation (Lijphart 1999: p.226), bills whose policy problem was mentioned in the government declaration are in fact more frequently challenged by constitutional courts than the other type (23.9 per cent compared to 17.3 per cent), but here again, the difference is statistically insignificant.

Intervening Contextual and Intra-Parliamentary Variables

A number of variables may strengthen or weaken the degree of association between dependent and independent variables. Given the fact that our analyses focus on the bivariate relationship between a single independent variable and a large number of dependent variables, we cannot use classical multivariate techniques for reporting in a concise way the impact and interaction effects of contextual, country effects and other variables on the bivariate relationships discussed above.

One could even argue that the relations between inclusion in the government declaration and most of the dependent variables mentioned above may be spurious, given the fact that these association could be due to their co-variation with a third variable, that is the scope and importance of bills. Bills included in the government agreement tend to be more important bills in terms of scope and political priority, and the latter feature may explain their different treatment by the legislature. Lacking indicators for political priority, we only ran an exploratory control for the scope of a bill, expressed in terms of pages, using partial correlations (results not reported in detail). All the relations that were significant (0.05) in simple bivariate correlations are equally significant when controlled for scope.

Furthermore, the policy content of the bill makes little difference and is not significant: of the working time/contract bills, 54.4 per cent were mentioned in the agreement, benefits slightly (but not significantly) more (58.8 per cent). A separate series of analyses for these two content groups is, therefore, not warranted.[22]

As far as structural and contextual factors are concerned, one could argue that the use and prominence of government agreements differs strongly between countries (compare Müller and Strøm's (2000) distinction between tight and loose agreements) and will affect the impact of the inclusion of problems in the

22 The category 'Unsuccessful' bills figures much less (23.1 per cent) than the other two types of bills (working time/contract plus benefits) (42.8 per cent) on the government agreement, which is probably the main reason why they failed. Given the fact that, for many unsuccessful bills, failure arrived early in the legislative process, and thus that for most variables used in the bivariate analysis of the other two types of bills data is missing, a separate bivariate analysis of unsuccessful bill in relation to inclusion in the government declaration has not been made.

agreement on the subsequent legislative process.[23] There is, in fact, large variation between countries: bills of which the problem matter was mentioned in government declaration constitute less than 20 per cent of the overall number of bills examined in France, Iceland, Ireland, Norway, Spain, Sweden and Italy; while they are mentioned far more often (that is about half or more of the bills) in Belgium, Austria, Denmark, Finland, Germany, Greece, Portugal, Luxembourg and the UK. To some extent, this corresponds to the use and size of government agreements and policy dependency on this document, but there are noticeable discrepancies, like the Netherlands, the champion of long coalition agreements and prolonged policy negotiations (Müller and Strøm 2000), but with still less than a third of bills analyzed that could be traced back to the government agreement.

Once again, using partial correlation to control for the impact of use of coalition agreements, all the relations that were significant in simple bivariate correlations prove equally significant when controlled for a dummy variable regarding commonality of the use of agreements.

Other contextual-structural and intraparliamentary institutional variables[24] that are of theoretical relevance to government/opposition relations and legislative procedure, also failed to produce new relations or refute significant ones found before, except in a handful of cases, but the increase in the strength of the partial correlation was usually less than 0.05, and never exceeded 0.10. Hence, the results of the bivariate analyses, indeed, seem rather robust.[25]

---

23 In Austria, Belgium, Finland, Iceland, Ireland, Luxembourg, the Netherlands, Norway, Portugal and Sweden, half or more of the post-war coalition governments concluded a government agreement.

24 Parliamentary versus (semi-) presidentialism, government constraints, corporatism, economic integration, federalism, cabinet type, electoral system and party system fragmentation. Intraparliamentary arrangements include governmental control of committee chairs, a variety of measures of plenary and committee autonomy developed by Döring (1995e) and Mattson and Strøm (1995), openness of committees, and timing of committee stage vis-à-vis plenary deliberation.

25 New significant relations ($p > 0.05$) occur only when controlling for:
consociational democracy: bills included in the agreement receive more committee minority reports; this relation also becomes significant when one controls for plenary agenda autonomy, but in both cases the gain in strength is marginal and the partial correlation does not exceed 0.09);
the degree of restriction of committee deliberations by preceding plenary sessions: a positive but weak relation appears between taking a final vote and the inclusion of a bill in the agreement ($r = 0.12$);
degree of political autonomy of the judiciary: a positive but weak relation ($r = 0.13$) appears between taking the inclusion of a bill in the agreement and constitutional challenge; the same association occurs when controlling for the degree of bicameralism.

Conclusion

Drawing from the 'stagist' approach to policy agenda setting on the one hand, and from principal-agent theory applied to (parliamentary) parties and cabinets on the other, we formulated a number of hypotheses with regard to the impact of government agreements on the procedural features, timing, success, actor involvement, et cetera in the legislative process. To a large extent, the empirical analyses produced statistically significant confirmation of these hypotheses. Bills whose policy problem was mentioned in the government declaration/agreement (in comparison to those whose topic was not mentioned):

- tend to be richer in terms of size, content and complexity,
- are less subjected to a plenary reading and vote before the committee phase,
- are more often treated by committees that are chaired by a majority MP,
- are more often submitted to a committee vote,
- face more different forms of committee dissent or plenary obstruction,
- have a lower approval rate in the plenary,
- yield stronger voting discipline amongst majority and opposition MPs.

However, and quite contrary to our expectations, they are treated slower in terms of the time lap between the moment of the first formal introduction of the bill until final promulgation.

Hence, the fact that a policy matter is mentioned in the government declaration or agreement has a significant impact of the passage of legislation, in terms of stages, conflictuality, timing, success, venues open to veto players and other sources of influence, et cetera. This conclusion also holds good after controlling for a wide variety of intraparliamentary institutional as well as wider contextual factors.

Thus, governments, and their loyal troops in parliament, devote more effort and resources for guaranteeing the smooth passage of bills that are the subject of promises they made at the beginning of their term of office. This general policy statement not only serves as a policy agenda, but also as a contract, holding government and individual ministers accountable to parliamentary parties, intraparty bodies, and eventually the voters.

Table 2.1 Summary Table to Correlational Analyses

	Relation	Independent Variable Successful Bills mentioned in the Government Declaration? Yes	No	Significance	Hypothesis
Dependent variables					
Size and scope of bills					
- pages in official publication	more	14.2	7.1	0 003	confirmed
- characters in official publication	more	39,550	21,668	0 000	confirmed
- articles	more	25 1	17 2	0.032	confirmed
- subheadings	more	7.1	4.7	0 115	insignificant
- modified clauses to existing bills	more	18 2	11.1	0 024	confirmed
- references to existing bills	more	5 4	2 9	0.020	confirmed
Legislative initiation					
- by government	more often	92.6%	90 1%	0.236	insignificant
Subjection to supplementary phases					
Subjection to plenary reading (in 8 countries where optional)	less often	51.1%	72 1%	0 070	confirmed
Subjection to vote after optional plenary reading	less often	89.3%	72 9%	0 003	opposite
Referral to committees					
- to only one committee	more often	77.7%	81 8%	0.275	insignificant
- average number of competent committees	lower	1.50	1 40	0 480	insignificant
Subjection to multiple plenary readings after committee stage (n of readings)	less often	1.56	1 61	0.502	insignificant

Government control over committee in terms of:					
- committee chair (11 countries)	more often	78.2%	69.9%	0.057	confirmed
- specific rapporteur (12 countries)	more often	87.2%	82.4%	n.a.[1]	
- reporting chair (11 countries)	more often	73.1%	61.5%	0.352	insignificant
Degree of partisan conflict					
- submittal to					
Vote during committee stage	more often	59.7%	52.8%	0.260	insignificant
Final plenary vote	more often	78.9%	78.3%	0.882	insignificant
- minority reports	more often	30.3%	25.6%	0.460	insignificant
- other forms of dissent	more often	53.9%	39.9%	0.004	confirmed
- attempts to oppose final plenary adoption	more often	26.0%	14.2%	0.033	confirmed
- support in vote after 1st plenary reading	less	63.0%	85 1%	0.000	confirmed
- support in final committee vote	less	78.4%	79.2%	0.832	insignificant
- % Yeas provided by majority MPs	more	84.3%	77.3%	0.042	confirmed
- % voting rebellion	less	17.0%	23.5%	0.063	confirmed
- support in final plenary vote	less	77.7%	85.2%	0.005	confirmed
- (near) unanimous support	less	37.3%	60.0%	0.007	confirmed
Hearings					
- held Yes/No	less often	21.1%	19.0%	0.635	insignificant
- number of hearings held	fewer	2.2	1.1	0.063	opposite
- % private hearings	less	77.9%	81.4%	0.579	insignificant
- ministers heard	less often	64.5%	31.1%	0.003	opposite

[1] Significance test not available for multiple response variables.

<u>Speed legislative process</u>					
- days introduction Z promulgation	less	208.4	192.7	0.672	insignificant
- days introduction Z end committee stage	less	126 6	136 2	0 770	insignificant
- days end committee stage Z plenary vote	less	24.0	13 9	0.189	insignificant
- days plenary vote Z promulgation	less	57 8	42 9	0.194	insignificant
- plenary debate decisive reading (days)	less	1.4	1.1	0.012	opposite
(hours)	less	6.7	3.0	0 000	opposite
<u>Role Second Chamber</u>					
Modification	less often	66.4%	69.7%	0 546	insignificant
Mode of modification					
- modification by amendment second chamber	less often	85.7%	58.9%	0 001	opposite
- number of navette rounds	fewer	2.1	2 8	0.130	insignificant
- referral to conference committee	less often	10 7%	39 7%	0 001	confirmed
- modified by conference committee	less often	71.4%	31 3%	0 048	opposite
<u>Challenge in constitutional court</u>	more often	23 9%	17.3%	0 171	confirmed

Chapter 3

The Life and Times of Bills

Rolf Becker and Thomas Saalfeld

Introduction

Time is one of the scarcest resources in modern parliaments (Döring 1995c; Riescher 1994; 1997). Western European constitutions typically limit the lives of parliaments – and the governments they select – to a maximal 'constitutional inter-election period' (CIEP) of three to five years (Laver and Schofield 1990: p.64). The time available for the introduction and passage of new policies is limited, even where pending bills can be carried over at the end of a legislative term. Majorities are interested in getting their manifesto pledges on the statute book in time to claim credit for them at the next election. In parliamentary systems the control of time in the chamber is therefore a significant power resource enjoyed – to varying degrees – by parliamentary majorities and the governments they support. Minorities may not be able to muster enough votes to stop bills, but they may have varying degrees of delaying powers enabling them to extract concessions from majorities attempting to get on with their overall legislative program.

A parliament's 'procedural efficiency' in legislation – the speed of the legislative process – is a matter of considerable practical importance, especially 'where quick interventions of the state are required' (von Beyme 1998: p.143). Issues such as agenda control (for example, Döring 1995c), discount rates, inter-temporal collective action problems (Elster 1989: pp.18-23), the importance of time for coalition bargaining (Lupia and Strøm 1995) or, more generally, the tactical use of time in bargaining processes (Doron and Sened 2001: pp.10-11) have been increasingly recognized in formal theories of political processes. Yet, despite its importance and obvious implications for legislative and regime performance on the one hand and the theory of parliamentary institutions on the other, the lack of suitable data has been an obstacle to systematic comparative studies of the dynamics of the legislative process for a larger number of parliaments in the past. The few existing investigations are usually based on highly aggregated measures of central tendency (for example, the average duration of the legislative process in days) for a single parliament, often over time (see, for example, Griffith and Ryle 1989: p.290, p.473; Schindler 1994: pp.862-863; Van Schagen 1997: p.116). Although such studies provide very useful insights, they have little to say about the *process* of legislation, let alone the institutional sources of cross-national and diachronic variations in the speed of legislation.

Table 3.1 Legislation on Working Conditions, Working Hours and Social Security Benefits in 17 Western European Countries, 1981-1991 (bills with valid time references only)

National parliament[1)]	Number of successful bills drawn at random	Number of failed bills selected by country experts	Total number of bills included	Median time in the legislative process (in days)	Median time of successful bills in legislative process (in days)	Significance and direction of cross-national differences[3)]
Austria	34	9	43	54	52	+
Belgium	34	10	44	178	176	n s
Denmark	32	10	42	70	65	+
Finland	34	10	44	80	79	n s
Germany	24	4	28	127	114	Ref Cat
Greece	14	8	22	162	75	n s
Iceland	26	10	36	59	50	+
Ireland	22	6	28	32	27	+
Italy	14	7	21	620	263	–
Luxembourg	28	7	35	318	292	–
Netherlands	31	5	36	378	324	–
Norway	30	13	43	83	71	n.s
Portugal	12	10	22	379	254	–
Spain	15	10	25	228	222	n s
Sweden	36	10	46	101	92	+
Switzerland	15	3	18[2)]	400	393	–
UK	33	9	42	219	218	n.s.
Total	575	141	443[2)]	128	106	

Source: SPPL – own calculations

Notes:

1) For the purposes of our analyses, France had to be excluded, because much of the required information on the timing of different parliamentary stages was missing.

2) For Switzerland, the sum of successful and failed bills does not add up to 18 because of two missing values. This is also the reason for the difference in the 'Total' row.

3) Effect of country dummy variables on the hazard rate of duration and success. Germany is used as the reference category (Ref. Cat.), because the length of the process (127 days) is almost identical with the overall median (128 days). + = legislative process significantly faster compared to Germany (at the 5 per cent level), – = legislative process significantly slower than in Germany (at the 5 per cent level). N.s. = not significant (at the 5 per cent level).

The present chapter provides a comparative analysis of the dynamics of the legislative process in 17 Western European parliaments from the formal initiation of bills to their promulgation (for a list of national parliaments and number of bills included see Table 3.1). The 'biographies' of a sample of bills will be examined using techniques of event-history analysis (a) charting the dynamics of the legislative process both across the life-times of individual bills and different political systems and (b) examining whether, and to what extent, parliamentary rules and some general regime attributes influence the dynamics of this process, speeding up or delaying the passage of legislation.

Given the small number of bills analyzed and the focus on some quite specific policy areas, we do not wish to put too much emphasis on cross-national variations at this stage. Nevertheless, Table 3.1 does provide some tentative evidence of significant differences. Using the Federal Republic of Germany as reference category, we estimated the effect of dummy variables for individual countries on the hazard rate of the successful conclusion of the legislative process. In five out of 16 parliaments, the legislative process was significantly faster and more likely to be successful than in Germany at the 5 per cent level of statistical significance. In five parliaments it was significantly slower and/or a bill was less likely to be passed successfully. Given these statistically significant cross-national differences we expect both general regime attributes and parliamentary procedures to have at least some impact on the dynamics of the legislative process.

Transaction Costs and the Dynamics of the Legislative Process

There is a considerable body of theoretical literature reflecting the growth of legislation as a policy instrument since the 19th century both in quantitative terms and importance (compare Mantl 1995: p.26). As a result of this expansion of legislative activity, parliaments – constitutionally the most important law-making bodies in parliamentary democracies – have increasingly come under pressure, especially since the end of the Second World War. Despite improvements, parliaments have been more constrained in their responses to this growth than executives. Time pressure has become a serious professional and personal problem for many members of parliament individually (for the German Bundestag see Patzelt 1993: pp.410-413). As individuals, members of parliament have responded to these pressures by an increasing degree of professionalization; at the organizational level there have been improvements in parliamentary resources including funds for personnel, policy advice and access to electronic information systems. In most parliaments the efficiency of parliamentary work has been improved through the establishment and systematization of committee systems, which provide a division of labor and allow chambers to process a number of legislative proposals simultaneously and subject them to specialized scrutiny. Yet the downside of specialization in parliamentary and party committees has been a hierarchization of parliamentary life (for example, growing influence of parliamentary experts and managers; for an analysis of the German example compare Schüttemeyer 1994) and the sort of agency problems between committee specialists and the chamber as a whole described by Keith Krehbiel (1991).

A great deal of literature has analyzed the *consequences* of the growing reliance on, and expanding volume of, legislation for parliamentary organization and the performance and accountability of governments. A much smaller amount of systematic research has sought to explain the volume, nature, dynamics and speed of legislation as *dependent variables* (compare, however, discussions in von Beyme 1998; Döring 1995c). Recent developments in the study of legislative organization and performance have focused on the transaction (including information) costs of legislative activity as an explanation for institutional choice and legislative performance (compare, amongst others, Epstein and O'Halloran 1999; Krehbiel 1991). We build on this body of scholarship and consider the dynamics of the legislative process as a function of the transaction costs of legislation, which, in turn, are (amongst other factors) a function of institutional constraints, including the number of relevant decision makers with veto powers or the ability to inflict opportunity costs on the parliamentary majority. Transaction costs can be defined as 'anything that impedes the specification, monitoring, or enforcement of an economic transaction' (Dixit 1996: p.38). Decision making in parliaments can be compared to economic transactions in that it combines (a) potential *gains from exchange* between politicians (for example, beneficial policies that increase the welfare of citizens and re-election chances) and, hence, incentives for cooperation with (b) strong elements of inter-party (electoral) and intra-party *competition* entailing incentives to behave opportunistically.

Buchanan and Tullock (1962: pp.68-69) provide a relevant and plausible intuition about the link between key features of the political system and the transaction costs of decision making by arguing that decision-making costs – time and effort needed to reach an agreement – increase with the number of actors whose consent is required. Based on such a framework, we could generate first hypotheses for the study of the dynamics of the legislative process. We would, for example, expect the cohesiveness of the government to have a systematic impact: For example, the smaller the number of coalition parties and/or relevant factions within government parties, the more likely are government majorities to function as unitary actors in parliamentary systems, the higher will the scope for transaction-cost saving 'majoritarian decision making' (Scharpf 1997a: pp.151-170) and the speedier the legislative process. However, as Buchanan and Tullock also point out, the number of decision makers with veto powers simultaneously influences the 'external costs' of decision making – or agency costs of representation in Brennan and Hamlin's (2000: pp.159-169) formulation: The lower the number of actors whose consent is required for a decision, the higher the external risks and potential costs for those affected by, but not participating in, a decision. This suggests that, from a normative perspective, neither an extremely low nor an extremely high number of veto points is desirable. These arguments are familiar and do not need to be dwelled on here (see Buchanan and Tullock 1962; Sartori 1987; Brennan and Hamlin 2000).

George Tsebelis (2002) goes one step further and provides a theory linking the number of veto players in a political system to its ability to change the policy status quo. Parts of the logic of his argument can be applied to our study of the dynamics of the legislative process, although we are not primarily interested in changes of the legislative status quo, but in the speed in which such changes are accomplished. Tsebelis (1995a: p.301) defines a veto player as 'an individual or collective actor whose agreement (by majority rule for collective actors) is required for a change in policy' and distinguishes between two main types of veto players: (a) *Partisan veto players* are the parties forming a government. Tsebelis specifies the 'micro-mechanisms' to support his theoretical model in which the number and cohesion of, as well as the ideological distance between, partisan veto players are crucial predictors of the possibility to change the legislative status quo. (b) In addition, *institutional veto players* including second chambers or directly elected presidents with significant veto powers can be relevant veto players. Tsebelis's theory is the most precise and elaborate formulation of a body of scholarship on 'veto players', 'veto points', 'veto gates' or 'veto offices' (see, for example, Cowhey and McCubbins 1995) so far, although the terms are often used interchangeably and more liberally than in Tsebelis's work: In a wider sense, which we are employing here, they may also include powerful interest groups, especially in countries with neo-corporatist arrangements, independent central banks, the army, the courts (particularly constitutional courts), constitutionally required super majorities and referendums (for example, Schmidt 1997: p.227).

In the context of the present study, there are good reasons to conceptualise 'veto players' somewhat more liberally than Tsebelis does: Time is a scarce resource in parliamentary life. Therefore legislation always involves opportunity costs for re-election seeking and policy-pursuing politicians: 'The more legislative time taken up refining any one piece of legislation, the less time for introducing other legislation or influencing the administration for existing legislation' (Horn 1995: p.13). Minorities that can use parliamentary procedures to obstruct majority/government legislation may therefore be able to inflict potentially considerable opportunity costs on the majority. Philip Norton (1999) speaks of parliamentary procedure as a 'hidden power' that Members of Parliament and minorities may have – even in the British parliament where government control of the parliamentary agenda is extreme (for example, one should not underestimate the effects of the delaying powers of the House of Lords, which Tsebelis would not count as a veto player). To the extent that minorities can prevent majorities from monopolizing the parliamentary agenda, they may be able to *de facto* exercise a veto, and decision making by majority vote may have to be replaced by negotiated agreement (Scharpf 1997a: pp.116-150) between government and minority groups (with likely implications for the dynamics of the legislative process). Based on these considerations, four broad hypotheses can be formulated:

HYPOTHESIS 1: In analogy to Tsebelis's (1995a: p.297) argument, *we test whether the number of partisan veto players affects the speed of the legislative process negatively.* We expect that the larger the number of partisan veto players (that is, the number of parties in a government coalition) the slower the legislative process and the higher the probability that a bill will fail in the legislative process.

HYPOTHESIS 2: Following Tsebelis's (1999) argument, *we hypothesize that the ideological range of a government coalition will tend to affect the speed of the legislative process negatively.* The stronger the ideological differences between the relatively most 'extreme' government parties on the left and the right of the political spectrum, the more time will be needed to agree on a common policy between all partisan veto players, the slower will be the legislative process.

HYPOTHESIS 3: The logic of Buchanan and Tullock's (1962) collective decision-making theory leads us to *expect the legislative decision-making costs to increase (and the speed of legislation to decrease) with the number of veto points outside the legislature that* parliamentary minorities *can utilize to block, delay or influence policy.* Systems with a large number of veto points outside the parliamentary arena offer more leverage to parliamentary minorities than systems with no or only a few veto points. In the former, parliamentary minorities have a wider choice of strategies to overturn parliamentary majority decisions after the passage of a bill. The more such veto points are available to minorities, the more incentives majorities will have to seek compromises with minorities during the passage of a bill and the larger the amount of time likely to be needed for the passage of legislation (if it is contentious).

HYPOTHESIS 4: *We expect the existence and strength of procedural veto opportunities enjoyed by parliamentary minorities* within the chamber *to affect the speed of the legislative process negatively.* We are mainly examining the extent to which the government and/or parliamentary majority can control the parliamentary agenda both on the floor and in committee. Some parliaments offer minorities very few veto and delaying powers. Others offer minorities considerable powers to co-determine the agenda both on the floor of the chamber and in committee. The existence of such minority powers can be expected to delay the passage of legislation. We also expect the authority of committees to determine their own agenda independent of the government/ majority to affect the speed of the legislative process negatively.

Data and Research Design

The legislative process proper usually begins with the formal introduction of the bill in parliament. In bicameral systems, most bills can usually be introduced in either chamber. Formal introduction often takes the shape of a 'first reading' followed by a stepwise process of deliberation. Often, the general principles of a bill are discussed and decided on, before Members of Parliament focus their attention on questions of detail. This stepwise procedure usually finds its expression in a number of further readings, which are usually interrupted by the detailed examination of a bill in committee. In some parliaments (for example, the German Bundestag) this committee stage takes place before second reading, in which many parliaments decide on the objectives and principles of the bill. In other parliaments (like in the British House of Commons) the floor majority decides on the main principles in a second reading, before it sends it to a committee thus restricting the possibilities of changes at the committee stage to questions of detail (of course the 'devil' may be in the detail). The third reading on the floor of the House usually deals with the amendments proposed at committee stage. This stage ensures that the floor majority remains in overall control of the bill and allows for final amendments, before the chamber decides on the final shape of the bill as a whole, usually in a final-passage vote or a number of votes. In bicameral systems, a similar process then ensues in the other chamber. If there is disagreement between the majorities in the two chambers, a 'ping-pong type' process might ensue in 'navette systems', while other parliaments may use a conference committee to resolve the differences. Alternatively, one chamber (usually the directly elected one) can overturn the veto of the other chamber after a certain period and/or provided certain majority requirements are fulfilled (compare Tsebelis and Money 1997).

Of course we are aware of the fact that the legislative process proper is usually preceded by a *pre-legislative stage* of policy gestation, formulation and initiation, in which Western European parliaments as political bodies are rarely the main actors. This stage is dominated by the government, ministerial administrations, interest groups, think tanks and other experts, although political parties inside and outside parliament may also play an important role. After a bill's formal passage through parliament, it usually enters what we might refer to as a '*post-legislative*' stage. It usually requires the signature of the head of state, before it can be promulgated. Some heads of state have certain veto powers or powers to delay the enactment of a bill. In some systems, the bill may be challenged in, and thrown out by, a constitutional court. In some countries (for example, Germany), parliamentary minorities may be able to use the constitutional court as a veto point where a bill can be stopped or delayed. The post-legislative stage also encompasses the phase of implementation. In some federal systems (especially in Germany), the implementation of many bills may be left to sub-national tiers of government, especially the federal states and their bureaucracies. Again, control of such sub-national tiers of government may provide parties, which are in a minority at the national level, with important veto powers. This may have reverberations for the legislative process itself as national governments anticipate such problems and may have incentives to engage in time-consuming bargaining with minority parties at the national level in order to ensure a speedy implementation of legislation. In the present chapter, our attention is focused strictly on the process from a bill's formal introduction to its promulgation (that is, including formal assent, for example, by the head of state), although the data set used does contain some information in the pre- and post-legislative stages.

In the present study, the legislative process in parliaments will be treated both as a single unit ('episode') and a multi-stage process broken down into several intervals. In the latter case (multiple-episode models), the legislative process will be analyzed in four different stages, (1) a pre-committee stage in the (temporally) first chamber, (2) a committee stage in the first chamber, (3) a post-committee stage in the first chamber and (4) the deliberations in the (temporally) second chamber and between the chambers in the case of disagreement in bicameral legislatures. These four episodes provide a simplified sequential model representing key elements of the legislative process described above; they are designed to accommodate the entire variety of different processes in the parliaments included as these processes are not completely uniform (for example, there may be one or two readings before committee stage, depending on the parliament). The deliberations in the second chamber will be treated as a single episode, because the total number of bills failing in the (temporally) second chamber is very low (see Figure 3.3). In the following, we are distinguishing between the time a bill is pending in the 'first' and 'second' chamber. In the terminology employed for the purposes of this work, the terms 'first' and 'second' refer merely to the temporal order in which a bill is introduced in one of the chambers of a bicameral system. They do not say anything about the preponderance of one chamber over the other.

The analyses of this process in the 17 Western European parliaments are based on data collected for the comparative project 'study of the Parliamentary Passage of Legislation, 1981-1991' (SPPL) on which this volume is based. The data set contains detailed information on the legislative process for 494 successful acts of parliament and 156 bills that failed in the legislative process in 18 Western European parliaments between 1981 and 1991. The bills deal with issues of working time and working conditions as well as social security legislation. The successful bills were identified using the very comprehensive labour and social security law data base NATLEX compiled by the International Labour Office (ILO) in Geneva (for a description of the data base and the sample see Scholz and Trantas 1995). To eliminate one source of sample selection bias, a random sample of these successful bills drawn from NATLEX was supplemented by 156 bills from the same policy areas that failed in the legislative process. These bills were selected by the country experts who collected detailed data on both the successful and failed bills.[1] Apart from a vast amount of information on the nature and history of each bill as well as the political circumstances of its introduction, the data set contains – for most cases – the precise dates for their passage through the various stages of the legislative process. It is therefore possible for us to reconstruct the 'biographies' of individual bills at all their major stages. Due to missing values the sample for our descriptive analyses is 639 bills and for the more complex event-history analyses 597 cases. Unfortunately, data on France could not be used for the purposes of our analyses, because many of the temporal data we require are

1 It would have been desirable to introduce weights ensuring that the ratio of successful to unsuccessful bills in our sample is proportional to the ratio in the population. At the time of writing it turned out to be extremely difficult to obtain such data for all parliaments in our sample. We (Becker and Saalfeld 2003) intend to pursue this issue in further analyses.

missing. In practice, therefore, our investigation is restricted to 17 Western European countries.

In order to test *Hypotheses 1 and 2*, a number of variables were created and added to the SPPL data set. First, we established for each individual bill the party composition of the government at the time of the bill's formal introduction and hence the *number* of partisan veto players at this point in time (for the testing of Hypothesis 1).[2] In a second step (in order to test Hypothesis 2), we calculated the *ideological range* between the parties in government using Laver and Hunt's (1992) data about the ideological position of political party leaderships on a single left-right continuum during the late 1980s. Laver and Hunt's data are based on expert interviews for 17 out of 18 party systems in our study (the exception being Switzerland, for which data are missing). We used Laver and Hunt's first (most salient) ideological dimension, which was 'increase services vs. cut taxes' for 16 out of 17 cases. Only for Luxembourg the most important dimension was 'pro public ownership', which we used in this case because of its greater salience. The ideological range for single-party governments was recoded as '0'. For all other cases, the range was calculated by subtracting the score on a twenty-point scale of the relatively most left-wing party from the relatively most right-wing party in the coalition.[3]

In order to estimate the cumulative effect of the number of institutional veto points outside parliament – but available to parliamentary minorities seeking to increase their political leverage (*Hypothesis 3*) – we use Schmidt's (1997: p.252) additive six-item index of constraints on government (with a range of 1-5 in our sample of countries). Low values indicate no or few institutional constraints on the government; high values indicate numerous and more severe constraints. This index is based on the non-weighted summation of the following dummy variables: Government constrained by membership of the European Union (yes=1),[4] degree of territorial centralization (federal system=1), supermajorities required for constitutional amendments (1 for particularly high thresholds), powerful second

2 If a bill was introduced between the termination of one and the formation of the next cabinet, it was attributed to the earlier cabinet (which usually stayed in power in a caretaker function). This applied only to a very small number of bills when the government formation process took a relatively long time, for example for the cabinets under Goria in Italy 1987-88 and between two cabinets formed by Ruud Lubbers in the Netherlands in 1989.

3 Tsebelis (1999: pp.606-607) arguably provides a more sophisticated composite index of inter-party differences based on standardized averages derived from Laver and Hunt's scales and two further sources (compare Tsebelis 1999: p.599). We decided not to use it, because Tsebelis's data set does not include values for Iceland and Switzerland. (There may be a valid constitutional argument to exclude Switzerland, but we nevertheless decided to include the country for the purposes of this study, which deals with a large number of constitutional variables other than partisan veto players.)

4 Adjustments were made for countries that were not members of the European Community at the time of the formal introduction of a bill.

chamber (yes=1), independent central bank (yes=1), extensive use of referendums (yes=1).[5]

An important set of independent variables used to test *Hypothesis 4* refers to the structures and institutional rules of the respective parliaments, which may provide minorities with a veto over procedure in the legislative process that can be converted into influence over the substance of a bill. Based on Döring's (1995c) work we distinguish the extent to which the parliamentary timetable and hence the legislative process is centralized (that is, the number of parliamentary 'veto players' reduced) and controlled by the parliamentary majority (that is, usually a government majority). Following the logic of Buchanan and Tullock's analysis (see above), our working hypothesis would be that the more centralized the control is in the hands of the government majority, the better the survival chances for government bills and the speedier the process of legislation.

One independent variable in this context is the extent to which the control of the floor agenda is centralized, especially in the hands of the government or majority. We use Döring's (1995e: p.684) index measuring each parliament's authority to determine the plenary agenda independent of the government. This index is based on factor scores (for explanations see Döring 1995e). The higher the index scores the stronger the opportunities of parliamentary *minorities* to influence the floor agenda. With very high scores, minorities may be vested with significant veto powers preventing the government from setting the agenda unilaterally. The higher the index scores, therefore, the slower should be the speed of legislation.

We shall also investigate the importance of time limits for the legislative process. In particular, is there a *principle of discontinuity* where a bill 'dies' if it is not passed within a legislative term. Our expectation would be that the existence of discontinuity helps to speed up the legislative process. The existence of deadlines will have an impact on the bargaining process. We know from bargaining theory that the player who controls the agenda and is in a position to make the last offer shortly before a deadline is in a very strong bargaining position vis-à-vis other players (Rasmusen 1989: pp.280-281). Therefore, the existence of discontinuity in the legislative process will tend to strengthen whoever controls the parliamentary agenda. We should expect the speed of the legislative process to vary systematically with the rigidity of the time limit in parliaments with a principle of discontinuity. For example, the pressure on legislators is higher in the British case with one-year legislative sessions (during our period of observation) than in Germany, where the principle of discontinuity also applies, but the legislative session is a full four-year parliamentary term or in the Netherlands, where bills can be carried over to a new parliament. Therefore, the legislative process in Britain should be speedier than in Germany; the German process, in turn, should be speedier than the one in the Netherlands. Information on discontinuity rules is

5 A more satisfactory approach would have been to introduce dummy variables for the existence of certain institutional veto points. This approach was tested in an earlier version of this paper. However, due to missing observations and other problems, this approach led to the loss of too many cases.

provided by Döring (1995c: p.242). Based on this information, we created a dummy variable comparing the effect of Category I ('Bills die at the end of session [6 months – 1 year]') as the strictest form of discontinuity rule with a reference category collapsing Döring's Categories II ('Bills lapse at the end of legislative term of 4-5 years'), III ('Bills usually lapse at the end of legislative term but carrying over possible') and IV ('Bills never die [except when rejected by a vote]'). For some analyses we distinguished between all three categories, using category III as the reference group.

Committees usually play an important part in the legislative process. Therefore, it seems useful to supplement the first two variables on agenda control on the floor with at least one variable capturing the extent of majority agenda control in committees. We use Mattson and Strøm's (1995: p.299) index scores measuring the committees' authority to determine their own agenda independent of government control. Similar to the variable measuring control of the floor agenda, we would expect a speedier legislative process with better success chances for bills where the committee's independence is low.

Control variables

In addition to the variables that are of substantive interest, the models estimated below include a number of other variables, which are not of primary concern for the purpose of this chapter, but which are likely to have a systematic and predictable impact on the speed of the legislative process: the initiator of the bill, its length and the point in the legislative session at which the bill is introduced. Where we look at individual stages of the legislative process, we also control for bills whose committee stage was taken in a 'Committee of the Whole House', whose decisive reading was before committee stage and which were subject to restrictive rules invoked by the majority. In bicameral parliaments we also control for the chamber in which the bill was first introduced. These influences are to be controlled for statistically in order to estimate the net effect of the substantive variables more accurately.

First, we distinguish between bills that were introduced by the government or a government parliamentary party and bills that were not. We expect government bills to go through more speedily and with higher success chances than other bills, because governments control the agenda. Second, we control for the length and complexity of the law using the number of articles/clauses of the bill as a proxy measure. The longer and more complex the text of the bill, the longer the legislative process is predicted to take. Data on both control variables mentioned above are included in the SPPL data set. Third, we created a variable measuring the time difference between a bill's formal introduction and elections to the next parliament. This control variable is used to account for the fact that bills tend to get rushed through parliament towards the end of a parliamentary session, especially in parliaments where the measure is lost if it is not passed within the respective session. The electoral dates were extracted from Keesing's Contemporary Archives.

The following control variables are mainly relevant to our study of the individual stages of the legislative process in what we refer to as a 'multiple-episode design' (see above). The data for all these control variables are included in the SPPL data set. In order to avoid misleading parameter estimates, we created a dummy variable for bills that were first introduced in the Upper House assuming that this could have a delaying effect on the passage of a bill in the temporally second chamber (in this case, the Lower House).[6] While we expect bills first introduced in, and passed by, the Lower House generally to go through the temporally second chamber relatively quickly (although we are aware that this need not always be the case), we predict the process in the temporally second chamber may be more long drawn-out, if the elected Lower House is the temporally second chamber in the sequence of the legislative process.

We assume that all stages of the legislative process will be affected by a parliament's decision to take the committee stage in a Committee of the Whole House, that is, in practice, the plenary (although the rules of procedure may be different from plenary sessions). In particular, we expect the committee stage to be longer than in a regular legislative committee. Therefore a dummy variable was created for bills whose committee stage was taken in a Committee of the Whole House.

There is also a possibility that the length of committee stage and the duration of the preceding plenary stages are affected by the question whether or not the decisive plenary reading takes place before or after committee stage. In order to maintain comparability of the 'life cycles' of bills in different parliaments with different institutional arrangements, we simply distinguished between a pre-committee, committee and post-committee stage. This might lead to misleading estimations for some of the individual stages of the legislative process if we did not control for the timing of the decisive plenary reading. Therefore we created a dummy variable for bills whose decisive reading was before committee stage.

Finally, we assume that the duration of the process and the effectiveness of agenda control may be influenced by the question whether or not the majority actually invoked restrictive procedures (such as allocation of time motions) in order to control the parliamentary agenda. To be sure, the mere existence of such rules may have an impact in itself, influencing the strategic options available to minorities, but the actual use of such procedures remains a factor that needs to be controlled for. We therefore created a dummy variable, which takes a value of one if the government invoked a restrictive rule asserting its agenda control during at least one decisive plenary reading.

---

6 In order to be able to compare the sequence and temporal dynamics of the legislative process, we did not eliminate bills that were first introduced in the Upper House. Instead, we decided to include a variable controlling for the possible effects of this factor on other (substantively more interesting) institutional variables.

Methods

The SPPL data allow the reconstruction of event histories, that is, they provide a longitudinal record of the occurrence of events such as the passage of a bill at a particular stage of the legislative process. These event histories allow dynamic longitudinal analyses with the help of techniques often referred to as survival and event-history analysis (Blossfeld and Rohwer 1995; Tuma and Hannan 1984). For each bill and each stage (episode) of the legislative process, the starting and end time (in days) are recorded. For each bill, we have information at what stage of the legislative process and on what day a bill passed to the next stage or failed. These events allow to determine the structure of the legislative process. In addition, event-history analysis allows to estimate the impact of institutional rules, structures and events in the 'biography' of a bill on the probability for it to be passed or to fail at any point in time. Duration dependence at the individual stages of the legislative process allows to identify mechanisms (a) speeding up or delaying legislation and (b) influencing the probability of success or failure.

While the results of comparative-static analyses depend on the particular point in time at which a particular event is observed, techniques of survival and event-history analysis permit us to model dynamic processes, that is, temporal sequences of states and events, which are contingent on each other. In the context of the present study, the duration of the legislative process (our dependent variable) is often measured using measures of central tendency, while other variables may have to be measured at a particular point in time such as the beginning of the legislative term. Subsequent changes and the institutional dynamics occurring within the lifetime of a parliament (for cabinet duration see, for example, Lupia and Strøm 1995) cannot be taken into account adequately (see Blossfeld and Rohwer 1997).

Our analysis treats legislation as a stochastic process. The occurrence of relevant events such as the passage or failure of a bill is not deterministic, but probabilistic. The conditional probability of an event occurring in a particular interval – for example the success or failure of a bill at committee stage – can be expressed as a 'transition rate'. Changes in transition rates indicate causal effects (Blossfeld and Rohwer 1997: p.369; Coleman 1981: p.16).

The transition rate describes the following basic causal effect:

$$\Delta X_t \rightarrow \Delta \Pr(\Delta Y_{t'}), t < t'.$$

A change in the time-dependent covariate X_t will change the probability (ΔPr) that the dependent variable $Y_{t'}$ will change in the future ($t < t'$). A relatively simple descriptive technique is 'survival analysis', which helps to estimate the duration of a bill in the legislative process from its introduction to its successful adoption or failure. It also allows the production of graphic illustrations of the respective survival function. This non-parametric method enables us to compare the development and speed of processes in different phases and contexts. Especially the Kaplan-Meier estimation is appropriate for such purposes. This method estimates the median time until an event occurs in a given time interval as well as statistics for the significance of differences between the survival functions for different groups (for example, parliaments or systems of government).

For more complex analyses we are going to use multivariate models. In order to describe the distribution of durations and events, the transition rate $r(t)$ is defined as the limit of the conditional probability for an event to occur, that is, under the condition that a particular event has not yet occurred in the interval $t, t + \Delta t$:

$$r(t) = \lim_{\substack{\Delta t \to 0 \\ \Delta t > 0}} \frac{P(t \leq t + \Delta t \mid T \leq t)}{\Delta t}$$

where $r(t)$ (sometimes also referred to as $\lambda(t)$) is the transition rate or hazard rate, that is, the probability that an individual (in our case a bill) experiences an event (for example, the failure of a legislative proposal) in the interval from t to $t + \Delta t$, provided the individual is at risk at time t. In our context, the relevant event is the survival of a bill from its formal introduction to its successful passage (dependent variable). Those bills that failed in the process remain in the analysis and are treated as censored cases. The transition rate $r(t)$ is a mathematical function of time accounting for the fact that most transition rates vary across time – they can be said to be 'time dependent' (Rohwer 1994: p.89). In our survival analyses we treat the transition rate only as a descriptive method for a risk set (for example, a number of bills that are still 'at risk' of failing to be passed) at time t.

In order to estimate the impact of any covariates, a baseline hazard rate needs to be specified. This requires a theoretical expectation about the distribution of the probabilities of an event occurring over time. The general transition rate can be estimated by a class of different models, some of which are usually referred to as 'semi-parametric', some of which are termed 'parametric' models (compare Blossfeld and Rohwer 1995). This chapter will rely on parametric models. A further distinction can be made between single-episode and multiple-episode models. In the former case, the entire legislative process will be analyzed as a single 'window' of observation. No distinction will be made between different stages of the legislative process. The statistical model will be specified as a log-logistic one assuming a bell-shaped distribution of the hazard rate specified above:

$$r(t) = \frac{ba^b t^{b-1}}{1 + (at)^b}$$

With $b \leq 1$ for the independent variables, the hazard rate declines monotonously, with $b > 1$ it rises monotonously and declines monotonously after reaching a maximum. Due to the sometimes very short duration of the process in individual stages of the multiple-episode models, we have chosen to use an exponential model for the multiple-episode estimations, that is, we assume a constant risk for each episode and proportional risks for the total legislative process. The hazard rate can be specified as follows:

$$r(t \mid x(t)) = \exp(\beta' x(t)),$$

where $x(t)$ is the time-dependent vector of the exogenous covariates. This model specification has proved to be useful in a number of social-scientific investigations (see Browne et al. 1984; King et al. 1990), although alternative models have now become common in the study of coalition duration (see Warwick 1994).

Findings

The empirical analyses in this chapter focus on the time each bill in our sample spends at each stage of the parliamentary deliberation process. In order to make adjustments for the different procedures in each of our 17 Western European parliaments, a common simplified 'grid' of four legislative stages had to be developed (see above). In the following, we distinguish between the time a bill is pending in the 'first' and 'second' chamber. As noted above, the terms 'first' and 'second' refer merely to the temporal order in which a bill is introduced in one of the chambers. The focus of our analysis then remains on the first chamber where we distinguish between a pre-committee (including all readings before the committee deliberations), a committee and a post-committee stage (including all readings and report stages after committee deliberations). Given the general empirical dominance of the (temporally) first chamber (see below), the passage through the second chamber is not broken down into different episodes.

The Lives and Times of Bills: Infant Mortality and Ageing Processes

Let us first get some general idea about the dynamics of the legislative process in all 17 parliaments treating it as a single episode. Figure 3.1 presents the survivor function for all our – successful and unsuccessful – bills in the areas of working hours, working conditions and social security benefits. In our case the survivor function is the probability that a bill is in the legislative process at any given point in time starting with its introduction. It demonstrates clearly that the likelihood of success and the speed of the process are not random, but highly time-dependent. During the first four months the share of bills pending in the legislative process declines strongly. After that phase, the dynamic is clearly reduced, which is expressed in a much 'flatter' slope of the curve. It can be surmised that delays are increasingly likely for complex or contentious bills as the duration of the process increases. The critical phase in the 'biography' of most bills is usually the early stages of their 'lives'. This is illustrated in Figure 3.2, which plots the hazard rate for successful and failed bills. The hazard function for successful bills is bell shaped and follows a log-logistic pattern. The hazard rate for failed bills, by contrast, decreases monotonously like the Weibull or Gompertz-Makeham distributions. Successful bills display a stronger dynamic. In the first four months the conditional probability of a bill passing all parliamentary hurdles increases quickly. Afterwards, the success rate decreases. With increasing duration (tenure) of a pending bill, failure becomes likelier. Because of the considerable dynamic during the first months, we expect interesting institutional variations between different sub-populations and phases of the legislative process.

Let us now turn to the multiple-episode perspective. Figure 3.3 is based on the full risk set of 575 bills (that is, excluding cases with missing values) and illustrates the simplified model of stages of the legislative process used in our chapter. It provides information about how many bills entered a particular stage, how many were passed and how many failed (in absolute numbers and as percentage) at the respective stage. Out of a total of 575 bills introduced 434 (75.5 per cent) were ultimately passed by parliament, 24.5 per cent failed. In bicameral parliaments the (temporally) first chamber is the decisive hurdle for the vast majority of bills. Only 5.1 per cent of the 277 bills going to the (temporally) second chamber failed there.

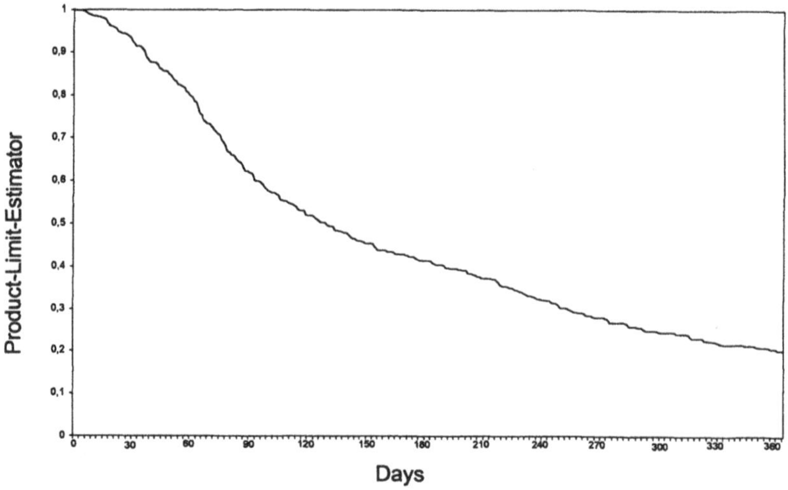

Figure 3.1 Survivor Function of Bills in 17 Western European Parliaments (1981-1991)

Source: SPPL – own calculations

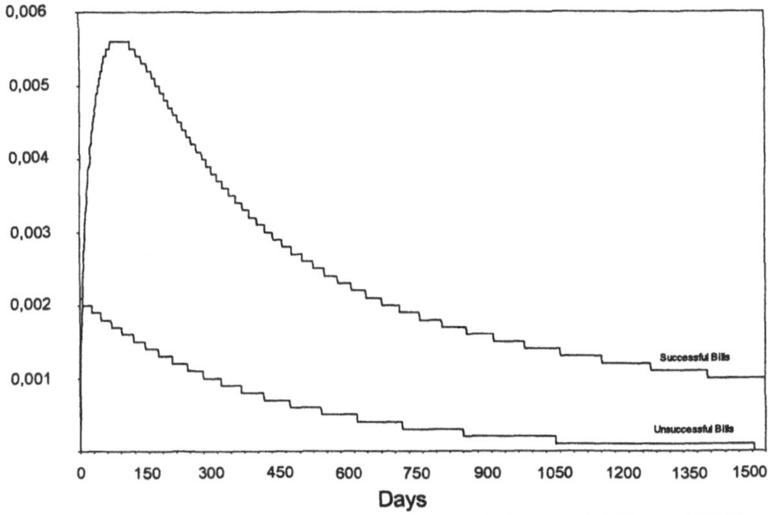

Figure 3.2 Hazard Functions for Success and Failure of Bills in 17 Western European Parliaments (1981-1991)
Source: SPPL – own calculations

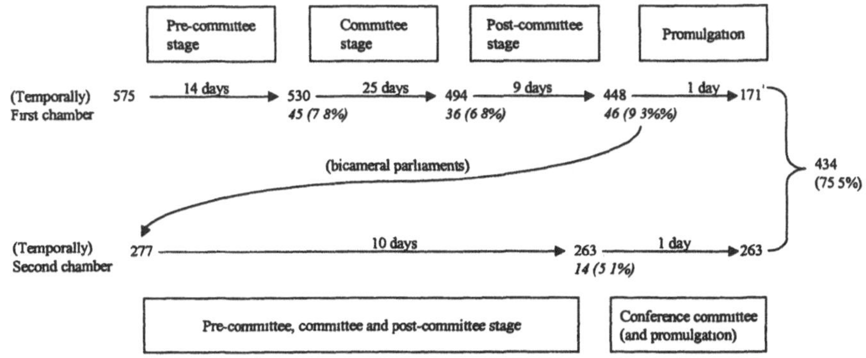

Median duration for the entire process 128 days

Complete-case analysis In italics Bills failing at each stage as number and percentage of all bills entering that stage Time median of days.

Figure 3.3 The Legislative Process in 17 Western European Parliaments (1981-1991)
Source: SPPL – own calculations

More than 7 per cent of the 575 bills failed before they reached committee stage in the first chamber. A further 6.8 per cent failed during committee stage in that chamber; more than 9 per cent of all bills failed after committee stage. For 171 bills introduced in unicameral parliaments, this constituted the end of the parliamentary process. The remaining 277 bills introduced were in bicameral parliaments and had to overcome the hurdle of deliberations in the (temporally) second chamber. Only 14 out of 277 (5.1 per cent) of those bills going to the second chamber failed there. None of the bills in our sample failed in a conference committee or because a head of state refused to give assent to the bill ('conference committee and promulgation').

Figure 3.3 also provides information on the median duration of the different stages of the legislative process. The median for the entire process is about 128 days, that is, 50 per cent of the 575 bills were passed within slightly more than four months. The fact that median duration of the individual stages (14 days for the pre-committee stage, 25 days for the committee stage and 9 days for the post-committee stage of the first chamber; 10 days for deliberations in the temporally second chamber and one day for conference committee deliberations and promulgation) indicates that a great deal of time is 'lost' *between the different stages*. The aggregate median duration of the individual stages is 59 days, 69 days less than the median value for the entire legislative process. In practical terms this means that 'streamlining' procedures in committees and other devices to control time during legislative deliberations would not necessarily cut down the time needed for legislative deliberations. More time seems to be lost, for instance, while bills were 'waiting' to be dealt with by a committee. The experience of British parliamentarism shows that a great deal of delays may actually be a result of inadequate drafting by the government requiring adjustments during the parliamentary process rather than inefficient parliamentary structures as such (Constitution Unit 2000: p.1).[7] Also, in some parliaments there is a required minimum time between the different stages (for example in the United Kingdom). If parliamentary reformers wanted to speed up the legislative process, (further) centralization of agenda control might not always be the most efficient way of achieving speedy legislation. General improvements in timetabling or 'programming' may be more effective.

These simple descriptive findings allow some interesting conclusions. First, the greatest dynamic in the 'biography' of bills is at the early stages. The durations in the different phases and the survival chances resemble patterns of infant mortality in biology or the 'liability of newness' frequently found in organizational studies (compare Hannan and Freeman 1989). From the perspective of procedural efficiency the legislative process seems to be relatively 'rational' in most cases of our sample. Bills with low survival chances (for example private members' or

---

7 The authors of this report of the London-based Constitution Unit, a leading constitutional-reform think tank, elaborate: 'The summer's pile up of bills is the worst that Whitehall insiders can remember ... Who is really to blame? Perhaps the Lords could streamline their procedure, and this is likely to be reviewed in the near future ... But the originators of the logjam are the government. They plan each session's legislative programme in Cabinet committee, which is where collective discipline has broken down. Bills are allowed into the legislative programme which are insufficiently prepared, and then subjected to rafts of government amendments as they go through parliament.'

opposition bills) tend to fail at a relatively early stage of the legislative process allowing more time for the deliberation of bills that actually stand a chance to be passed.

Explanatory Variables

The following tables (3.2-3.11) provide the unstandardized coefficients for multivariate single-episode analyses estimating multivariate log-logistic models for the various independent variables (covariates) described in the third section as well as estimations for the individual stages of the legislative process (multiple-episode analyses).

Table 3.2 Effects of Partisan Veto Players on the Success of Legislation on Working Conditions, Working Hours and Social Security Benefits in 17 Western European Countries, 1981-1991 – Log-logistic model (single episode-estimates; in parentheses: standard error of β-coefficients)

Independent Variables	Model 1a	Model 2a
Constant	-5.5138***	-5.4845***
	(0.1818)	(0.1679)
Bill initiated by government or government party	1.0510***	1.0423***
	(0.1598)	(0.1601)
Length of bill	-0.0025*	-0.0025*
	(0.0012)	(0.0012)
Time until the end of CIEP	-0.0010***	-0.0010***
	(0.0001)	(0.0001)
Number of parties in government	0.0320†	
	(0.0358)	
Ideological distance between veto players		0.0139
		(0.0144)
Time dependence	0.5082***	0.5088***
	(0.0398)	(0.0398)
Chi²	274.4	274.4
Degrees of Freedom	4	4
Events	434	434
Number of Cases	575	575

* $p \leq 0.05$; ** $p \leq 0.01$; *** $p \leq 0.001$; † $p \leq 0.1$

Source: SPPL – own calculations

Partisan Veto Players (Hypotheses 1 and 2) Model 1a (Table 3.2) estimates the effect of four covariates on the hazard rate of a bill's successful passage treating the entire legislative process as a single episode. Three of these covariates are to control for the effects of general characteristics of the respective bill, which may have a strong influence on the dependent variable, but are not of major substantive interest in terms of the veto player model on which our hypothesis is based. These covariates are a dummy variable with a value of '1', if the bill in question was introduced by the government or a government party, the word count of a bill as a measure of its length and complexity and the timing of a bill, that is, the temporal proximity of its formal introduction to the end of the CIEP (see above).

Treating the entire legislative process as a single episode, Models 1a and 2a confirm our expectations as far as our three control variables are concerned. They all have a significant influence on the hazard rate, and this influence is in the expected causal direction (Table 3.2).[8] Positive signs indicate higher speed as well as higher chances of successful passage. Negative signs indicate the opposite. Thus, if the government introduces a bill, its success chances are (unsurprisingly) significantly higher than those of non-government bills, and government bills have a better chance to get passed quickly. The complexity and length of a bill is significantly – and, as expected, negatively – related to both the chances of passage and the speed of the process. The same is true for the period between a bill's formal introduction and the end of the CIEP: The longer this time (in days), the slower the process and the lower the chances of successful passage. It is worth pointing out at this stage that the impact of these control variables remains relatively stable throughout this chapter whatever the model specification and, at least to a very large extent, irrespective of whether we analyze the process in a single-episode or a multiple-episode design.

However, the variable that interests us most in theoretical terms, the number of partisan veto players and the maximal ideological range between them, does not have a significant negative influence on the hazard rate of successful passage at a 5 per cent level of significance. Whether a bill is introduced under a one-party government with an ideological range of zero or a multi-party coalition cabinet with a considerable ideological range does not have any significant impact on the likelihood of a bill's successful passage, or indeed on the speed of passage, if we look at the entire legislative process (one episode).

---

8 The estimated beta coefficients are difficult to interpret. For a more intuitive interpretation we first need to calculate the (natural) antilog of the estimated beta coefficient (=alpha coefficient). In a second step we subtract 1 from the alpha coefficient and multiply the result by 100. The result is the probability that a one-unit increase of the independent variable accelerates a process by the calculated rate. Let us consider the estimated beta of -0.0025 for the control variable 'Length of bill' as an example: The antilog of -0.0025 is 0.999. From this value we subtract 1. The result is -0.00249. If we multiply this value by 100, the result is -0.249. This means that each additional clause (the unit of the independent variable) reduces the probability of a bill's successful passage in any given time interval by 0.249 per cent.

Table 3.3 Effects of the Number of Partisan Veto Players on the Success of Legislation on Working Conditions, Working Hours and Social Security Benefits in 17 Western European Countries, 1981-1991 – Log-logistic model (multiple episode-estimates; in parentheses: standard error of β-coefficients)

Independent Variables	Stage 1 Pre-Committee	Stage 2 Committee	Stage 3 Post-Committee	Stage 4 2nd Chamber	Log-Likelihood
Reference model without	-3.8575***	-4.6349***	-3.4307***	-3.5865***	-4801.8210
covariates	(0.0568)	(0.0614)	(0.0654)	(0.0774)	
Model 1b					
Constant	-4.1088***	-3.7822***	-5.3023***	-2.7745***	-4458.7055
	(0.1914)	(0.2493)	(0.2778)	(0.3892)	
Bill initiated by government	0.6586***	0.2183	1.5625***	0.6858*	
or government party	(0.1586)	(0.1773)	(0.2395)	(0.2916)	
Length of bill	-0.0040*	-0.0057*	-0.0040†	-0.0021	
	(0.0018)	(0.0021)	(0.0024)	(0.0024)	
Time until the end of CIEP	-0.0012***	-0.0014***	-0.0002	0.0001	
	(0.0001)	(0.0001)	(0.0002)	(0.0002)	
Bill first introduced in Upper	-0.7523**	0.1238	-0.2957	-0.4893*	
House	(0.2135)	(0.2097)	(0.2309)	(0.2415)	
Committee stage in	2.2074***	0.1212	0.4865**	1.9289***	
Committee of the Whole	(0.1613)	(0.1715)	(0.1795)	(0.2164)	
House					
Decisive reading before	-0.6316***	0.2776	0.3519*	-1.4646***	
committee stage	(0.1743)	(0.1714)	(0.1784)	(0.2024)	
Number of parties in	0.2184**	-0.0423	0.3714***	-0.4147***	
government	(0.0632)	(0.0669)	(0.0592)	(0.0716)	

$p \leq 0.05$; ** $p \leq 0.01$; *** $p \leq 0.001$; † $p \leq 0.1$
Source: SPPL – own calculations

As mentioned above, the one-episode perspective refers to the entire legislative process from a bill's formal introduction to formal assent. One of the main findings of section 5.1 is, however, that bills 'spend' more time pending between than within the individual legislative stages. Event-history analysis allows us to examine the individual stages of the legislative process using a technique usually referred to as episode splitting. Table 3.3 (Model 1b) presents the estimates of the impact of each covariate used in Model 1a on the speed and success chances of all bills in the respective risk set during each of the main stages of the legislative process defined in the third section of this chapter. In order to control for the effect of potentially important institutional 'deviations' from the simplified sequential model of the legislative process we are including the three control variables discussed above in section 3.

The variable 'number of parties in government' does not have the expected effect in the chamber where the bill was first introduced. There are significant effects for the pre-committee and post-committee stages, but the sign is not in the expected direction. Only for the (temporally) second chamber, we find a significant delaying effect of an increasing number of partisan veto players.

The variable 'ideological distance between partisan veto players' is an alternative operationalization of partisan veto players. Table 3.4 is an attempt to test Hypothesis 2 in a multiple-episode design. The maximal ideological distance between partisan veto players does have the expected delaying influence in three out of four stages now (except in the post-committee stage of the temporally first chamber), although the parameter estimates are statistically insignificant at the five per cent level. Only at the committee stage, the estimated coefficients are at least significant at the 10 per cent level. We therefore find little evidence to support Hypotheses 1 and 2. Once a bill has completed the pre-parliamentary stage and reaches the parliamentary stage, the differences between coalition partners seem, on the whole, to have been ironed out in conflict management bodies, and coalition governments are virtually as cohesive as single-party governments. Nevertheless, there are at least three general lessons from these findings, which will resurface throughout the remainder of this chapter:

- Variables that have no significant effect on the overall process may have a significant effect on the individual episodes (here: stages) of the legislative process and *vice versa*.
- The two main independent variables do not have a uniform impact for all stages. There may be stages of the process where the respective variable has a significant accelerating impact, stages where the impact is insignificant and stages where the same variable has a significant delaying impact. These findings, which will re-surface in other models below, point to different 'logics' of decision making at different stages, especially in committee and on the floor of the chamber, which may not be captured very well by our fairly general veto players model. In other words, the same variables may accelerate the legislative process on the floor of the chamber, but slow it down in committee or *vice versa*.

Table 3.4 Effects of the Maximum Ideological Distance between Partisan Veto Players on the Success of Legislation on Working Conditions, Working Hours and Social Security Benefits in 17 Western European Countries, 1981-1991 – Log-logistic model (multiple episode-estimates; in parentheses: standard error of β-coefficients)

Independent Variables	Stage 1 Pre-Committee	Stage 2 Committee	Stage 3 Post-Committee	Stage 4 2nd Chamber	Log-Likelihood
Reference model without covariates	-3.8575*** (0.0568)	-4.6349*** (0.0614)	-3.4307*** (0.0654)	-3.5865*** (0.0774)	-4801.8210
Model 2b					
Constant	-3.7124*** (0.1568)	-3.7204*** (0.2085)	-5.0432*** (0.2748)	-4.2722*** (0.3158)	-4474.7179
Bill initiated by government or government party	0.7098*** (0.1614)	0.2443 (0.1766)	1.6302*** (0.2409)	1.2051*** (0.2786)	
Length of bill	-0.0042** (0.0017)	-0.0050* (0.0022)	-0.0068** (0.0024)	-0.0014 (0.0022)	
Time until the end of CIEP	-0.0011*** (0.0001)	-0.0015*** (0.0002)	0.0001 (0.0002)	0.0001 (0.0002)	
Bill first introduced in Upper House	-0.4682* (0.2018)	0.0200 (0.2027)	-0.0128 (0.2267)	-0.8403** (0.2341)	
Committee stage in Committee of the Whole House	2.0655*** (0.1565)	0.0607 (0.1685)	0.4337* (0.1775)	2.1947*** (0.2158)	
Decisive reading before committee stage	-0.8582*** (0.1724)	0.2095 (0.1707)	0.3203† (0.1767)	-1.0206*** (0.2067)	
Ideological distance between partisan veto players	-0.0035 (0.0222)	-0.0423† (0.0235)	0.1684*** (0.0232)	-0.0188 (0.0298)	

$p \leq 0.05$; ** $p \leq 0.01$; *** $p \leq 0.001$; † $p \leq 0.1$
Source: SPPL – own calculations

The Sum of Institutional Veto Points (Hypothesis 3) Model 3a in Table 3.5 tests the hypothesis that the sum of veto points or veto players in a political system has a cumulative delaying effect on the legislative process. The more institutional veto points (assuming that the scope for conflicts of interest between them will increase with their number), the more difficult is any change of the status quo and the slower is the process of legislation. The Schmidt index we are using here as an operationalization reflects the extent to which Western European states are generally subject to constitutional constraints (defined by their general ability to veto or delay government policy). Table 3.5 (Model 3a) shows that the number of institutional veto points has no significant impact on the speed and success chances of legislation, if we treat the legislative process as a single episode. Since there is very little change in the estimates for our control variables, we are not commenting on them in this or indeed in the following sections. The results can be viewed in Table 3.5 and have been commented on in section 5.2.1.

Table 3.5 Effects of Sum of Institutional Veto Points on the Success of Legislation on Working Conditions, Working Hours and Social Security Benefits in 17 Western European Countries, 1981-1991 – Log-logistic model (single episode-estimates; in parentheses: standard error of β-coefficients)

Independent Variables	Model 3a
Constant	-5.4864***
	(0.1666)
Bill initiated by government	1.0533***
or government party	(0.1593)
Length of bill	-0.0027*
	(0.0012)
Time until the end of CIEP	-0.0011***
	(0.0001)
Sum of institutional veto points	0.0412
	(0.0394)
Time dependence	0.5084***
	(0.0398)
Chi²	274.6
Degrees of Freedom	4
Events	434
Number of Cases	575

* $p \leq 0.05$; ** $p \leq 0.01$; *** $p \leq 0.001$; † $p \leq 0.1$
Source: SPPL – own calculations

If we break the legislative process down into its main stages, the picture is, once again, more complicated. An increasing number of veto points significantly (but unexpectedly) accelerates the speed and success rate of a bill at the pre-committee and post-committee stages of the deliberations in the chamber where the bill was first introduced. It has no significant impact on the committee stage and the passage in the second chamber. It is once again intriguing that the signs and significance of the parameter estimates change across the different stages of the legislative process. Again, a static theoretical framework as sketched above does not offer a 'neat' explanation of the dynamics of the legislative process.

Table 3.6 Effects of the Sum of Institutional Veto Points on the Success of Legislation on Working Conditions, Working Hours and Social Security Benefits in 17 Western European Countries, 1981-1991 – Log-logistic model (multiple episode-estimates; in parentheses: standard error of β-coefficients)

Independent Variables	Stage 1 Pre-Committee	Stage 2 Committee	Stage 3 Post-Committee	Stage 4 2nd Chamber	Log-Likelihood
Reference model without covariates	-3.8575*** (0.0568)	-4.6349*** (0.0614)	-3.4307*** (0.0654)	-3.5865*** (0.0774)	-4801.8210
Model 3b					
Constant	-4.1672*** (0.1738)	-3.8240*** (0.2174)	-5.2802*** (0.2723)	-4.1741*** (0.3800)	-4467.2028
Bill initiated by government or government party	0.6701*** (0.1578)	0.2222 (0.1777)	1.6269*** (0.2321)	1.2485*** (0.2664)	
Length of bill	-0.0042* (0.0019)	-0.0055* (0.0021)	-0.0059* (0.0026)	-0.0017 (0.0022)	
Time until the end of CIEP	-0.0014*** (0.0002)	-0.0013*** (0.0002)	-0.0003 (0.0002)	0.0001 (0.0002)	
Bill first introduced in Upper House	-0.7551** (0.2012)	0.1080 (0.2042)	-0.0169 (0.2146)	-0.7871** (0.2359)	
Committee stage in Committee of the Whole House	2.3806*** (0.1640)	0.1419 (0.1631)	0.2959 (0.1785)	2.1455*** (0.2253)	
Decisive reading before committee stage	-0.9402*** (0.1583)	0.3253* (0.1603)	0.0118 (0.1647)	-1.0511*** (0.2200)	
Sum of institutional veto points	0.3129*** (0.0560)	-0.0374 (0.0635)	0.4038*** (0.0598)	-0.0752 (0.0984)	

p ≤ 0.05; ** p ≤ 0.01; *** p ≤ 0.001; † p ≤ 0.1

Source: SPPL – own calculations

The Impact of Procedural Veto Opportunities in Parliament (Hypothesis 4) A parliament's authority to determine the plenary agenda independent of the government and/or majority is inversely related to a quick passage of legislation. In other words, the stronger the government's control over the plenary agenda, the speedier the process and the higher the general success chances of bills (even after controlling for government bills). This is in line with our theoretical expectations.

The result holds both for the single-episode (Table 3.7, Model 4a) and the multiple-episode design (Table 3.8, Model 4b). In the multiple-episode design, the extent of the chamber's independence from government agenda control on the floor of the chamber is negatively related to speed and success at all four main stages. Thus, government control of the floor agenda does speed up the legislative process and improves the survival chances of a bill.

We also expect a strict discontinuity rule to have a positive impact on the speed of legislation. The parameter estimates for the single-episode design suggest that a restrictive discontinuity rule (bills 'die' at the end of a legislative term of 6 to 12 months) does have a significant positive impact on speed and success rate of the overall legislative process (Table 3.7, Model 5a) when compared to bills introduced under a less restrictive or no discontinuity rule. For the multiple-episode estimations we created two dummy variables, one for a strict discontinuity rule (bills 'die' at the end of a legislative term of 6-12 months) and one for a less restrictive rule (bills 'die' at the end of a legislative term of 4-5 years).

Bills introduced under no discontinuity rule are the reference category. Our estimates for the impact of the strict rule on the dynamics of the legislative process are entirely consistent with our expectations at all main stages, although the impact is insignificant for the post-committee stage in the (temporally) first chamber (Table 3.9, Model 5b). As expected, the results for the less restrictive rule are slightly less clear-cut. For the very restrictive discontinuity rule, for instance, bills passed under a slightly less restrictive rule (bills die after 4-5 years) are significantly quicker and more successful in terms of the pass rate as compared to bills introduced under no discontinuity rule. But the result for the post-committee stage is highly significant and negative, which is inconsistent with our expectations.

Table 3.7 Effects of Different Forms of Agenda Control in the Plenary on the Success of Legislation on Working Conditions, Working Hours and Social Security Benefits in 17 Western European Countries, 1981-1991 – Log-logistic model (single episode-estimates; in parentheses: standard error of β-coefficients)

Independent Variable	Model 4a	Model 5a	Model 6a
Constant	-5.3672*** (0.2289)	-5.7627*** (0.2334)	-5.2530*** (0.2241)
Law initiated by the government or government party	0.6898*** (0.2172)	0.7903*** (0.2116)	0.4812* (0.2134)
Length of law	-0.0034* (0.0016)	-0.0027 (0.0015)	-0.0037* (0.0015)
Time until the end of CIEP (in days)	-0.0004* (0.0002)	-0.0001 (0.0002)	-0.0004* (0.0002)
Bill first introduced in Upper House	0.0113 (0.2303)	-0.2471 (0.2238)	0.0023 (0.2218)
Committee stage in Committee of the Whole House	0.1891 (0.1514)	0.3251* (0.1534)	0.1877 (0.1487)
Decisive reading before committee stage	-0.2877† (0.1641)	-0.5781** (0.1805)	-0.2102 (0.1539)
Parliament's authority to determine plenary agenda independent of government	-0.1263† (0.0724)		
Maximum life of a bill (6-12 months)		0.7013*** (0.1676)	
Invocation of restrictive rule during decisive plenary readings			0.7715** (0.2001)
Time dependence	0.4753*** (0.0492)	0.4996*** (0.0492)	0.5096*** (0.0495)
Chi^2	135.69	149.83	145.52
Degrees of Freedom	8	8	8
Events	280	280	280
Cases	315	315	315

$p \leq 0.05$; ** $p \leq 0.01$; *** $p \leq 0.001$; † $p \leq 0.1$

Source: SPPL – own calculations

Table 3.8 Effects of Different Forms of Parliamentary Agenda Control in the Plenary on the Success of Legislation on Working Conditions, Working Hours and Social Security Benefits in 17 Western European Countries, 1981-1991 – Log-logistic model (multiple-episode estimates; in parentheses: standard error of β-coefficients)

Independent Variables	Stage 1 Pre-Committee	Stage 2 Committee	Stage 3 Post-Committee	Stage 4 2nd Chamber	Log-Likelihood
Reference model without covariates	-3.7733*** (0.0574)	-4.6612*** (0.0623)	-3.3489*** (0.0655)	-3.5920*** (0.0776)	-4682.4614
Model 4b					
Constant	-2.9307*** (0.2005)	-3.3870*** (0.2327)	-3.8095*** (0.3093)	-4.2905 (0.2740)	-4341.4760
Bill initiated by government or government party	0.2296 (0.1655)	0 2776 (0.1862)	1.4903*** (0.2427)	1.4397*** (0.2694)	
Length of bill	-0.0040** (0.0019)	-0.0050** (0.0020)	-0.0063** (0.0025)	-0.0035† (0.0023)	
Time until the end of CIEP	-0.0012*** (0.0001)	-0.0012*** (0.0002)	0 0002 (0.0002)	0.0002 (0.0002)	
Bill first introduced in Upper House	-0.5060* (0.2015)	0.2303 (0.2008)	0.1738 (0.2219)	-0.7156*** (0.2343)	
Committee stage in Committee of the Whole House	2.1974*** (0.1758)	0.7496*** (0.1837)	0.8109*** (0.2066)	2.4475*** (0.2353)	
Decisive reading before committee stage	-0.7447*** (0.1702)	0.6172** (0.1705)	0.7315** (0.1958)	-0.5925† (0.2352)	
Invocation of restrictive rule during decisive plenary readings	-0.1537 (0.2196)	0.9183*** (0.2106)	0.5679** (0.2068)	0.5417 (0.2945)	
Parliament's authority to determine floor agenda	-0.0003** (0.0001)	-0.0009*** (0.0002)	-0.0011*** (0 0002)	-0.0005** (0.0002)	

$p \leq 0.05$; ** $p \leq 0.01$; *** $p \leq 0.001$; † $p \leq 0.1$
Source: SPPL – own calculations

Table 3.9 Effects of Different Forms of Parliamentary Agenda Control in the Plenary on the Success of Legislation on Working Conditions, Working Hours and Social Security Benefits in 17 Western European Countries, 1981-1991 – Log-logistic model (multiple-episode estimates; in parentheses: standard error of β-coefficients)

Independent Variables	Stage 1 Pre-Committee	Stage 2 Committee	Stage 3 Post-Committee	Stage 4 2nd Chamber	Log-Likelihood
Reference model without covariates	-3.7733*** (0.0574)	-4.6612*** (0.0623)	-3.3489*** (0.0655)	-3.5920*** (0.0776)	-4682.4614
Model 5b					
Constant	-3.8309*** (0.1950)	-4.7448*** (0.2696)	-4.3508*** (0.3458)	-4.8160*** (0.3242)	-4257.8123
Bill initiated by government or government party	0.3233* (0.1694)	0.3213† (0.1905)	1.5012*** (0.2505)	0.3501 (0.2995)	
Length of bill	-0.0052** (0.0020)	-0.0045* (0.0022)	-0.0056* (0.0025)	-0.0037 (0.0028)	
Time until the end of CIEP	-0.0009*** (0.0001)	-0.0012*** (0.0002)	0.0003 (0.0002)	-0.0004* (0.0002)	
Bill first introduced in Upper House	-0.6028** (0.2058)	0.2403 (0.2136)	-0.1180 (0.2264)	-0.3229 (0.2761)	
Committee stage in Committee of the Whole House	2.0329*** (0.1550)	-0.0472 (0.1783)	0.5106* (0.1967)	1.6039*** (0.2152)	
Decisive reading before committee stage	-1.5868*** (0.1987)	-0.0565 (0.1845)	-0.6616* (0.2482)	-1.1153*** (0.2847)	
Invocation of restrictive rule during decisive plenary readings	-0.2014 (0.2191)	0.9619*** (0.2107)	0.7321** (0.2151)	0.2052 (0.2946)	
Discontinuity rule					
6-12 months	1.4723*** (0.1918)	0.6561** (0.2179)	0.3420 (0.2643)	1.7742*** (0.3661)	
4-5 years	0.9953*** (0.1382)	1.1948*** (0.1735)	-0.6727** (0.1750)	2.4236*** (0.2744)	

$p \leq 0.05$; ** $p \leq 0.01$; *** $p \leq 0.001$; † $p \leq 0.1$
Source: SPPL – own calculations

Table 3.10 Effects of Different Forms of Parliamentary Agenda Control on the Success of Legislation on Working Conditions, Working Hours and Social Security Benefits in 17 Western European Countries, 1981-1991 – Log-logistic model (single episode-estimates; in parentheses: standard error of β-coefficients)

Independent Variable	Model 7a	Model 8a
Constant	-5.5918*** (0.2207)	-5.4447*** (0.2269)
Law initiated by the government or government party	0.7880** (0.2104)	0.7042*** (0.2188)
Length of law	-0.0022 (0.0015)	-0.0031† (0.0016)
Time until the end of CIEP (in days)	-0.0005* (0.0002)	-0.0004* (0.0002)
Bill first introduced in Upper House	-0.0644 (0.2136)	-0.0309 (0.2280)
Committee stage in Committee of the Whole House	0.3749* (0.1534)	0.2079 (0.1527)
Decisive reading before committee stage	0.1744 (0.1727)	-0.2540 (0.1723)
Committee's authority to determine its own agenda independent of government	0.3108*** (0.0714)	
Committee deliberations restricted by preceding plenary vote		0.0895 (0.1579)
Time dependence	0 5105*** (0.0497)	0.4730*** (0.0493)
Chi²	150.64	132.97
Degrees of Freedom	8	8
Events	280	280
Cases	315	315

$p \leq 0.05$; ** $p \leq 0.01$; *** $p \leq 0.001$; † $p \leq 0.1$
Source: SPPL – own calculations

Finally, we tested the impact of 'invocation of restrictive rule' on the speed and success of the legislative process as an independent variable in the single-episode model and as a control variable in the multiple-episode model. As expected, the legislative process overall tends to be speedier and the success chances of bills tend to improve, if and when restrictive rules such as 'guillotine' or 'closure' motions are used at a decisive stage of the plenary deliberations (Table 3.7, Model 6a). As can be seen in Table 3.9 (Model 5b) the invocation of such a rule speeds up the legislative process especially at the committee and post-committee stages of the temporally first chamber.

Let us now turn to the question of agenda control in committee. Models 7a and 7b (Tables 3.10 and 3.11) refer to the committee's authority to determine their own agenda independent of government. Based on our theoretical reasoning, we would expect a high level of committee independence be related to slower passage and *vice versa*. The opposite is the case: In the single-episode design (Table 3.10, Model 7a), higher levels of committee independence in setting their own agendas tend to lead to speedier passage of a bill overall. These findings are largely confirmed when we apply a multiple-episode design (Table 3.11, Model 7b) with the exception of the committee deliberations themselves. The difference between committees with a large degree of autonomy in setting their own agenda and those with a lower degree of autonomy is statistically insignificant at the 5 per cent level. In practical terms this means: if committees have the right to determine their own agenda, this will make no (statistically) significant difference to the speed of committee deliberations and the success chances of bills at this stage (stage 2). However, there may be clear 'efficiency gains' on the floor of the chamber. That is, parliaments with committees that are allowed a relatively high degree of independence in setting their agenda is not more or less 'efficient' in their committee deliberations, but the overall process will be speeded up significantly.

In sum, a higher degree of committee autonomy in controlling their agendas will not inevitably lead to a slower legislative process. This may be so for a number of reasons: (a) Committees may use their powers to conduct hearings and the cross-examination of witnesses more effectively and therefore reduce the need for late amendments. (b) Although committees may enjoy a high degree of independence according to the parliamentary rules of procedure, they may in fact be tightly controlled by the parliamentary parties, which delegate and instruct their members on the committee. That is, formal committee independence may lead to overall efficiency gains, if certain specialized tasks can be delegated to them and the linkage between committees and parliamentary parties remains close.

Table 3.11 Effects of Different Forms of Parliamentary Agenda Control in Committee on the Success of Legislation on Working Conditions, Working Hours and Social Security Benefits in 17 Western European Countries, 1981-1991 – Log-logistic model (multiple-episode estimates; in parentheses: standard error of β-coefficients)

Independent Variables	Stage 1 Pre-Committee	Stage 2 Committee	Stage 3 Post-Committee	Stage 4 2nd Chamber	Log-Likelihood
Reference model without covariates	-3.7733*** (0.0574)	-4.6612*** (0.0623)	-3.3489*** (0.0655)	-3.5920*** (0.0776)	-4682.4614
Model 7b					
Constant	-3.4835*** (0.1739)	-4.1324*** (0.2024)	-4.6758*** (0.2853)	-4.5465*** (0.2757)	-4344.6821
Bill initiated by government or government party	0.4253** (0.1721)	0.3727† (0.1909)	1.7841*** (0.2456)	1.2909*** (0.2656)	
Length of bill	-0.0026 (0.0017)	-0.0058* (0.0021)	-0.0036 (0.0024)	-0.0027 (0.0023)	
Time until the end of CIEP	-0.0009*** (0.0001)	-0.0013*** (0.0002)	0.0002 (0.0002)	0.0001 (0.0002)	
Bill first introduced in Upper House	-0.6053** (0.2016)	0.1494 (0.2075)	-0.1707 (0.2256)	-0.9611*** (0.2397)	
Committee stage in Committee of the Whole House	2.0784*** (0.1602)	0.2534 (0.1602)	0.0261 (0.1813)	2.3534*** (0.2202)	
Decisive reading before committee stage	-0.7451*** (0.1615)	0.3409* (0.1633)	0.3118† (0.1684)	-0.5862* (0.2355)	
Invocation of restrictive rule during decisive plenary meeting	-0.0091 (0.2163)	0.6509** (0.2113)	0.9586*** (0.2199)	0.7185* (0.3049)	
Committee's authority to determine their own agenda	0.2512*** (0.0587)	0.0696 (0.0938)	0.7850*** (0.0946)	0.4337** (0.1461)	

$p \leq 0.05$; ** $p \leq 0.01$; *** $p \leq 0.001$; † $p \leq 0.1$
Source: SPPL – own calculations

Conclusions

In this chapter we describe the 'life cycles' of bills in 17 Western European parliaments, the area of working time and working conditions and estimate the effect of a number of institutional variables on the dynamics of legislative process. Theoretically, the chapter was guided by a conceptual framework derived from a veto-points framework and some simple intuitions about the transaction costs of decision making. The chapter seeks to contribute to a better understanding of a number of empirical questions:

1. A better understanding of the temporal dynamics of the legislative process and their institutional determinants may contribute to an empirically richer discussion about the procedural efficiency of parliaments and possibilities of institutional design and reform.
2. The study of the temporal dimension of strategic choice in the context of parliamentary systems of government is still in its infancy. The study of the stability of government coalitions has provided compelling evidence that the choices of actors may be highly time-dependent, especially with regard to the electoral cycle (Diermeier and Stevenson 1999; Lupia and Strøm 1995; Warwick 1994; Wiberg 1991; more generally, Riescher 1994; 1997).
3. Event-history analysis allows us to estimate the hazard rate of the successful passage of a bill. Not only can we estimate the chance of a change in the legislative status quo at any point in time, we can also estimate how long a change in the status quo will take. Another advantage of the use of event-history analysis gives us the possibility to work at the level of individual bills (rather than aggregates such as average values for a cabinet or legislative term) and use episode-splitting to determine changes in the hazard rates across different stages of the legislative process as well as the changing impact of certain independent variables across these stages. Finally, and crucially, event-history analysis allows us to control for the time dependence of hazard rates of successful passage.

Even a superficial comparison between traditional empirical studies of the time budgets and procedural efficiency of Western European parliaments on the one hand and the event-history analyses presented in this report on the other, demonstrates the usefulness of the chosen methodology and its potential to model parliamentary processes more accurately than in the past. Success and failure of parliamentary bills are not distributed randomly. Their time dependence cannot be adequately modelled with aggregate measures such as the average length of the legislative process per parliament or cabinet. The chances of a bill to 'survive' and succeed tend to be determined in the first months of its 'life'. If a bill survives the first months of the parliamentary process, it is increasingly likely to succeed or to be stopped by obstructionist and delaying tactics. This must have significant implications for the parliamentary strategies chosen by the initiators and opponents of legislation, which could not be explored further in this chapter.

As conceptualized in our paper, the veto-points framework allowed us to generate a number of plausible predictions about the impact of general regime attributes, actor constellations and parliamentary procedures on the hazard rate of the successful passage of legislation. The main adjustment we made was to relax Tsebelis's (2002) relatively precise but restrictive definition of 'veto player' in order to capture the possibility for parliamentary actors without formal veto powers to invoke constitutional constraints outside the chamber or use delaying powers within the chamber thereby increasing the opportunity costs for the majority to such an extent that they may *de facto* enjoy veto powers. The German parliamentary opposition in periods when the government does not control a majority in the Bundesrat is a case in point.

On the whole, our models estimating the influence of partisan and institutional veto players on the hazard rate of successful legislation (that is, changes of the status quo) do not provide strong support for the veto players' framework as an explanation for the dependent variables studied here (Hypotheses 1-3). If we divide the process into different episodes, a more nuanced picture emerges. The most important general point, which requires further reflection, is that the estimated coefficients for the single-episode models may differ radically from those estimated for the multiple-episode models. These findings are not easily reconciled with the general veto players' framework we are using, which is largely insensitive to the time dependent nature of some of the phenomena studied here. In a future chapter (Saalfeld and Becker 2003) we will juxtapose the veto players' framework with an alternative model based on agency theory in an attempt to develop a model with a more satisfactory empirical fit.

The models testing the role of agenda control by the parliamentary majority and the scope for minorities to *de facto* instrumentalize parliamentary procedures as veto opportunities (through delay in a situation of scarce time) are more encouraging, although they are by no means unequivocal (Hypothesis 4). On the whole it is possible to say that the stronger the majority's powers to control the legislative agenda (and the more limited the scope for minorities to use delaying tactics), the higher the chance for the legislative process to be concluded successfully and speedily. The conclusion that the procedural efficiency of the legislative process can be speeded up simply by centralizing the agenda-setting powers in the hands of governments even further would be premature, however. Our descriptive analyses show that, on average, legislative debates on the floor of the 17 parliaments and in committee tend to be quite short compared to the time 'lost' *between* the different stages of the legislative process. Careful timetabling of the different stages may be a much more effective way of speeding up the process than reducing minority rights. Also, our multiple-episode estimations show that a chamber which entrusts its legislative committees with a great deal of autonomous control over their own agenda may reap net 'efficiency gains', rather than losing speed. This, again, is a finding which is difficult to reconcile with the simple theoretical framework we have used here. These findings lead us to new substantive and theoretical questions, which we shall attempt to pursue in future work.

Chapter 4

Committee Effects on Legislation

Ingvar Mattson and Kaare Strøm

Modern parliaments have many functions, only one of which is to legislate. Yet, when parliaments legislate (as indeed when they perform many of their other key functions), they typically do a significant part of their deliberation within parliamentary committees. Indeed, committees are widely recognized as important arenas of legislative deliberation. In his classic and often-quoted study, Woodrow Wilson (1885) equated congressional government with committee government. Wilson, of course, was referring to the federal institutions of the United States, and students of politics have long recognized that American-style presidential government enhances the power of legislatures and legislative committees. Yet, legislative committee power is by no means strictly a function of presidential government. As Laundy (1989: p.96) notes: '[a]ll Parliaments work to a greater or lesser extent through committees.' Even in many parliamentary systems, assembly committees seem to be important forums for policy making. At the same time, the literature is replete with references to the decline of parliaments and the weakness of their oversight capacity.

What legislative roles do European parliamentary committees actually play, and how does this square with our understanding of parliamentary politics (see Strøm 2000)? These are the questions that will be at the forefront of our attention in this chapter. We shall examine the role of committees in European parliaments, and particularly their involvement in the industrial relations legislation with which this book is concerned. We begin by surveying the committee systems of Western European polities. We then discuss the role of such committees in parliamentary democracies and develop three perspectives on the role of parliamentary committee: the arena perspective, the universalist perspective, and the partisan perspective. These perspectives, all of which are well represented in the literature on legislative politics, yield widely different understandings of the importance of committee deliberations and the interests that such institutions serve. Finally, using our available data, we begin to explore the fit between such theoretical understandings and the real world of European parliamentary committees.

Why Committees?

A legislative committee is a subgroup of legislators, normally groups entrusted with specific organizational tasks. Parliamentary committees are rarely mandated by constitution; yet they almost invariably exist. Within their areas of responsibility, parliamentary committees are often vested with decision-making privileges. These privileges deserve our attention, since they modify the decision-making principle of one person, one vote.

In the great majority of modern legislatures, members are elected equal. All members, regardless of, say, the pluralities by which they gained election, have the same rights and privileges. With rare exceptions, voting rules in legislatures are egalitarian and 'undifferentiated', as each legislator's vote counts as much as that of any other. Such egalitarian principles, which are often constitutionally entrenched, commonly go far beyond simple voting rules. Fundamentally, legislatures are *collegial*, rather than hierarchical, organizations. They are thus unlike bureaucracies or military services, in which some individuals have the authority to command others.

Yet, in reality there are all kinds of differences between members. Such differences take two general forms: *hierarchy* (vertical differentiation) and *specialization* (functional or horizontal differentiation). These forms of differentiation are rarely laid down in the constitution, yet they can be found with amazing regularity and in intricate detail. We can think of them generally as forms of *legislative organization*. Krehbiel (1991: p.2) defines legislative organization as: 'the allocation of resources and assignment of parliamentary rights to individual legislators or groups of legislators.' Legislative organization defines a set of *privileged groups*, that is, subgroups of parliamentarians with specific powers, and a set of *procedures* that specifies the powers of these subgroups with respect to the functions that legislatures perform.

Committees are critical parts of the organization of most legislatures. And if we believe that such organization generally serves some purpose, then we must also ask to what end parliamentary committees are established. There are essentially two answers to this question. In one view, committees are merely an arena or setting in which legislators conduct some of their political activities. For example, committees may be an important arena in which legislators pursue their strategies of credit-claiming, self-advertising, and blame-avoidance (Mayhew 1974). In this perspective, committees do not have agency, and they may not be important loci of actual political decision making. We shall refer to this view of parliamentary committees as the *arena* perspective.

In the second view, committees are organizations to which legislators delegate certain tasks, not just a stage upon which they play. Thus, parliamentary committees are *agents* of the legislators, or of some subgroups of them. In this *delegation* perspective, legislators invest in committees and subject their political fortunes to the results that they produce. Committees, then, are not simply a backdrop to various parliamentary activities. They are structures that legislators erect at some cost to themselves, and which coexist uneasily with the basic egalitarian principles of democratic representation. To understand the rationale behind this organization of their work, we must therefore look to the legislature itself, and to the interests of its members.

Delegation is common in all sorts of social situations, for example, when individuals consult a medical doctor or a lawyer to help them with medical or legal concerns, respectively. Agency theory, which describes situations in which one party (an *agent*) acts on behalf of another (the *principal*) (see, for example, Lupia and McCubbins 2000; Aghion and Tirole 1997; Kiewiet and McCubbins 1991), tells us that delegation takes place because the agent has information, skills, or simply time that the principal lacks. When the principal is a group, rather than an individual, delegation could also be a response to the problems of preference aggregation or collective action that afflict collectivities. Such motivations for delegation apply in politics as well as in other spheres of life.

There are three main tasks that legislators may delegate to committees. One is the detailed crafting of legislation. The second is the fine print of the budgetary process. The third is oversight of the executive branch. In the rest of this chapter, however, we shall focus on the first of these tasks: the crafting of legislation.

To the extent that they perform these activities, parliamentary committees can be understood in large part as agents of other collective entities. But exactly who are their principals? And what are the motivations behind delegation to parliamentary committees? Legislative politics scholars have developed a more or less formalized literature that attempts to address precisely these questions. According to this literature, the principals of committees are either all legislators, or those that belong to the parliamentary majority (which in parliamentary democracies typically also means the party or parties that control the executive branch). In other words, committees either serve the interests of all legislators, or those of a dominant coalition within parliament. Since parliaments typically make most decisions by (most often simple, occasionally absolute or qualified) majority vote, the dominant coalition in parliament will most often have to be a majority coalition, sometimes a qualified majority coalition. We shall refer to the theoretical approach that sees committees as agents of all parliamentarians as a *universalist* perspective, whereas the alternative is a *partisan* perspective. Thus, delegation to committees may be driven by a universal interest, or more narrowly by the interests of the dominant party or coalition.

Universalist Perspectives

Let us now consider more specifically the rationale for delegation to committee. A basic tenet of universalist theories is that hierarchy and delegation afford certain economies of operation. Division of labor, such as a committee system permits, creates obvious opportunities for legislative efficiencies. The greater the number of committees, the more parallel tracks of deliberation the legislature possesses. Given the perennial scarcity of time, numerous committees therefore facilitate legislative productivity. This is, of course, most clearly the case with those stages of the legislative process that take place in committee, rather than on the floor. All else equal, the larger the number of committees and the greater the part of the legislative process they perform, the higher the potential output of parliament, and the greater these economies of operation.

Economies of operation are a broad and widely accepted understanding of the rationale for parliamentary committees. Within this general framework, however, students of parliamentary committees emphasize different gains from trade that committees make possible. One such variant is primarily concerned with mutually advantageous logrolls among members with different preferences over different policy dimensions. The second variant is more concerned with the collective gains that can result from investment in information. We shall discuss these variants in turn.

Distribution

Early neo-institutional analyses of legislative institutions, at first almost exclusively focused on the United States Congress, gave pride of place to committees. This literature emerged as an attempt to explain the apparent stability of legislative policy choices. This stability appeared to contradict the devastating 'chaos results' in the social choice literature (for example, McKelvey 1976), which suggest that legislative majorities should be highly unstable and cyclical. The neo-institutionalists saw legislative structures such as committees as critical impediments to such chaos and sought their rationale in this feature.

Neo-institutionalists see legislators as involved in collective choice situations that involve both inescapable conflict over outcomes and prospects for gains from trade (Shepsle and Weingast 1994). The latter gains stem from the fact that legislators have different policy goals, for example because their respective constituencies differ. Members from rural districts are driven by the force of electoral competition to care much more about farm subsidies and much less about urban transit than representatives from major cities (Mayhew 1974). Such policy differences, which are particularly likely in single-member district systems or in very diverse societies, may induce legislators to engage in *logrolls*, such as 'pork barrel' projects (Baron 1991). The rural member votes for urban transit in exchange for farm support, and vice versa. The rationale for legislative committees and various other legislative structures, then, is to enforce such logrolls. Committees enable members to make credible commitments by assigning 'property rights' over specific policy areas. The members of the agriculture committee get to make farm support policy, whereas the members of the transportation committee are empowered to choose mass transit programs. For committees to serve this function, several conditions must hold. Committees must enjoy some institutional advantages within their respective jurisdictions, such as proposal or gate-keeping powers, restrictive amendment rules, effective oversight functions, etc. Moreover, non-committee members need to show deference to committees in floor voting. Finally, members must have a way to secure their preferred committee assignments (Shepsle 1978; Shepsle and Weingast 1994).

This perspective suggests autonomous committees with broad policy-making privileges. Policy making should be decentralized and governed by restrictive rules. And committees should consist of 'high demanders' of whatever benefits the committee provides. Defense committees should be hawkish, social affairs committees spendthrift with welfare benefits, agriculture committees generous to farm interests, and so forth. As a result, the legislature should spend more in each policy area than the median member would prefer. Thus, while distributive universalism brings mutual benefits to the participating politicians, it may produce collectively inefficient budget-busting policies.

Information Acquisition

The distributive perspective on legislative organization has been challenged by authors who stress the critical role of information uncertainty in policy making (Gilligan and Krehbiel 1989; Krehbiel 1991). They remind us that the legislative majority routinely chooses all committee powers and voting rules and similarly approves all committee assignments. If these powers and assignments systematically thwarted the majority's will, then the members should not rationally adopt them. Thus, they argue, there is no reason to think that the legislative majority would put up with committees consisting of 'high demanders' that produce unattractive budget-busting legislation.

Gilligan and Krehbiel instead stress the advantages that information provides. As even the casual observer knows, the most well-intentioned pieces of legislation occasionally lead to results that no one anticipated or wanted. But legislators can mitigate some of this uncertainty through policy specialization. This is an indirect benefit that specialization may engender, especially under permanent committees with fixed jurisdictions and stable memberships. Through specialization, and at some cost to themselves, committee members can gain private information about policy consequences. The trick for the legislature as a whole is to induce members to take the trouble to acquire such expertise. This desire to foster specialization explains deference to committees on such matters as seniority privileges and restrictive rules.

The informational perspective implies that members should receive committee assignments that allow them to specialize at low cost, for example because of their professional training (medical personnel on health committees, lawyers on judiciary committees) or other prior experience. These members may occasionally also be high demanders, but latter fact is not the reason they are chosen. On the contrary, the confidence that a committee enjoys increases with the heterogeneity of the policy preferences of its members. If radicals and conservatives on the committee agree, then floor members can safely defer to their recommendations.

The Partisan Perspective

Both the distributive and the informational perspective emphasize the gains to all legislators from specialization. An alternative view of legislative organization sees committees as instruments of narrower, partisan interests. The relationship between disciplined political parties and legislative committees is an old one in the literature on legislative committees. Shaw (1979: p.394) concludes that they are inversely related: 'Where the committees are strongest ... one finds the lowest level of party control over the committees.' While parliamentary systems thus tend to foster cohesive parties, powerful committees are especially likely to be found in presidential regimes as well as in parliamentary systems where no single party dominates.

Cox and McCubbins (1993), however, challenge the conventional association between parties and committees, arguing instead that committees are extensions of party power. Parties arise to solve various 'collective dilemmas' legislators face, and committees are simply the extensions of their power. Following Mayhew (1974), Cox and McCubbins stress the legislators' reelection motive. Since voters rely on party identification, legislators can benefit from the collective reputation their party provides. At the same time, each legislator seeks to improve his or her prospects by tailoring the party line to the district interest and by delivering benefits that the constituents value. The collective dilemma is that such 'entrepreneurship' debases the party label, making it a less valuable cue for the voters. The legislators seek to solve this problem by delegating authority to party leaders empowered to enforce discipline on ('whip') the members. Legislative committees are part of this authority structure. Cox and McCubbins see legislative committees as the instruments of the majority party, and more specifically its leadership.

Expectations

Let us now see what implications these models of legislative organization have for our understanding of the role of legislative committees in the European parliamentary democracies with which this book is concerned. In the arena perspective, we expect parliamentary committees to be relatively 'cheap' organizations, in which few investments have to be made. They are simply there to provide a 'soap box' for parliamentarians who wish to advertize themselves to their constituents. Consequently, we expect to see little institutional elaboration and no extensive deliberation in committee.

Alternatively, parliamentary committees may be vehicles of delegation. In a distributive or partisan model, there is thus active delegation and investment in committees, for which parliamentarians are willing to pay a price. The difference is that in the distributive world, all legislators benefit from committee deliberation. We therefore see signs of cross-partisan investment in committees, and committee deliberation should in itself promote consensus and deference to committee decisions and compromises. In the partisan perspective, on the other hand, committees serve the dominant coalition in parliament, which typically means the executive coalition.

It makes sense to think that either universalist or partisan delegation may be found in parliamentary as well as presidential systems. Yet, the forms that such delegation takes may be a little more complicated. Under presidentialism, committees are supposed to serve either the collective interests of all legislators (universalism) or those of the controlling legislative majority. In parliamentary systems, we may similarly distinguish between parliaments in which committees serve the interests of a broad or even universal coalition of parliamentarians, and those in which they serve a mere (minimal winning?) parliamentary majority.

Yet, identifying this partisan majority may not be straightforward. Cox and McCubbins' partisan perspective is informed by the United States Congress, which is almost strictly two-party. In the extension of these ideas to multi-party parliamentary democracies, the theory must be modified by the fact that the parliamentary majority that the committees serve does not necessarily consist of a single, majority party but may be whatever coalition controls the parliamentary majority. Moreover, under minority governments, it may be even more difficult to identify the partisan majority (Strøm 1990), as the cabinet party (or parties) then by definition does not control such a parliamentary majority. Consequently, the identity of the committees' partisan principal may be less obvious. Moreover, under minority government, committees may not be facing a homogeneous or coherent principal, and deference might therefore be less likely.

The amount of investment in committees will also depend on the availability of alternative mechanisms of policy deliberation and coordination. Under strong and cohesive partisan majorities, committees may conform to the partisan model if the ruling majority prefers to use these committees for policy deliberation. But if the ruling party instead prefers to delegate such tasks to the cabinet or to the party organization, parliamentary committees may rather resemble the arena model.

Under coalition government, the role of the parliamentary committees similarly depends a great deal on whether these committees are the prime arenas of intracoalitional policy coordination. There are several institutional circumstances under which they may not be. In some coalitional systems, policy coordination takes place before governments are formed, in negotiations between party leaders over a detailed coalition agreement that then forms the policy contract of the governing coalition. This has been especially common in consociational countries such as Belgium, the Netherlands, and Austria, but also in Italy (see Strøm and Müller 1999). Again, when such ex ante agreements have been struck, the incentives to delegate to parliamentary committees should be reduced. But not all coalitional systems coordinate policy in this way. In some, governing coalitions are relatively fluid, sometimes corresponding to the presence of minority governments. In some of those systems, parliamentary committees may play a particularly important role in the construction of ad hoc legislative majorities. Denmark and the other Scandinavian countries may be the best examples. In such situations, we would expect delegation to parliamentary committees to be prominent and generally to conform to a universalist model. Deference to the same committees should then follow.

Finally, even arenas outside the parliamentary chain of delegation may greatly affect the role of committees. Under corporatism, policy coordination (at least in areas such as labor market policy) often takes place prior to parliamentary debate and in forums that primarily include non-parliamentarians. These consultations, we expect, often tie the hands of parliamentarians and render committee deliberation less useful and more constrained. Consequently, committees may become arenas in which little is invested.

The role of parliamentary committees should have 'downstream' consequences for the bills that pass through them. If parliamentarians invest heavily in universalist committees, then they should tend to defer to them ex post. Consequently, we should see little conflict or obstructionism at the final floor stage of deliberation or beyond. On the other hand, we expect committees engaged in partisan advocacy to be distrusted by the opposition, which might well engage in dilatory or obstructive procedures against the committee's recommendations. Thus, under a universalist model, the more committee deliberation a bill has undergone, the less obstruction there should be. Under partisan circumstances we might expect the opposite relationship: the more committee deliberation, the greater likelihood of obstructionism on the part of the opposition. Finally, if the committee is simply an arena, we expect little deference and no systematic effects of committee deliberation.

Parliamentary Committees: A Survey

In the remainder of this chapter, we shall examine the manner in which committee deliberation was used in the legislative consideration of the bills with which this project is concerned. In this empirical investigation of the structures, procedures, and powers of West European parliamentary committees, the neo-institutional premises outlined above will serve as our guide. We shall examine the role that committees played in the deliberation of each bill, as well as the consequences of that treatment. We shall focus especially on the deference that was granted to the main legislative committee to which the bill was assigned. The rationale for this focus flows directly from the theoretical arguments we have reviewed above.

Data

The data for 18 West European parliaments cover parliamentary committees engaged in the fulfillment of constitutional parliamentary duties (such as legislation, budgeting and/or control of the government) and focus on those with law-making functions. We ignore committees established to direct the parliamentary administration or to organize the work of the assembly, or to perform other duties in the management of the assembly (for example, library matters). Nor do we cover extraparliamentary committees to which Members of

Parliament belong (Schnellknecht 1984: p.90) or 'parliamentary delegations' (for example, delegations to the EU or EFTA).

The main source of legislative information is the data bank on industrial relations legislation compiled under the direction of Herbert Döring. The analysis is a continuation of our earlier study on committees in Western Europe (Mattson and Strøm 1995) but includes behavioral data on 650 bills in the field of labor market and social security benefits policy, mainly from the 1980s. The bills in the data set were randomly selected from three populations: 1) labor market laws, 2) social security benefits bills and 3) unsuccessful bills from both policy areas considered during the same period. An overview of the data set is presented in this volume's Introduction.

Let us begin with a brief survey of the role that committees play in the politics of modern Western European democracies. Table 4.1 presents a condensed overview of the features of these parliamentary committee systems. Note the substantial variation in the roles that committees play across the parliaments of Western Europe. We have previously divided the features of these committee systems into structures, procedures, and powers, respectively, and Table 4.1 follows this analytical structure. Thus, this table surveys the types of committees that dominate the legislative process in these 18 countries and provides numbers on the committees that most interest us here, namely those that are involved in scrutiny of pending legislative proposals. In cases of bicameralism, Table 4.1 reflects the properties of the lower house.

Procedurally, European parliamentary committees select their chairs in various ways. Some are majoritarian, which is to say that all or most committee chairs represent the governing or majority party or parties. In other countries, committee chairs, as well as memberships, are proportionately distributed among the parties. Moreover, committee chairs may be selected either by the committee itself or by the house as a whole. It is often held that one of the most crucial features of parliamentary committees is whether they deliberate on legislative bills before or after the most important plenary debate on the bill. Most parliamentary committees deliberate before plenary debates, and indeed this particular sequence is typically considered a necessary condition for effective legislative committees. Nonetheless, four Western European countries (Denmark, Ireland, Spain, and the United Kingdom) refer bills to committee only after the main plenary debate.

Committees meet more or less regularly, and they may or may not conduct hearings. Over time, hearings do in fact seem to have become more common. As Table 4.1 shows, there are various rules regulating ordinary meetings as well as hearings. Such meetings may be public or private, they may or may not be open to legislators who are not members of the committee in question, and committees in different countries vary in their powers to summon witnesses or demand documents from government officials or private citizens. More fundamentally, committees differ in the discretion with which they can amend, or even initiate, legislative bills. In a few countries, committees are authorized to initiate bills in their own right. In most European parliaments, however, committees can only

Table 4.1 Parliamentary Committees in Western European Systems (Lower House)

	Committee type	Number of Permanent, Specialized Committees	Chairs	Committee Stage in Legislative Deliberation	Meetings	Legislative Authority	Hearings	Agenda Control	Drafting Authority
Austria	Permanent and specialized	17	Mainly majoritarian, selected by committee	Before plenary stage	Various non-members permitted to attend	Can initiate or redraft bills	Private; committee can summon witnesses and demand documents	0.5	0.87
Belgium	Permanent and specialized	11	Proportional, selected by committee	Before plenary stage	About half of all meetings are public	Can redraft bills, but not initiate	Public or private; committee can invite witnesses and demand documents	-0.17	1.21
Denmark	Permanent and specialized	22	Proportional, selected by committee	After plenary stage	Open to committee members and certain other MPs	Can propose amendments, but not redraft or initiate	Private; committee can summon witnesses and request documents	1.84	-1.71
Finland	In practice, permanent and specialized	12	Proportional, selected by committee	Before plenary stage	Closed	Can redraft bills, but generally not initiate	Private; committee can invite witnesses and demand documents	-1.23	0.88
France	Mostly large, permanent and specialized	6	Mainly majoritarian, selected by committee	Before plenary stage	Open to all MPs	Can propose amendments, but not redraft or initiate	Private; committee can summon witnesses and demand documents	0.29	-0.93
Germany	Permanent and specialized	19	Proportional, selected by committee	Before plenary stage	Open to all MPs	Can redraft bills, but not initiate	Public or private; committee can invite witnesses and request documents	0.32	0.09
Greece	Mostly large, permanent and specialized	6	Majoritarian, selected by committee	Before plenary stage	Open to all MPs	Can redraft bills, but not initiate	Private; committee can invite witnesses and request documents	-0.25	-0.50
Iceland	Permanent and specialized	9	Mainly majoritarian, selected by committee	Before plenary stage	Closed	Can initiate or redraft bills	Private; committee can invite witnesses and request documents	1.12	0.52
Ireland	No permanent and specialized committee; committees used sparingly	None	Majoritarian or by agreement, selected by	After plenary stage	Ad hoc committees open to public	Can propose amendments, but not redraft or initiate	No hearings	-1.89	-1.19

Italy	Mostly large, permanent and specialized	13	Majoritarian, selected by house	Before plenary stage	Open to all MPs	Committee members can initiate or redraft bills	Public or private; committee can invite witnesses and request documents	-0 48	-0 34
Luxembourg	Permanent and specialized	19	Proportional, selected by committee	Before plenary stage	Closed	Can redraft bills, but not initiate	Private; committee can invite witnesses and demand documents	-0 78	0 97
Netherlands	Small, permanent and specialized	29	Proportional, selected by committee	Before plenary stage	Generally open to public	Can propose amendments, but not redraft or initiate	Public or private; committee can invite witnesses and request documents	0 96	-1 62
Norway	Permanent and specialized	12	Proportional, selected by committee	Before plenary stage	Closed	Can initiate or redraft bills	Private; committee can invite witnesses and request documents	-0 33	0 21
Portugal	Combination of permanent and specialized, and ad hoc	12	Proportional, selected by committee	Before plenary stage	Open to all MPs and the mass media	Can propose amendments, but not redraft or initiate	Normally private; committee can summon witnesses and request documents	0 60	-0 24
Spain	Generally permanent and specialized	11	Proportional, selected by committee	After plenary stage	Open to all MPs and the mass media	Can redraft bills, but not initiate	Public or private; committee can summon witnesses and demand documents from some sources	0 31	0 67
Sweden	Permanent and specialized	16	Proportional, selected by committee	Before plenary stage	Closed	Can initiate or redraft bills	Public or private; committee can invite witnesses and demand documents from government officials only	0 88	1 08
Switzerland	Generally permanent and specialized	12	Proportional, selected by bureau	Before plenary stage	Closed	Can initiate or redraft bills	Public or private; committee can invite witnesses and demand documents from government officials only	0 22	1 20
United Kingdom	Ad hoc committees and select committees for scrutiny	None	Mainly majoritarian, selected by house or speaker	After plenary stage	Open to public	Can propose amendments, but not redraft or initiate	No hearings	-189	-1 19

Source: Mattson and Strøm 1995

deliberate on bills referred to them by the house in which they function. Again, the power of committees to amend these bills differs. In some cases, committees can redraft, merge, or substitute bills and are thus not required to report the original bill to the floor. In other cases, committees can propose amendments or substitutes but are also required to report the original bill to the floor.

Finally, Table 4.1 reports the two summary measures of committee power that we developed in our previous study (for details, see Mattson and Strøm 1995: pp.298-300). These entries represent factor scores from a factor analysis of five measures of committee power, in which we utilized an orthogonal (varimax) rotation technique. The two dimensions represented here accounted for 65 per cent of the variance in committee power. Higher scores represent greater committee power.

Committee Referral

Do parliamentary committees matter? If they do: how and why do they affect the legislative output?

A first and necessary condition for committees to matter is that bills actually go to committee on their way through the legislative process. Thus, our first indicator of committee influence is simply whether or not bills are referred to a committee for scrutiny, or whether alternatively the plenary (or the Committee of the Whole House) deals with the matter without any committee's advice. In our SPPL sample of legislative bills, 591 of the bills, or 91 per cent, were actually referred to committee. In only 59 instances (9 per cent) were committees not heard. This would seem to confirm that the vast majority of bills are indeed referred to committee, and that the first condition for committee influence thus seems to hold. However, since the bills in the SPPL data set are not a random sample of parliamentary bills introduced in their respective countries, interpretive caution and further scrutiny are warranted.

If we concentrate on bills subsequently adopted by parliament, we find that 95 per cent were scrutinized in committee, which is slightly higher than for unsuccessful bills. We could also examine whether bills that by objective criteria appear more important are also more likely to go to committee. As elsewhere in this volume, we have used inclusion in the Blanpain Encyclopaedia as an indicator of importance. However, there is no difference in committee referral between objectively important vs. unimportant bills. In both cases, about 95 per cent of all bills were referred to committee.

There is, however, clearly some institutional variation among the countries under study. In some parliaments, for example, the Swedish Riksdag, committee referral is compulsory according to formal statutes, namely the Riksdag Act. In other cases, such as the Danish Folketing, such procedures are not compulsory, but informal norms ensure that in practice almost all bills are referred to committee. Yet there are parliaments in which bills are not always scrutinized in committee. In our data set, that includes the German, Greek, Irish, Luxembourg, Spanish and

British parliaments. In Ireland, only 6 per cent of the relevant bills were referred to committee. Though the correlation is not perfect, the set of countries in which referral is not universal also tends to have less powerful committees (Mattson and Strøm 1995: p.299). Among the countries above, all but Spain and Germany cluster among those with the least powerful committees. In the remainder of our analysis, we shall focus on the 591 bills that were actually referred to committee.

Another indicator of the significance of committee deliberation is whether bills are referred to only one or to multiple committees. There may of course be different reasons for multiple referrals. Some may be due to particularly broad bills that clearly crosscut the jurisdictions of two or even more committees. In other cases, the cause may instead be a lack of deference to (trust in) a particular committee. Though we cannot guarantee that all our cases fit into the latter, rather than the former, category, it is indeed this latter rationale that is especially important for our purposes. And the fact that our bills have been drawn from a specific and common policy area should help reduce the incidence of the former motivation for multiple referrals.

Table 4.2 Share of Bills Referred to One and Only One Committee, by Country

Country	Bills referred to one committee (%)	N
Austria	100	45
Belgium	91	44
Denmark	100	42
Finland	11	44
France	83	42
Germany	3	29
Greece	95	19
Iceland	100	37
Ireland	100	2
Italy	0	35
Luxembourg	100	31
The Netherlands	100	37
Norway	100	43
Portugal	59	22
Spain	100	18
Sweden	100	49
Switzerland	67	18
UK	97	34
Total	78	591

As shown in Table 4.2, 78 per cent of our bills were referred to one committee only, indicating that the most common institutional solution is to give a single committee deliberative monopoly. Yet, there is substantial cross-national variation. In about half of the countries, every bill was referred to one committee only. Then there are some countries, such as Greece and the United Kingdom, where single referral is by far the dominant pattern, but where occasional deviations occur.

Finally, in some countries multiple referrals seem either obligatory or at least the dominant practice. Thus, in Italy and Germany exclusive referrals hardly ever occur. Finland also comes close to this pattern and we assume that this can be explained by the important role of the 'Grand Committee' in the Eduskunta. As shown in Figure 4.1, the largest number of committees to which any one bill was referred was nine, which happened to one bill in Belgium and another one in Italy. Whereas all Italian bills were considered in committee, not a single bill was referred to one committee only. In Ireland, on the other hand, only two bills (6 per cent) went to committee, in both cases exclusive referrals.[1]

Exclusive referrals are one of the traditional cornerstones of the distributive perspective on legislative organization. Exclusive 'ownership' of bills in a particular issue area is one way in which committee 'property rights' are expressed and sustained. At first glance, multiple referrals would therefore seem to indicate weaker committees less capable of controlling legislation in their respective policy areas. Yet, cross-national variations could simply reflect differences in the ways bills are crafted. Perhaps countries in which legislation is broadly framed and packaged also tend to have multiple committee referrals? If so, there may still be inter-committee coordination and log-rolling that allow each committee to have a predictable and recognizable impact on the final legislation. At a minimum, however, such coordination requires an arena outside the legislative committees themselves. Most likely, that arena for coordination will be the parliamentary party groups or a coalition committee comprising the ruling parties. If committees, working jointly on the same bills, are significant in the legislative process, it is likely that they function as extensions of the same political party or parties. It is thus difficult to imagine strong committees without either monopoly property rights over bills or partisan coordination.

---

1 Both these countries have reformed their committee systems since the period covered by our research.

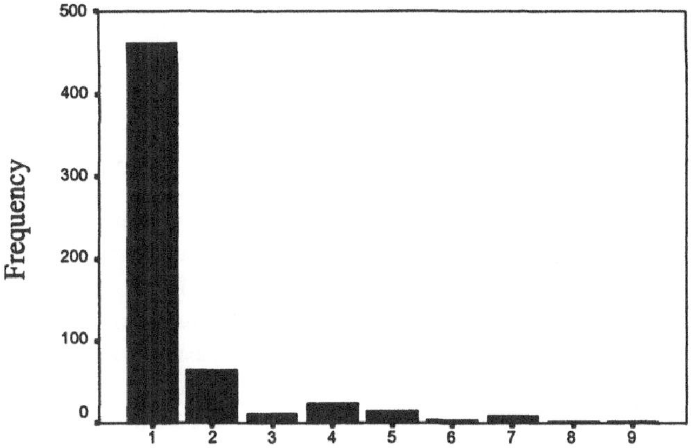

Figure 4.1 Number of Committees to which Bill was Referred

Commitment to Committee

Investment in committees is crucial to any argument why they matter in parliaments. If the legislators in plenary session (the 'floor') make no investment in the committee considering a bill, then what is the purpose of committee scrutiny in the first place? We know that parliamentarians in many countries spend a great deal of their time on committee matters, that they often care a great deal about committee assignments, and that they often spend long years on the same committee, acquiring specialized knowledge about an often very limited range of political issues. If such behavior consistently and systematically went unrewarded, then no rational legislator would make such an investment of his or her time, and the effectiveness of any system of committee scrutiny would unravel.

Yet, investment in committees is hardly uniform or absolute. Few parliamentarians are willing to abdicate totally their control over policy issues outside the jurisdiction of the committee(s) to which they are assigned, and we expect that their willingness to defer could depend on a whole range of factors dealing with the bill at hand as well as their political environment.

To conceptualize and measure investment in committees, we use two admittedly imperfect indicators: (1) the length of committee deliberation, and (2) a categorical variable that measures whether during committee deliberation bills were subject to either hearings or subcommittee deliberation. A minimum duration of deliberation is at least a necessary, though hardly sufficient, condition for serious committee involvement. Similarly, hearings or subcommittee deliberations are presumably at least positively correlated with the seriousness of committee scrutiny. If either of these forms of deliberation occurred, then we count that as evidence of delegation and investment in the relevant committee(s).

Consider first the former indicator. The average total time for committee scrutiny in our sample is 113 days, or less than three months. The maximum is as high as 2148 days, or more than five years, a record set in Luxembourg. At the other end, there are cases in which committees have delivered their reports on the very same day that the committee deliberation began, which makes it difficult to believe that the committees in question actually had any impact in those cases.

The duration of committee deliberation varies cross-nationally, with the highest mean of 470 days (or more than one year) in Switzerland. That figure contrasts starkly with that of Greece, where the committee stage on average takes only three days. These countries are exceptional, and others, such as Germany and Finland, are closer to the mean. The contrast between Switzerland and Greece does suggest that the length of deliberation may be systemically related to regime type, in a way that is not consistent with the partisan perspective. Greece is one of the most majoritarian polities in Western Europe, with strong political parties and virtually no history of coalition government. Switzerland, at the other extreme, is the only country in this sample in which the cabinet is not accountable to the parliamentary majority, and it is also one of extremely stable and inclusive multi-party (specifically, four-party) government. Thus, parliamentary committees seem to play a more substantial role in 'universalist' Switzerland than in 'partisan' Greece. More generally, we note that the average length of committee deliberation is slightly correlated with our measure of drafting authority reported in Table 4.1 (Eta = 0.11).

Thus, we find it plausible to think that the length of committee deliberation to some extent reflects committee strength. Yet, there may well be circumstances in which the duration of committee deliberations is an inadequate measure of the investment made in committees. Committees might from time to time give priority to particular bills for reasons that have little to do with the deference that the floor is willing to grant the committee. Moreover, the duration of committee deliberation may reflect the tempo of legislative work in general, and perhaps also whether the committee in question handles bills in a serial fashion or considers several simultaneously. Moreover, it is probably unwarranted to suggest that a committee that deliberates for two years enjoys more deference than one that deliberates for one year only. Yet, some length of deliberation is at least a necessary condition for committee investment. It is difficult to believe that such short deliberations as happen in Greece can signify any serious dedication to committee scrutiny.

Table 4.3 Duration of Committee Deliberation by Country

Country	Average number of days (mean)	Standard deviation	N
Austria	19	75	40
Belgium	71	99	30
Denmark	57	80	33
Finland	120	228	39
France	–		–
Germany	113	135	26
Greece	3	5	19
Iceland	58	67	27
Ireland	50		1
Italy	267	338	27
Luxembourg	321	462	29
The Netherlands	–		–
Norway	45	62	42
Portugal	235	227	19
Spain	106	50	18
Sweden	38	76	47
Switzerland	470	558	18
UK	48	52	33
Total	113	236	448

A large and professional committee staff can to some extent compensate for committee members' lack of time. Western European parliamentary committees are normally assisted by a secretariat. Only for 19 per cent of the bills in our sample did the committee thus not enjoy the assistance of full-time staff members. Yet, most committee staffs are small, with an average size of two professional persons. Again, there is cross-national variation. Italy stands out with an average of seven staff members per committee, followed by Sweden with five. Committees in Austria, Iceland, and Ireland had to deliberate without the support of any full-time staff members.

Our second indicator of investment is a categorical variable that measures whether during the committee stage bills were subject to either hearings or subcommittee deliberation. We count either of these forms of deliberation as evidence of delegation and investment in the relevant committee(s).

Table 4.4 Investment in Hearings or Subcommittees by Country

Country	Investment 2 (%)	N
Austria	9	45
Belgium	0	35
Denmark	23	42
Finland	0	44
France	0	42
Germany	70	27
Greece	100	19
Iceland	38	37
Ireland	100	1
Italy	80	35
Luxembourg	11	27
The Netherlands	0	37
Norway	0	43
Portugal	82	22
Spain	83	18
Sweden	18	49
Switzerland	22	18
UK	6	34
Total	25	575

In total, about one out of four bills were scrutinized through hearing or subcommittee. As Table 4.4 demonstrates, in Greece and Ireland all bills that went to committee were subjected either to subcommittee scrutiny or to hearings. Yet, neither of these two parliaments is generally considered to house strong committees. The Irish case is easily explained, as Table 4.4 reports on a single bill, and all others were not referred to any committee at all. Greece has only a few large committees, but judging from our data, they usually arrange hearings (no subcommittees were involved in our sample). In five countries, Belgium, Finland, France, The Netherlands, and Norway, there were no subcommittees or hearings. One explanation is institutional differences. For instance, in Norway it is not possible to establish parliamentary subcommittees (C.f., Table 4.1).

Do our two investment variables measure the same thing? Our analysis of variance indicates a positive and significant correlation between the two variables, but this association is only modest.[2] Such a correlation also stands to reason. When a committee invests in hearings or subcommittee scrutiny, the duration of deliberation will most probably increase.[3] In broad terms we thus believe that the two indicators measure the same thing, but neither of them is as compelling as we ideally would have liked.

Committee Dynamics: Level of Conflict and Fate of Bill

Finally, what effects do committees have on legislation? Does it matter whether and how intensively they are involved? As shown in Table 4.5, the evidence is not overwhelming, as the overall fate of bills hardly correlates with the role of committees. Among successful bills in our sample, 25 per cent were subjected to hearings or subcommittee. The corresponding figure for unsuccessful bills is 27. This result is certainly contrary to our expectations, since it suggests that in aggregate we cannot reject the 'null hypothesis' that parliamentary committees are mainly arenas for grand-standing which enjoy little or no deference from the floor.

We argued above that the partisan and universalist perspectives yield conflicting predictions concerning the level of interpartisan conflict in committees, a subject that has been analyzed by Damgaard and Mattson in this volume. According to their measurement of conflict, conflict exists if a nay vote has been registered during the committee stage, or if a minority report has been attached to the committee report, or if another committee dissent was recorded. When none of these three conditions apply, the case has been classified as consensual. As is shown in Table 4.5, the level of conflict appears not to be correlated with committee investments. This result, if it can be generalized, would tend to contradict the partisan perspective.

Table 4.5 also reports whether committee investment correlates with the formal authority and resources of committees. We expect a positive correlation, and indeed we find that permanent committees (which are generally more resourceful) enjoy significantly greater investment than ad hoc ones. With respect

---

2 Eta squared = 0.022, F = 9.9 (p = 0.002), observed power = 0.880, logit = – 75.8 (for Invest 1 = 0, that is, no investment is made in hearing or subcommittee), t = – 3.1.

3 Due to missing observation, however, the two variables are not based on exactly the same set of bills. We lack data from two countries, France and the Netherlands, on duration but are able to include them with respect to the qualitative variable.

to committee authority, the picture is a bit more complicated, as committees with medium levels of formal authority seem to enjoy the greatest level of deference. This somewhat puzzling result may be due to the fact that relatively few systems fall into the highest category on formal authority.

Table 4.5 Investment in Hearings and Subcommittees by Various Independent Variables

Independent variable		Investment (%)	Total N	Cramer's V	sign. (p)
Did bill pass?	Successful	25	575	.016	.699
	Unsuccessful	27			
Conflict	Consensus	26	539	.013	.766
	Dissensus	25			
Ad-hoc committee?	No, permanent	28	568	.128	.002
	Yes, ad hoc	8			
Committee rights for initiatives	no rights	8	575	.326	.000
	right to consolidate and split bill	39			
	right to initiate legislation	32			
	both (2+3)	0			
Pure parliamentary system?	No	4	575	.233	.000
	Yes	30			
Corporatism	Lowest	49	575	.392	.000
	1	28			
	2	0			
	Highest	10			

Finally, Table 4.5 reports on whether committee investment is associated with larger regime characteristics such as semi-presidentialism or corporatism. Indeed, investments appear to be correlated with, and can thus probably be explained by, such political features. Table 4.5 reveals that committees make investments in political systems that practice pure parliamentarism and have a low degree of corporatism. The former result may reflect a tendency for policy bargaining in semi-presidential systems to take place in extra-parliamentary settings. The latter finding conforms to our expectation that under corporatism deliberation is similarly displaced from the parliamentary arena.

Conclusion

Committees are among the most important internal arenas of contemporary European parliaments. Yet, they may be more than simply arenas. In this chapter, we have argued that parliamentary committees may also be prominent organizational vehicles of delegation inside parliaments. Parliaments use committees not just as soapboxes, but also as instruments for legislation, budgeting, or oversight of the executive branch. Here, we have focused upon their legislative uses. There are several theoretical perspectives in which parliamentary committees can be understood, including the arena, universalist, and partisan models.

These perspectives have been developed within the Americanist literature on legislative organization. While we believe that they may also fruitfully guide our understanding of European parliaments, it is important to be mindful of the structural differences between presidential and parliamentary systems and among the latter. The functions of parliamentary committees depend on the strength and cohesion of governing coalitions, as well as on the availability of alternative channels of policy coordination.

The data that we have examined permit us a preliminary opportunity to evaluate the roles of European parliamentary committees in light of the existing models. And while our understanding is still very incomplete, it appears that no single model accounts for the full range of parliamentary committees in Western Europe. Under systems approximating the Westminster model, committees are often not much more than arenas, as governing parties delegate policy coordination to the cabinet instead. Under systems of stable, pre-negotiated majorities (the Netherlands or Austria, for example), committees conform better to the partisan model, except that the party in question is an executive coalition of several political parties. Finally, where governing coalitions are fluid and ad hoc, as in Scandinavia, the distributive model may yield the most fruitful benchmark for understanding. Yet, a more complete understanding of this variation is well worth further study.

Chapter 5

Conflict and Consensus in Committees

Erik Damgaard and Ingvar Mattson

Introduction

Alongside performing several functions for their members, parliamentary parties and the whole parliament (Mattson and Strøm 1995), parliamentary committees are often considered to be vital co-operative structures. Fostering a communitarian atmosphere among members, committees may be conducive to frequent negotiations, accommodation and agreement. A 'face-to-face' decision-making forum can serve to promote unitary and integrated policy communities within parliaments. As such, a committee can function as an arena where conflict is resolved through a compromise (Mattson 1996: p.61).

Giovanni Sartori has even claimed that committees in general represent the optimal decision-forming units, since they operate on the basis of a well-established yet highly flexible operational code of reciprocal compensation. The operational code allows for a reasoned and discussed elaboration of matters, and makes it possible to consider unequal intensity of preferences. Decision making in committees thus reflects the very essence of democratic decision making, complementing pure majority rule where politics has a tendency to amount to a zero-sum game (Sartori 1987: Chapter 8).

In a similar vein, but from another analytical point of departure, John Lees and Malcolm Shaw have argued that it is precisely in the small, face-to-face group where crucial decisional and deliberative interaction occur in organizations. It is committees that provide this forum in parliaments (Lees and Shaw 1979: p.4).

Not only may parliamentary committees function as an arena for conflict resolution between parties, they may also function as a method of breaking deadlock between the two houses of bicameral parliaments.[1] Among the countries under study, conference committees may be called in France, Germany, Ireland

1 However, our data does not provide support for this proposition. Out of a total of 650 bills there are only 40 cases of bills being submitted to conference committees. Of these 40, in only 16 cases was conflict between the chambers resolved in the conference committees. Thus in 24 cases, conflict was not resolved. Due to the small numbers, one should, however, not exaggerate the implications of this finding.

(available but rarely used), and Switzerland (Tsebelis and Money 1997: p.55 et passim; compare Tsebelis and Rasch 1995).[2]

The literature often describes consensual committees as well functioning entities promoting influence for the whole parliament. The implication is that we should expect a positive correlation between strong committees, consensus in committees and strong parliaments (compare Rommetvedt 1998). Yet, we also know that in many parliaments, committees have only a marginal role in the decision-making process. In fact, if 'a strong committee is one that has a significant independent impact on public affairs' (Shaw 1998: p.237), there may not be many such committees outside of the U.S.A. One reason as to why this should be, is that in Western Europe, parliamentary party groups clearly constrain the behavior of committee members (Damgaard 1995).

Comparative studies have shown that committee systems vary between parliaments (Mattson and Strøm 1995). Indeed, committees also tend to vary within a parliament (Fenno 1973; Mattson 1996). The aim of this study is to map the occurrence of dissent in parliamentary committees, and to explain the variation of committee consensus and conflict.

Theoretical Perspectives on Unanimity and Conflict in Committees

Sartori gives an apt characterization of committees in general, which therefore also applies to standing parliamentary committees in particular: Committees are small, *interactive, face-to-face* groups, characterized by durability. Moreover, they are highly *institutionalized*, which entails that as distinct, specified groups, they have certain tasks assigned to them. Finally, committees are confronted with a *flow of decisions* (Sartori 1987: p.228).

Given these characteristics, Sartori claims that decisions in committees are most often reached with unanimity. Even if the pertinent rules formally prescribe majority rule as a proper procedure, decisions are not ordinarily brought to a vote. Yet, according to Sartori, this is not because the members actually agree:

> Committees generally end up with unanimous agreement because each component of the group expects that what he concedes on one issue will be given back, or reciprocated, on some other issue (Sartori 1987: p.229)

Compensation can be explicitly negotiated, that is, through logrolling, but can also be expressed in terms of anticipated reactions. The negotiators deduce the reactions of counterparts in advance. Since this is a tacit understanding, Sartori calls it an operational code. This reciprocity must not be immediate but can be deferred, as is probably often the case.

Robert Axelrod's seminal study on the rise of co-operation is also valuable in this context. Axelrod employs game theory in The Evolution of Co-operation in order to demonstrate that a co-operative strategy ('tit-for-tat') is rational in certain

2 This particular committee form, however, will not be dealt with in the present analysis.

circumstances. Axelrod's primary objective was to investigate the conditions under which co-operation will emerge in a world dominated by egoists and lacking a central authority. In Axelrod's computerized tournament of the prisoners' dilemma game the 'tit-for-tat' strategy triumphed. This was due to the fact that the actors involved sought to plan for the future, which Axelrod called the 'shadow of the future'. He concluded that co-operation will emerge when the game is iterated and the players are uncertain as to exactly how many iterations there will be. Non-co-operative strategies, including cheating and similar tactics, are not the optimal choice in situations where the parties are likely to encounter one another again (Axelrod 1984).

The emphasis on rational action and utility maximization has long been the subject of extensive scholarly criticism. The main tenet of this criticism is the argument that human nature is far more complex and multifaceted than is allowed for in rational choice models. More specifically, critics contend that the models have not been able to resolve the problem of balancing present and future utility; have neglected the factors of uncertainty and risk in their calculations; and have disregarded the costs of decision-making calculations. Although recent theories within the rational choice school have sought to address these weaknesses, the insufficiencies of the models have paved the way for alternative approaches.

Although reciprocity may in fact constitute a motivated, rational strategy, and can be rationally justified, as has been claimed by Sartori, it can also be regarded as a powerful social norm within the group. Attitudes among group members fuel and nourish emotional reactions such as embarrassment, anxiety, guilt and shame which a person may experience at the prospect of violating the norms. If an individual disrupts the co-operative pattern, he will be socially admonished, and the resulting sanctions can be quite severe (Elster 1989: pp.99-100). Overwhelming empirical evidence indicates the existence of a social norm of reciprocity, as has been pointed out by Lawrence C. Becker (Becker 1986: p.346). A group whose members interact frequently and continuously, and whose interaction spans the indefinite future develops norms. All groups who share a common history, and who have tasks assigned, comprise an informal social organization which generally includes a norm of reciprocity.

In addition, the incentives to conform to a uniform code of behavior are more potent in smaller systems, such as committees, than in larger ones. Norms are more readily communicated in smaller groups where violations are highly visible and sanctions can be implemented without difficulty. Moreover, if group composition is homogeneous, which is more likely to be the case in smaller groups, conflicts can be expected to be less frequent than in larger systems (Dahl and Tufte 1973: pp.92-93; compare Dahl 1971: p.37).

Consensus tends to emerge from an integrated committee. Members of different parties who must work harmoniously together frequently converge around a joint approach to a given issue. Consequently, parliamentary committees are often able to produce reports unanimously approved without a vote. Each side may, in such cases, have compromised its party-political stance in order to produce this result. Thus, committee loyalty substitutes or complements party loyalty.

However, the key to co-operative decision making in committees in Sartori's model is not integration by norms in the sociological sense, but rather by rational choice. In contrast to majority decisions, decisions in Sartori's model of committees are positive-sum games. Over the last three or four decades, social choice theory has revealed several fundamental problems associated with aggregating preferences in voting bodies such as parliaments (Rasch 1995; Sen 1988; Nurmi 1991). Given that an operational code of deferred rather than immediate reciprocal compensation is established, it is, however, possible to heed different preference intensity among the participants (Sartori 1987: Chapter 8; compare Buchanan and Tullock 1962). Decisions by committees allow for preference orderings and encourage agreements based on second or third preferences (Sartori 1987: Chapter 8).

Thus, unanimity and/or co-operative conflict-solving strategies are probable, since Members of Parliament may in fact gain from mutual agreements in committees. The legislators are involved in collective choice situations with inescapable conflict over outcomes and as well as prospects for gains from trade (Mattson and Strøm 1995). In game theory terminology, the game is assumed to be neither a pure co-ordination nor a constant-sum game – which would have entailed that the actors benefit from bargaining. The gains from trade between legislators stem from their heterogeneous preferences, which in turn may derive largely from the electoral connection. Legislators have different policy goals since the interests of their respective electorates differ. For instance, members from constituencies with high unemployment are more inclined to vote for subsidies for the unemployed than are members from constituencies with low unemployment. Other considerations aside, they are compelled to adopt a particular stance by the sheer force of electoral competition (Mayhew 1974). Such differences in policy objectives are most likely in single member district systems or in highly heterogeneous societies.

Given diverse preferences, legislators may have a collective interest in logrolling deals. However, collectively beneficial logrolling may easily fail where the exchange is not concomitant (Weingast and Marshall 1988). Due to difficulties in enforcing such deals, representatives may easily find themselves confronting collective action problems such as the prisoners' dilemma. According to several Neo-institutionalists, this forms the basic rationale for legislative committees. Committees enable members to make credible commitments because they assign property rights over specific policy areas to various subgroups of legislators (Shepsle 1978; Shepsle and Weingast 1994).

The gain from trade is a clear possibility in a bargaining situation. The coincidence of co-operative and conflictual elements, in conjunction with interdependent decisions, characterizes a bargaining situation (Schelling 1960: pp.5-6; Jönsson 1990: p.2). In a negotiation, two or more parties seek to build conflicting standpoints into a single decision. The desired result will be achieved if, for instance, the parties modify their preferences or take into consideration the asymmetric preference structure, thus initiating a positive-sum process (Zartman 1983: pp.9-15).

When dissensus threatens unanimity, negotiations may be expected to take place in the committees. Negotiation theory has established that negotiations are more effective in small groups, such as committees, than in larger ones, such as the chamber (Sjölin 1993: p.132; Scharpf 1993: p.30, p.36). Moreover, secret negotiations are more effective than open ones (Sawyer and Guetzkow 1965: p.492; Stenelo 1972: pp.62-64). The fear of losing face can impede progress toward agreement (Brown 1977). When parties commit themselves to a particular issue they thereby preclude the possibility of accommodation, making it difficult to slacken the commitment if the negotiations are public. Unlike chamber meetings, committee meetings can be held behind closed doors and members are thus free to express themselves without the subsequent risk of engaging in polemics that might obstruct successful negotiation.

Participants in democratic decision making can always fall back on the process of voting by the majority principle. However, in his argument for a theory of democracy, Sartori has emphasized that unanimity, negotiations, accommodations and compromises are all valuable components in a stable, functioning democracy (Sartori 1987). The Danish law professor Alf Ross made a similar point in his plea for democracy after the Nazi occupation during World War II, asserting that deliberations and negotiations should always take precedence over majority rule. A vote should be arranged only if and when negotiations fail (Ross 1967: p.139; compare Tingsten 1971). Sartori and Ross are both drawing on an established tradition within Liberalism, which emphasizes faith in rational communication and enlightened deliberation.

As has been demonstrated by both rational choice theory and sociological group theory, there are grounds for maintaining that, under certain circumstances, rational choices and/or social norms will lead to integrative and unitary decision making in committees. The very essence of permanent parliamentary committees is that they are durable and that they face a flow of issues upon which to decide. Members are aware of the fact that they are going to meet one another again. Theory indicates that unanimity is the normal, and in fact ideal, mode of decision making in committees. However, consensus, co-operation, and unanimity do not necessarily figure in this context. Members of certain committees opt for bargaining, accommodation and peaceful settlement of disputes, while others do not. When voting substitutes unanimity, Sartori rather provocatively concludes 'that a committee ceases to be a committee' (1987: p.230).

How, then, is decision making actually conducted in parliamentary committees? We shall now turn to the empirical sections of this study, first describing the patterns of co-operation and conflict.

Measuring Conflict and Consensus in Committees

The level of conflict or consensus can be, and indeed has been, operationalized in various ways. Klaus von Beyme (1998: pp.4-5), for example, enumerates the following possible indicators for the German parliament:

- amendments proposed in the committees and in the plenary sessions;
- length of debates in parliament and the importance of party leaders involved;
- use of roll call voting;
- margin of the majority;
- echo in the media (and sometimes in the streets by rallies of organized interests);
- use of conference committee to settle disputes between the Bundestag and the Federal Council and/or the opposition's attempt to stop a decision via a trial in the Constitutional Court.

As for the Swedish and Norwegian parliaments, Mats Sjölin (1993), Anders Sannerstedt (1992) and Hilmar Rommetvedt (1984) have measured the share of committee reports with dissenting minority reports attached to them. The results from these studies indicate a trend of an increasing level of conflict in both countries.[3]

Operationalizing conflict and consensus presents us with severe problems in comparative cross-country analyses. Measuring conflict as the frequency of minority reports has both advantages and drawbacks. Since the working of committees is the focus of our study, the procedure has a major advantage compared to most of the alternatives mentioned by von Beyme. If Sartori is right, and an operational code of reciprocation is at work, the committee should come to a single conclusion during the preparation. Unfortunately, in 5 of our 18 countries minorities do not have the right to deliver a minority report (see Mattson and Strøm 1995: pp.279ff).

Another possibility derived from the reasoning of Sartori would be to consider a formal vote as a sign of conflict. A vote in the committee could thus be an alternative indication of conflict, were it not for the unfortunate fact that the voting records of committees are only accessible for research in a few countries.[4]

Aside from minority reports and registered votes, there may be other, country specific, ways for committee members to air their discontent. We therefore asked the country specialists to indicate if any such discontent had been registered.

Pondering over the various possibilities for measuring conflict and consensus in committees, we eventually concluded that no single measure would cover all institutional variety in our selection of committee systems, and that a combination

3 For an empirical account of the level of conflict in the Nordic parliaments, see Damgaard (1992).

4 Voting record was accessible in only 43 per cent of the cases analyzed.

of them would be the best comprehensive solution. We have thus operationalized the level of conflict as a combination of three indicators in the following way:

Conflict exists *if* a nay vote has been registered during the committee stage, or *if* a minority report has been attached to the committee report, or *if* another committee dissent was recorded.[5] When conflict has not been indicated in any of these three instances, the case has been classified as consensual. A case has only been classified as missing if information is completely lacking in all of the variables considered. It turned out that 105 of the cases are missing according to our definition.

Our data set contains information on how 650 bills have been dealt with by 18 parliaments in Western Europe in the 1980s.[6] 608 of these bills were submitted to a committee for consideration. Our interest will of course be focused on these bills. For reasons related to the collection of data, it has been necessary to exclude the 42 French bills from our analysis. In sum, that leaves us with 503 cases for closer analysis.

We have excluded the committee stage in the upper house of bicameral parliaments and only analyzed the committees of the lower chamber. Although many of the bills in our data set have been considered by more than one committee in the lower house,[7] we have concentrated our analysis on the main committee. Thus, only one committee is considered for each bill in our analysis.

As we are interested in the functioning of committees as conflict-solving arenas, it is therefore particularly valuable to know of the level of conflict before a bill actually enters the committee stage in parliament. On considering the options made available in the data set, we were forced, reluctantly, to refrain from such an analysis. For similar reasons we also kept clear of looking into whether committee recommendations are accepted by the parliament and if the same structure of political conflict appears in plenary as appeared in the committee. This would have meant comparing committee recommendations with floor decisions, information which was simply not made available by the data set.

Empirical Findings: Signs of Conflicts

Our expectations from the theoretical argument outlined above were dashed when confronted with our own data. As shown in Table 5.1, conflict is indicated in more than half of the valid cases (58 per cent). To paraphrase Sartori: the parliamentary committees fail to function in dealing with more than every other bill!

5 We used variables V46-51, V80 and V82.

6 See the introductory chapter for a description of how data was collected and an overview of the data set. See also Scholz and Trantas (1995).

7 This was the case for 130 bills or 20 per cent of all bills in the data set.

Table 5.1 Number of Bills where an Act of Conflict has been Registered

	Count	Percent	Valid percent
Conflict	293	48	58
Consensus	210	35	42
Missing cases	105	17	
Total	608	100	100

We can thus conclude that conflict was frequently at hand in West European parliamentary committees in the 1980s, at least in the area of labor market policy. But was that a stable condition? A trend of increasing conflict (measured as existence of minority reports) has been found in earlier studies of committees in Sweden (Sannerstedt 1992) and Norway (Rommetvedt 1984), indicating an increasing level of conflict in the 1980s in these two countries.

As Figure 5.1 shows, conflict in committees reaches a peak in 1981 when 75 per cent of the bills were contested in the committees. The lowest indication is indicated for 1984 when conflictual actions have been registered in only 46 per cent of the cases. But apart from those two years, conflict never deviates with more than 10 per cent points from the statistical trend which is indicated in the figure as a regression line, somewhat increasing, but rather stable at just above 60 per cent.

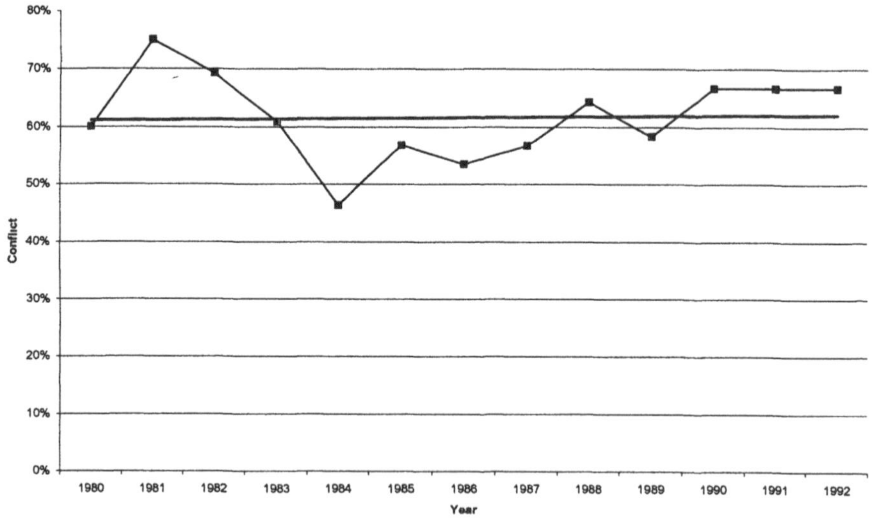

Figure 5.1 Conflict in Committees by Year
N=500 (1979 and 1996 (two cases) have been excluded)

Any conclusion to be drawn from the figure must be done so with caution since not only is the annual number of cases low, they also vary considerably over the years from 3 in 1992 to 60 in 1987. We are, nevertheless, inclined to conclude that the level of conflict has remained rather stable during the decade and that there is no indication of a general trend towards increasing conflict.

If there is no large variation over time, is there, then, a variation between countries? Table 5.2 indicates that there is, indeed, a rather large variation between the countries under study. The highest levels of conflict are found in Greece, Germany, and the Netherlands where more than 90 per cent of the bills lead to controversy during the committee stage, which could not be solved by the committees. The lowest levels are to be found in Italy and Spain.

Table 5.2 Number of Bills with Indicated Conflict by Country

Country	Consensus	Conflict	Total	Conflict (%)
Italy	24	0	24	0
Spain	17	1	18	6
Portugal	19	3	22	14
Ireland	3	1	4	25
Austria	26	15	41	37
Luxembourg	15	13	28	46
Finland	20	19	39	49
Iceland	15	15	30	50
Switzerland	8	10	18	56
Norway	15	28	43	65
Denmark	11	24	35	69
Sweden	15	34	49	69
United Kingdom	8	26	34	76
Belgium	8	27	35	77
Netherlands	3	33	36	92
Germany	2	26	28	93
Greece	1	18	19	95
Total	210	293	503	58

As for Italy, there is actually no single incident of conflict, which is probably astonishing for anyone familiar with Italian politics. The explanation for this is that labor market reforms in the 1980s were carried out in close co-operation between the government and the employers' and employees' organizations. The role of parliament was, in practice to rubberstamp the agreement after deals had been struck between the three parties. As a consequence of this, there was no room for maneuvers in the committees.[8] We must thus accept that the selection of labor market policy makes Italy a very special case in our context, and we must keep in mind throughout the rest of the chapter that in other countries, for example, Spain, the labor market policy may similarly not be representative of all policy areas with regard to the level of conflict analyzed here.

Explaining Variation in Conflict and Consensus

Looking beyond our first conclusion that conflict is somewhat more common in committees than consensus, we are also interested in the explanation for the variation in conflict and it is to this task that we now turn.

From our theoretical point of view, we can think about several possible explanations that should be explored. Before doing this, there are some key features of the committees that should be considered first. We should expect a face-to-face decision-making style to be more likely in small committees than in large ones. We would also think that secrecy rather than openness facilitates consensus in committees, as likewise a high degree of specialization also would. One would reasonably expect the operational code of reciprocity to be best nurtured in permanent committees than in ad hoc committees. At the same time permanent committees should also enhance the threat posed by the shadow of the future, as members are sure they will soon meet again in another matter. Further, a high number of substitutions is expected to work against consensus solutions.

In addition, we should also include an analysis of the type of bill under committee scrutiny and its history before it reaches the committee. A common sense notion would be that conflict should be greater when an important bill is scrutinized. We could also expect bills concerning benefits (and thus constituting sharp zero sum games) to create more conflict than regulatory bills. Further, the existence of a pre-parliamentary commission for preparations of bills might help to create consensus. Finally, we expect a governmental bill to be more partisan than had it been initiated by someone else, for example, the committee itself.

Going a step further, we consider a number of properties that are related to the actual powers of the committees. In Sartori's theory, there is a more or less outspoken assumption that since well functioning committees seldom vote, we could assume that strong (influential) committees are consensual. We should therefore expect that committees that have both a high degree of independence, are supported by a large staff, and arrange hearings are less struck by conflict than weak committees.

Finally we should also include country specific variables such as type of political system (consensual or conflictual, corporatism, et cetera). The reason for

8 We thank Professor Luca Verzichelli for providing us with this information.

this is that not only do we need to control for other variables, but also because there is a statistical indication on correlation between country and conflict. Cramer's V is 0.53 and highly significant ($p < 0.0005$) if we test the hypothesis that country is related to committee conflict.

The following two sections contain bivariate and multivariate analysis of conflict in committees.

Bivariate Empirical Analysis

It is reasonable to assume that the face-to-face style of decision making is fostered by small committees rather than large ones. Our first empirical test therefore include a test of that proposition.

Table 5.3 shows conflict by size measured as number of committee members. As can be seen in the table, there is no clear linear correlation. Against our expectations, the highest levels of conflict are to be found in committees with 11-40 and more than 51 members. Consensus, on the other hand, is especially frequent in committees with less than 10 and 41-50 members.

Table 5.3 Conflict by Committee Size (Number of Committee Members)

Size	Conflict (%)	N
1-10	48.9	45
11-20	59.1	215
21-30	61.3	137
31-40	59.1	44
41-50	28.6	21
51-	68.3	41
Total	58.3	503

Cramer's V = 0.151 ($p=0.042$)

In the hypotheses outlined above, we also expected that secrecy rather than openness facilitates consensus in committees. Table 5.4 corroborates the hypothesis. Conflict is more common than statistically expected in committees which are open to MPs, to the public and to the media. The dependence, however, is not significant on the 5 per cent level.

Table 5.4 Conflict by Committee Openness

Committee meetings	Conflict (%)	N
Closed	57.5	207
Open to MPs	68.3	104
Open to public and media	68.2	88
Total	62.7	399

Cramer's V = 0.111 (p=0.086)

For the operational code of diffuse reciprocation to work well, we assume that membership volatility should be low. Table 5.5 shows conflict in committees by number of substitutions in the committee during the period when the committee prepared its final report on the bill.

The table exposes that consensus is more frequent than expected when 1-10 substitutions have occurred and the same is true for conflict in the two other categories.[9] However, there is no clear linear dependence, as is affirmed by the highly insignificant Cramer's V. Therefore, number of substitutions will not be included in the multivariate analysis.

Table 5.5 Conflict by Substitutions

Substitutions	Conflict (%)	N
None	63.2	133
1-10	56.4	181
11 or more	61.8	55
Total	59.6	369

Cramer's V = 0.066 (p=0.448)

What about the effects of specialization on conflict? We assume that the number of committees is positively correlated to the opportunity for members to

9 A note of caution is well-deserved here, since the length of the period in which the bill was prepared varies between the cases.

specialize in their fields. Table 5.6 shows conflict by number of permanent committees in the respective parliaments (lower house).

Table 5.6 Conflict by Number of Committees

No. of committees	Conflict (%)	N
10 or less	69.0	87
11-20	51.0	345
21 or more	80.3	71
Total	58.3	503

Cramer's V = 0.23 ($p<0.0005$)

Here again there is no linear relationship between the two variables. Consensus is more frequent than expected when the parliament's lower chamber houses 11-20 committees, which is by far the most common number of committees in the data set. Conflict, on the other hand, is found in both the least as well as the most specialized committees.

We expect permanent committees to have fewer conflicts than ad hoc committees. In ad hoc committees, the committee is set up for a limited period of time and members frequently change their committee membership, which should decrease the possibility of establishing an operational code of deferred reciprocity. Table 5.7 shows that most of the bills that we study have been scrutinized by a permanent committee. Ad hoc committees were engaged in only 10 per cent of the cases. It also shows that our expectations are corroborated by the data. Most of the bills have been scrutinized by a permanent committee and in those instances 56 per cent created conflict compared to 84 per cent in ad hoc committees.

Table 5.7 Conflict by Ad Hoc Committees

Ad hoc committee	Conflict (%)	N
No (permanent)	55.8	441
Yes	84.3	51
Total	58.7	492

Phi = 0.177 ($p<0.0005$)

We have so far investigated the first category of variables with mixed or even discouraging results for the theory. Conflict is not unambiguously more probable in large committees or in committees with many substitutions. Neither is it clear that conflict is more probable in specialized committees than in committees with more general tasks. However, theory is supported with regard to two other variables. Conflict appears to be more probable in open committees than closed and in ad hoc committees.

We will now turn our attention to variables related to features of the bill and its history prior to committee scrutiny. From a common sense notion, we assumed in the above that important bills should be subject to more conflict than unimportant ones. But how can importance be measured? One advantage in selecting labor policy legislation as our field of study is that we can rely on earlier research and the existing expertise in the field. The Blanpain Encyclopaedia lists those labor market laws that are of importance in most of the countries under study (see Scholz and Trantas 1995).

Table 5.8 Conflict by Bills Mentioned in Blanpain's Encyclopaedia

Bill mentioned	Conflict (%)	N
Yes	75.0	44
No	56.6	459
Total	58.3	503

Phi = – 0.105 (p=0.018)

Table 5.8 shows that only 44 bills (8.7 per cent) in the data set are mentioned in the handbook, implying that only these are the important bills.[10] And indeed, it seems as if the common sense notion is corroborated. Important pieces of legislation do create conflict in committees.

Is there also a difference between regulatory bills and distributive bills? The hypothesis formulated above was that distributive politics is more conflictual than regulatory politics. We have a variable in the data set that indicates whether the bill refers to regulations on working hours and contracts or whether it refers to benefits. (Unsuccessful bills have not been attributed any value in this distinction.)

As is shown in Table 5.9, we must reject the hypothesis. To the extent that there is any relationship, the direction is actually the reverse of what was expected. Since the difference is so minor (and significance so low), we should, however, not conclude on any dependence.

Does it matter who initiates the bill? It is reasonable to expect that Government bills often have a partisan content, whereas initiatives from the

10 Note that unsuccessful bills may, for obvious reasons, not be mentioned as important laws in the Encyclopaedia.

committee itself are less partisan (but may be more particularistic, if the iron triangle is at work).

Table 5.9 Conflict by Type of Bill

Type of bill	Conflict (%)	N
Working time and conditions	61.7	235
Benefits	58.9	190
Total	60.5	425

Phi = -0.028 (p=0.564)

Table 5.10 Conflict by Initiator

Initiator	Conflict (%)	N
Government or minister	63.5	394
Parliamentary party	28.6	28
Individual MPs	44.6	74
Parliamentary committee	20.0	5
Total	58.3	501

Cramer's V = 0.215 (p<0.0005)

Table 5.10 shows that 4 out of 5 bills in the data set were initiated by the government. This is not surprising in itself, since most legislation is initiated by governments anyway. However, the data set also includes bills that did not pass through parliament. The balance between unsuccessful bills and successful bills is, however, not representative of the actual balance. The same can be said of the balance between governmental and other bills. Moreover, the formal possibilities for committees and individual members to initiate bills vary between the countries under study (Mattson 1995).

The table also indicates, which is more important for this context, that the answer to the question should be answered positively. It does matter who initiates the bill. Conflict is indicated in the committees much more often for governmental bills than for any of the other categories. We could possibly interpret the groups of initiators as categories in an ordinal scale, beginning with the most partisan issues and end with the less partisan, but any interpretation of it must be taken carefully. Since this is a doubtful interpretation of the variable, we will in the remainder of the chapter (that is, the multivariate analysis) only make a distinction between governmental and other bills.

We should also consider another aspect of the bill's history prior to the committee stage, namely, whether or not the proposals have been object to consideration in pre-parliamentary commissions before they were presented in the parliament.

Table 5.11 does indeed reveal that the history of the bill prior to committee scrutiny is of importance. Surprisingly, conflict appears more often in committees where a commission has previously been at work and their report has been made accessible or even if the commission worked behind closed doors. Consensus is more probable if there has been no pre-parliamentary commission at all.

Table 5.11 Conflict by Pre-Parliamentary Commissions

Pre-parliamentary commission	Conflict (%)	N
Yes, with a publicly accessible report	80.0	70
Yes, but secret	81.0	58
No	53.2	325
Total	60.9	453

Cramer's V = 0.251 ($p<0.0005$)

In sum, the second group of variables have shown conflict to be more frequent for important bills, governmental bills and bills that have been subject to a parliamentary commission of inquiry before the government presented its bill. We believe it would come as no surprise to anyone, if these three variables turned out to be correlated to each other. It is normally governmental bills that are preceded by a pre-parliamentary commission and in most countries and for most of the time it is the government that presents the most comprehensive and important pieces of legislation. And indeed, that is also the case. Only six out of 143 bills initiated by someone other than the government were preceded by a pre-parliamentary commission. Moreover, only four out of 172 bills other than governmental bills were mentioned in the Blanpain's Encyclopaedia. Our conclusion from this is that what matters is that the government is the initiator of the bill. As for regulatory or distributive pieces of legislation, we found no support for the hypothesis that distributive politics should be more conflictual than regulatory politics. At this stage we can draw an intermediate conclusion and reject this particular hypothesis irrefutably.

We will now turn to the third group of independent variables, namely those related to committee powers and independence. In the 1995 volume, Herbert Döring made a comparative study of governmental control of parliaments' agenda in the 18 West European parliaments (1995c, 1995e). Proceeding from his comparative analysis, but also drawing from variables by other contributors based on institutional data and thus summarizing a rich set of variables on institutional features, he constructed an index of independence by factor analysis (1995e). The analysis ended up with three factors, one of which was interpreted as the government's ability to control the agenda, so that the government's priorities took precedence in parliament's schedule. We will use the factor loading for each country on this factor for our purposes here. The more independent the parliament is from the government, the higher the factor loading. In Table 5.12, the index is cross tabulated with our dependent variable.

As can be seen in the table, the relation is the reverse of that which was expected. The more independent parliament is, the more probable it is that conflict has been registered during the committee stage.

Table 5.12 Conflict by Parliament's Independence (from Government Control)

Parliament's independence (factor loading)	Conflict (%)	N
< 0.0	51.4	144
0.0–0.5	51.4	216
> 0.5	75.5	143
Total	58.3	503

Cramer's V = 0.221 ($p<0.0005$)

A related question regards the committees' ability to control their own agenda. In the 1995 Döring volume, Ingvar Mattson and Kaare Strøm (1995) also constructed an index on committee agenda control (a subset of Döring's index on government's agenda control) following a factor analysis based on variables that indicated institutional committee powers.

Table 5.13 Conflict by Committee's Agenda Control

Agenda control (factor loading)	Conflict (%)	N
< -0.5	56.2	105
-0.49–0.00	60.3	121
0.01–0.5	49.5	105
> 0.5	63.4	172
Total	58.3	503

Cramer's V = 0.105 ($p=0.136$)

Table 5.13 shows no signs of linear correlation between the two variables and significance does not meet even the 10 per cent requirements. We are therefore inclined to conclude that parliament's ability to control the agenda independently from the government is more important that the committee's ability to control its own agenda. As we are dealing here with indexes that are extracted from factor analysis and then interpreted as indicators of independence for parliament and committees respectively, any conclusion must, however, be made with great caution.

We thus turn to a variable that is less vulnerable in this respect. In his study, Herbert Döring (1995c) also made a survey of the committees' ability to control their own timetable for scrutinizing a bill. The strongest position is held by committees where the plenary body can neither determine the timetable nor recall the bill from the committee.

Table 5.14 shows that conflict is most frequent where the committee has the strongest positions in this regard.

Table 5.14 Conflict by Committee's Timetable Control

Control of committee timetable	Conflict (%)	N
Bills tabled before committee constitutes agenda	59.7	77
Plenary body as directing authority with right to recall	40.0	195
Committees set agenda, plenary may recall	77.8	81
House may not reallocate bill to other committee	70.7	150
Total	58.3	503

Cramer's V = 0.312 ($p<0.0005$)

Another aspect of committees' strength is their rights to rewrite bills and to take initiatives of their own. Table 5.15 shows the committees rights in this respect as indicated by data from our last volume (Mattson and Strøm 1995: Table 8.4).

Table 5.15 Conflict by Committee's Rights for Initiatives

Control of committee timetable	Conflict (%)	N
No rights	77.1	109
Right to consolidate and split bills	60.1	193
Right to initiate legislation	45.7	162
Both (2+3)	48.7	39
Total	58.3	503

Cramer's V = 0.236 ($p<0.0005$)

Table 5.15 indicates that committees with strong rights experience fewer conflicts than the other way around.

Further, the size of the committee staff is a fairly straightforward indication on committee capacity and thereby independence.

The percentages in Table 5.16, in which v68 was recoded using percentiles, shows that there is no linear relationship between staff and conflict, even though Cramer's V is significant. Therefore, v68 will not be included in the multivariate analysis.

The final variable to be investigated in this group of variables is hearings. Some committees have the right to arrange hearings, summon ministers, civil servants, and experts, and the like, whereas other committees lack that right (Mattson and Strøm 1995). But to what extent are these rights used, and what is the relation to our dependent variable?

Table 5.16 Conflict by Committee Staff

Staff	Conflict (%)	N
0–1	58.3	199
2	73.0	126
3 or more	46.5	71
Total	60.9	396

Cramer's V = 0.192 ($p<0.001$)

Table 5.17 Conflict by Hearings

Hearings	Conflict (%)	N
Yes	81.4	86
No	57.3	314
Total	62.5	400

Phi = -0.204 ($p<0.0005$)

Hearings were arranged in 86 instances.[11] Table 5.17 shows a clear pattern. Conflict in committees is more probable if hearings have been held. This seems reasonable, since uncontroversial issues do not tend to need any complementary information. Moreover, hearings may often be used (especially by the minority) to 'announce' disagreements, since hearings have a potential to attract the interest of the media.

The third group of variables has, in sum, shown that conflict is more frequent in parliaments where the government does not control parliament's agenda and committees control their own timetable and have the right to take initiatives of their own. Conflict is also more frequent for bills when the committee has arranged a hearing during its scrutiny of them.

We are thus inclined to conclude that conflict is more associated with strong committees than it is with weak ones. This appears to be contrary to the expectations of Sartori but well in line with Rommetvedt's observations on Norway. When the Norwegian committees became more significant in the decision-making process, conflict increased (Rommetvedt 1984).

Finally, we will now analyze a group of variables related to the political system of the countries under study. We have already noted that certain country-specific features seem to be of importance and that we need to check for some factors that we assume could have an influence here.

Arend Lijphart and others have classified countries as conflictual or consensual. It goes almost without saying that we should expect a co-variation between conflictual systems and conflict in committees. In Table 5.18 we have used the Schmidt (1997) classification of consociational democracies.

Table 5.18 Conflict by Consociational Democracies

Consociational democracies	Conflict (%)	N
No	56.5	345
Yes	62.0	158
Total	58.3	503

Phi = -0.052 ($p=0.245$)

11 In 43 cases, hearings were not arranged because the committee lacks the right.

Surprisingly, we find the direction of the relationship to be the reverse of what one would expect. Table 5.18 shows that the probability for conflict increases as we move to the consociational democracies from the other systems. However, since the significance is low, we should only conclude by rejecting the hypothesis.

Another aspect of interest is whether the country is corporative or not. One would assume this to be especially important in the field of labor market policy, as illustrated by the Italian case (see not 8 above).

Table 5.19 Conflict by Corporatism

Corporatism	Conflict (%)	N
Lowest level	40.5	121
1	65.5	139
2	91.7	36
Highest level	58.0	207
Total	58.3	503

Cramer's V = 0.265 ($p<0.0005$)

In Table 5.19 the Lane-Ersson (1995) index of corporatism is cross tabulated with conflict. The table shows that consensus is most probably found in countries with the lowest level of corporatism. The highest level of conflict, 92 per cent of the bills, is found in the second highest level of corporatism. However, since the highest level of corporatism indicates only an average level of conflict, there appears to be no linear relation between the two variables.

Another important aspect of the political system that we should want to control for is the effective number of parties. The effective number of parties has been measured as defined by Müller and Strøm (2000).[12]

12 Information for Greece, Iceland, Spain and UK was calculated and inserted into the data set by the project management. Data for the other countries, except for Switzerland, where data was not available, were taken from Müller and Strøm (1997). We are thankful to Herbert Döring and his assistants for computing this and other variables in the data set. We are also indebted to Thomas Saalfeld and Rolf Becker for introducing some of the other variables.

Table 5.20 Conflict by Effective Number of Parties

Effective number of parties	Conflict (%)	N
Less than 3.0	61.2	139
3 to 5	57.8	204
More than 5.0	60.7	122
Total	59.6	465

Cramer's V = 0.031 (p=0.796)

Table 5.20 shows no clear pattern. It indicates that consensus is found more frequently than expected in countries with 3 to 5 parties, and conflict in the two other cases. From this table there seems thus not to be any linear dependence. This ocular observation of per cent figures in the crosstable is corroborated by the low Cramer's V and significance figures.

Two other important variables to check for are type of government and parliamentarism vs. presidentialism.

Table 5.21 shows type of cabinet based on Müller and Strøm (1997: Table 1 and 3). Table 5.22 is based on information from Schmidt (1997: p.223).

Interestingly enough, consensus is more often found if the government is a single-party majority government, than in any of the other three cabinet types. However, the observed numbers are close to the expected and significance is low. Moreover, the probability for conflict is higher in pure parliamentary systems of government. However, also in this case, significance is low.

Table 5.21 Conflict by Type of Cabinet

Type of cabinet	Conflict (%)	N
Coalition majority	61.2	245
Single-party majority	53.8	80
Coalition minority	68.1	47
Single-party minority	61.4	83
Total	60.7	455

Cramer's V = 0.078 (p=0.433)

Table 5.22 Conflict by Pure Parliamentarism

Pure parliamentarism	Conflict (%)	N
No	50.9	57
Yes	59.2	446
Total	58.3	503

Phi = 0.053 (p=0.231)

The final variable in this group of variables is the electoral system. We assume that the political system becomes more competitive and thus more conflictual if the voters have the chance to cast a vote for individual candidates as reported by Gary Cox (1997).

Table 5.23 Conflict by Electoral System

Candidate votes	Conflict (%)	N
No	49.3	136
Yes	61.6	367
Total	58.3	503

Phi = 0.111 (p=0.013)

And indeed, the hypothesis is corroborated by the data. Table 5.23 shows that conflict is found more often than statistically expected where the electoral system allows for candidate votes. It seems as though the electoral connection is at work. The competitiveness between members affects the function of parliament, just like Mayhew (1974) would have predicted.

In sum, the final group of variables seem to have little to contribute to our understanding of why conflict arises in committees. Only for corporatism and electoral system was a significant pattern discernible. What comes as more of a surprise here is that corporatism apparently does not moderate conflict in committees; and that, most interestingly, conflict is more frequently to be found in countries where candidate votes are possible. Having concluded the bivariate analysis, we now turn our attention to a multivariate analysis.

Multivariate Empirical Analysis

To get a firmer grasp of the variables that perform best in explaining committee conflict or consensus and controlling for the independent effects of other variables, we conducted a multivariate binomial logistic regression analysis (using SPSS) with conflict as the dependent variable.[13] We included the four sets of variables presented in the previous bivariate analyses, except for those variables that proved highly insignificant or did not show, inspite of their significance, a clear linear relationship in the bivariate analyses (number of substitutions, type of bill, staff). Variables were entered successively and block-wise into the regressions. We also

13 Conflict was attributed the value 1 and consensus 0. The independent variables are both continuous and nominal. In the bivariate analysis, the continuous variables were recoded into nominal variables with categories. However, the continuous variables were used in the logistic regression.

Table 5.24 Logistic Regression Models of Conflict in Committees
Coefficients are not standardized (Significance levels are given in parentheses)

	Model 1	Model 2	Model 3	Model 4
Committee size	0.07 (0.002)	0.04 (0.06)	0.07 (0.01)	0.10 (0.04)
Openness	-1.30 (0.00)	-0.84 (0.02)	-1.02 (0.01)	-1.05 (0.06)
Number of committees	0.18 (0.00)	0.14 (0.00)	0.16 (0.00)	0.11 (0.34)
Ad hoc	0.05 (0.94)	-0.31 (0.64)	0.10 (0.88)	0.83 (0.37)
Unimportance of bill		-0.13 (0.78)	-0.07 (0.89)	0.15 (0.78)
No pre parl commissions		-0.65 (0.01)	-0.59 (0.02)	-0.55 (0.03)
Government bill		1.10 (0.01)	0.98 (0.03)	0.83 (0.09)
Independence (from govt)			0.74 (0.00)	0.88 (0.00)
Committee hearings			2.03 (0.00)	1.60 (0.003)
Consociational				-0.15 (0.91)
Corporatist				0.26 (0.62)
Eff. number of parties				-0.38 (0.24)
Parliamentary system				0.60 (0.60)
Candidate vote				1.40 (0.02)
Constant	-1.50 (0.002)	-0.16 (0.90)	-1.66 (0.24)	-2.16 (0.41)
Log-likelihood	312.37	293.41	251.84	242.77
Nagelkerke's R^2	0.209	0.287	0.442	0.472
N	266	266	266	266

took into consideration the consequences of deploying variables with many missing cases.

Model 1 includes the critical variables for the theoretical assumptions outlined above (group 1 in the bivariate analysis). It explains about 21 per cent of the variance, as estimated by the Nagelkerke method. Moreover, it shows that open committee meetings reduce conflict whereas large committees and high numbers of committees facilitate conflict. Thus, the expected results appear for committee size and number of committees (specialization), but not for open meetings. On the whole we may therefore conclude that model 1 only provides limited support for the Sartorian argument.

As we go on to include variables from the second group of variables, the share of explained variance increases to almost 29 per cent. Model 2 shows that important bills, pre-parliamentary commissions and governmental bills all promote conflict in committees, but only the latter two significantly so. At the same time, we can still observe the effects of committee size, openness and number of committees. Model 3, which introduces committee characteristics (group 3 variables), explains 44 per cent of the variance. It shows that committee hearings increase the likelihood of committee conflict significantly, as does committee independence. Again, the significant effects of committee size, number of committees, pre-parliamentary commission, independence, and government bills are retained.

Finally, model 4 introduces political system variables (fourth group of variables) as control variables. Except for candidate vote, none of the system characteristics (consociational, corporatist, effective number of parties, and parliamentarism), have significant effects on the likelihood of committee conflict. At the same time, there remain significant effects of committee size in the first block of variables, of pre-parliamentary commissions in the second block, and of committee independence and hearings in the third block. These control variables, thus, do not reject promising results from individual data analysis of the SPPL dataset. Significant results from model 3 are, with the only exception of 'number of committees' neither reduced nor impaired if they are controlled for aggregate system properties. There is no reason for surprise that these system properties do not show a great deal of significance at all because they are constants within each country that show variation only between countries, that is between altogether no more than 16 cases. Model 4 explains 47 per cent of the variance.

Conclusions

We took the Sartorian notion of committees as our point of departure. Committees are small, interactive, face-to-face groups, characterized by durability. They are highly institutionalized, which entails, that as distinct, specified groups, they have certain tasks assigned to them. Committees are also confronted with a flow of decisions. Given these characteristics, Sartori claims that decisions in committees are most often reached with unanimity. Even if the pertinent rules formally prescribe majority rule as a proper procedure, decisions are not ordinarily brought to a vote. This is due to an operational code of reciprocation that exists in committees that function well. However, when voting substitutes unanimity, Sartori rather provocatively claims 'that a committee ceases to be a committee' (1987: p.230).

Faced with the empirical observations from 17 West European parliaments we are inclined to conclude that the parliamentary committees fail to be committees. That is at least as long as we keep the Sartorian notion of committees. We found indications on conflict in committees for 58 per cent of the labor market bills. Consensus prevailed in 42 per cent of the cases. It seems obvious that an understanding of parliamentary committees cannot be built solely on the Sartorian notion of committees.

We then proceeded with bivariate and multivariate analyses with the intention to explain the variation in conflict. The first group of variables to be tested was derived from the key elements of the Sartorian conceptualization of committees. We then added three other groups of variables for purposes of control. These were type of bill, committee strength and political system characteristics. Table 5.25 summarizes our analyses in a somewhat different way than was Table 5.24 above.

Instead of analyzing logit coefficients as in Table 5.24, we can also analyze our regression results in terms of risks or odds ratios. This enables us to interpret the results comprehensively and also improve the possibility to estimate the relative importance of the different independent variables (although odds ratios must, like unstandardized logits, be compared with caution). The question is about the risk for conflict associated with a given variable. Table 5.25 thus indicates the odds ratio for each of the significant (5 per cent level) variables in model 4.[14]

Table 5.25 Risk for Conflict in Committee

Variable	Odds ratio
Committee hearings	4.9
Candidate vote	4.0
Pre-parliamentary commission	0.6
Independence	2.4
Committee size	1.1

The risk for conflict is 4.9 times greater (change in odds) if the committee arranges a hearing during its deliberation than if it does not. If candidate votes are possible, the risk for conflict is 4 times greater than if it does not. The similar change in odds for pre-parliamentary commission is 0.6. The interpretation of the

14 That is, number of committees and effective number of parties have been excluded from the table but is still included in the model.

two continuous variables is as follows. By increasing the value for independence by 1 the change of odds ratio is 2.4 and for committee size it is 1.1.

In sum we can conclude that little is left to support the Sartorian argument when the critical variables are controlled for by other crucial variables. Conflict is fostered in committees that arrange hearings on the matter and where the election system allows for candidate votes. Hearings and, to some extent committee size, is coherent with a Sartorian notion of committees, but this is obviously not sufficient if one wants to understand the parliamentary committees in Western Europe.

It is apparent that the contexts of parliaments do have an impact on how the committees work. The political system in which the committees work is important. Mayhew's electoral connection seems to be at work. If candidate votes are possible, then level of conflict increases in parliament. We interpret this as a sign of increased level of competition among parliamentarians.

Our final observation that we want to emphasize is that conflict is more common in strong committees. In the outset of our article we pointed to the common notion – which is well in line with the Sartorian conception of committees – that connects strong committees with consensus. Hilmar Rommetvedt, however, had found that this was certainly not the case for Norway and we are inclined to broaden his conclusion to Western European parliaments. Conflict primarily occurs in strong committees.

Chapter 6

Controversy, Time Constraint, and Restrictive Rules

Herbert Döring*

The very notion of voting a bill under a 'restrictive rule' is well known for the US Congress. What may be less well known is the observation that it is also a fact of parliamentary life in Western Europe. While there is a wealth of in-depth studies of agenda control in the US Congress (Gilligan and Krehbiel 1989, Bach 1990, Binder 1997, Binder and Smith 1997, Dion 1998, Marshall 2002) to date there is only one comparative work (Huber 1992), which compares restrictive legislative procedures in the United States and France. The multinational team 'Parliaments and Majority Rule in Western Europe' attempted to redress this balance by focusing, among quite a few other aspects, on restrictive rules. From the SPPL data set it turned out that no less than 80 of 512 bills across 17 parliamentary democracies witnessed some kind of restrictive rule (amendment control or timetable control or vote of confidence procedure).[1] It goes without saying that there is one huge difference, all similarities notwithstanding, between restrictive rules in the US and Western Europe. In the presidential system of the US, it is some authority within the House that grants a restrictive rule on a bill. But in the parliamentary systems of Western Europe it is rather the executive itself, i.e., that part of parliament that happens to form the government of the day, that invokes restrictive rules. In some cases government imposition of restrictions occurs, as we shall see, without active consent of parliament.

Government imposition of restrictive rules in the procedure for passing legislation can be exercised in either of three different ways. (1) Government may impose a restrictive amendment rule. This instrument is possible only in a few countries of Western Europe, for example the package vote (*vote bloqué*) in France. (2) Government may limit the time available for discussion of a bill and fix a date in advance for final voting on the bill, no matter whether all of its clauses have been dealt with. This instrument also exists in only a few countries, for example motions of 'closure' or the British 'allocation of time order' also called

* My special thanks for statistical advice and assistance in data management go to Silke Hans and Jewgenij Sven Noth.

1 The different procedures for restrictive rules are explained in section 2.

the British-style 'parliamentary guillotine'. (3) Government may at any time link adoption of a particular bill to its own fate by making it a vote of confidence. This procedure makes the bill a take-it-or-leave-it or rather 'take-it-or throw-me-out' proposal. A well-known example for this confidence vote procedure is Article 49.3 of the French Constitution also called the French-style 'parliamentary guillotine'. This third instrument is ubiquitous in all parliamentary democracies (Huber 1996b, Diermeier and Feddersen 1998).[2] The 'confidence vote procedure' is, of course, not so much geared to staying in office as to restricting any changes to a bill. It therefore may justifiably be grouped under the heading of 'restrictive rules', too.

This chapter is studying government imposition of restrictive rules in the 17 parliamentary democracies contained in the SPPL data set not for purely descriptive reasons. From a theoretical angle it is also going to re-examine with bills as units of analysis a topic previously only explored with aggregate data (Döring 1995d, 1995e, 2001). The research question at issue is whether time constraints as well as controversy between government and opposition, notably towards the end of the legislative term, form an important and empirically provable rationale for government imposition of restrictive rules on bills in final voting. Readers may be cautioned at the outset here that the term 'controversy' is to signify not so much substantial policy disagreement but rather a rhetoric of conflict created for the purpose of impressing voters. The difference is perhaps best captured by John D. Huber's (1996a: pp.65-68, 75f) distinction between the two notions of 'policy conflict' on the one hand and 'controversy' and 'political cover' on the other.

Searching for correlations between time constraint, controversy and restrictive rules is tantamount to adding another rational choice point of view to a series of already well-received theories for imposition of restrictive rules. Based on neo-classical assumptions of 'cost and output' in law production, in the first book of the 'Parliaments and Majority Rule in Western Europe' research group Döring (1995b) and Henning (1995) arrived at a theoretical prediction properly formalized by Henning with the apparatus of formal logic as used by economists. This seemingly paradoxical, yet quite logical, prediction holds: the more a government, due to time-saving prerogatives of agenda control, is principally able to push many legislative measures through, the fewer, yet more controversial, bills it is actually inclined to submit to parliament (a theoretical explanation for this expectation will be given in section 1). In other words, there should be visible a negative correlation between high agenda control and average total volume of legislation, but a positive correlation between high agenda control and average controversy over bills.

Section 1 recapitulates in an introductory précis the Döring and Henning theory about the impact of agenda control, referring to the previously published formal model by Henning (1995). *Section 2* clarifies what different instruments for imposition of 'restrictive rules' actually exist in Western Europe and gives a brief

---

2 Even in Iceland, where Huber did not find any provision for such a rule in the Constitution or Standing Orders of parliament (Huber 1996b: p.271, Table 1), it was actually practiced in the SPPL data set.

overview of previous findings confirming on the basis of aggregate analyses the two predictions by Döring and Henning. In countries with an opportunity structure conducive to high government control of the agenda there are (a) on average fewer bills (Döring 1995c, Döring 1995d) and these bills are (b) comparatively more controversial as measured in means of divisions on bills by country (Döring 2001).

The proof of the pudding is, however, in checking those already published aggregate results with individual data. *Section 3* shows in bivariate analysis with individual bills in the SPPL data set: (a) there were more delaying attempts of opposition parties against government bills if and when a restrictive rule was imposed and (b) in case of a restrictive rule being imposed more often than not there was also time constraint visible in terms of fewer days until the end of the legislative term. It would be naïve, however, to assume from those bivariate correlations the Döring and Henning theory already to be 'proven'. The decisive question is whether these bivariate results will prove robust if controlled in multivariate analysis for the simultaneous impact of other, perhaps more promising, reasons for government imposition of restrictive rules.

Section 4, therefore, extracts from the rational choice literature about observable behavior of actors in parliaments a series of testable hypotheses. These hypotheses serve as controls for the Döring and Henning theory. *Section 5* then subjects all of those theories to logistic regression analysis of the likelihood of restrictive rules being imposed by governments in the procedure for passing legislation. It turns out that the Döring and Henning theory, which is the last one to be inserted into a series of logistic regressions, does add predictive value if all of the alternative theories are also retained in the logistic regression model.

A Theoretical Rationale to be Examined: Electoral Utility of Agenda Control Concerning Controversial Bills

Most rational choice studies on parliaments focus on 'policy conflict' instead of 'partisan conflict'. Yet time as a scarce resource is a neglected topic in most of those studies. The bargaining model by Baron and Ferejohn (1989) operates, however, with assumptions of urgency and open as well as closed amendment rules. But it differs from Döring and Henning in that it concentrates on policy conflict visible in amendment procedures, and not on partisan conflict. Furthermore, their 'logic does not focus on how restrictive procedures expedite processes by limiting dilatory tactics on the floor' (Huber 1996a: p.99). This is precisely the intention of Döring and Henning, who emphasize interactions between time constraint, controversy and agenda control. Working together at the Mannheim Centre for European Social Research, they developed in joint discussions two conjectures, subsequently formalized by Henning (Döring 1995b, Henning 1995):

A. In countries where institutional means for agenda control exist, a government will on average produce fewer bills than in countries with little or no agenda control.

B. In spite of producing fewer bills, those pieces of legislation will in high-agenda-control countries be on average more controversial than those in low-agenda-control countries. These two empirically examinable predictions about volume and contentiousness of legislation were arrived at in several steps under the following assumptions:

1. In parliamentary systems the government 'is the single producer of political decisions [...] analogous to the single firm in a natural monopoly' (Crain, Holcombe and Tollison 1979: p.54).

In parliamentary systems the choice of how many bills a parliament will consider is made by the government. Not only may it choose whether to produce laws or instead take recourse to government regulations. In those systems private member bills have no chances of success except when tolerated by government (for statistics on success rates of private member bills in Western European parliaments, see Andeweg and Nijzink 1995: p.171, Table 5.4, Mattson 1995: p.478, Table 14.6).

2. Even if government comes close to a monopoly in law production, oppositional deputies may kill government bills by using obstructionist tactics when time is running out towards the end of the legislative term.

There is a lot opposition parties can do in some systems to delay or even 'kill' bills if they are not passed before the end of the legislative term. Only if there is consensus between government and opposition are the transaction costs of passing bills low. Opposition parties may, for example, extend debate over a conflictual bill by occasional filibustering, which is possible in Finland (Arter 1984: p.280). They may delay final voting and prolong publicity-rousing debates in parliament by putting up amendment proposals that even obstruct government business if government has no powers to curtail debate.

3. The marginal costs of producing additional government bills tend to rise towards the end of the legislative term and will be higher for controversial bills than for consensual ones. Imposition of restrictive rules against delaying attempts by opposition parties lowers the marginal costs of producing additional bills for controversial bills more than it does for consensual bills.

In parliament, which is constantly pressed for time, the marginal costs of producing additional laws, even for a monopolist, cannot be modeled as a remaining constant over time, but are bound to rise as the legislative term progresses. In the large majority of political systems, pending bills lapse at the end of the session or legislative term if not voted upon. As a result they must be reintroduced all the way back at the start of the 'legislative obstacle course' (Olson 1980: p.350f.). Assumption 3 as well as the following assumptions are graphically visualized as a simplified scheme in Figure 6.1:

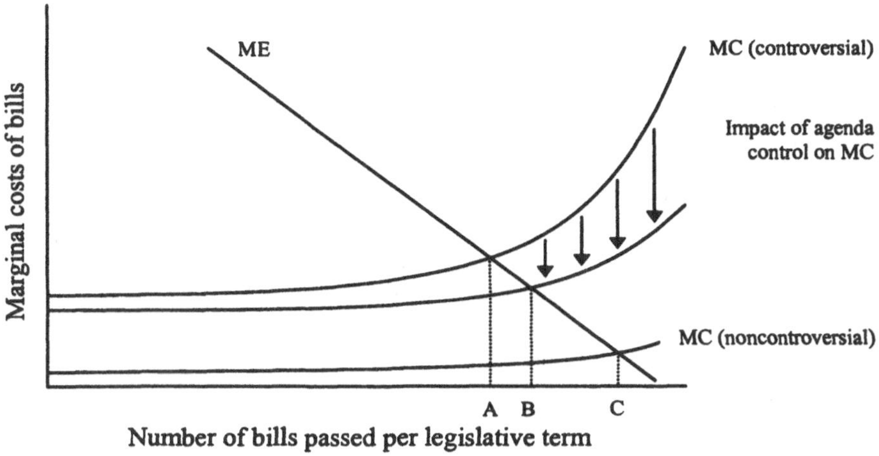

MC = Marginal costs
ME = Marginal evaluation

Figure 6.1 Impact of Agenda Control on Marginal Costs

Source: Döring 1995b: p.46

4. For reasons of electoral utility a government will prefer a controversial bill to a consensual one.

Controversial laws carry a higher electoral utility, the model assumes, because they elicit a higher political support response. In the game between the 'ins' and the 'outs' visible contestation between competing teams carries advantages in vote maximizing. Given the government can determine the agenda it 'will use the parliament for those matters that it considers of major importance and wishes to symbolize to the whole population' (Olson 1980: p.17f). One can, therefore, 'assume that disciplined parliamentary government, when pondering the utility of producing an additional bill, will, for reelection purposes, prefer a conflictual bill to a routine administrative technical bill' (Döring 1995b: p.45). But passing such conflictual laws also requires a higher amount of resources (time in the simplified model).

5. A government will normally produce more consensual than controversial bills because they are less cost-intensive. Given constant resources, a lowering of decision-making costs by agenda control works as an inducement to substitute controversial bills for consensual ones.

Lowering decision-making costs due to an invocation of instruments for agenda control works as an incentive for government to draft more conflictual bills (a move from point A to B in figure 6.1). However, even with agenda control controversial bills will still be more costly than consensual ones. Because resources for overall law production are assumed to remain constant and limited, the hypothesized substitution effect of controversial for uncontroversial bills must lead to an adjustment of the number of uncontroversial bills (a move from point C into the direction of point B in figure 6.1). Henning separated agenda control into a substitution effect and scale effect (Henning 1995: p.613, Figure 13.1), from which the following prediction is derived: In the 'monopolistic mix' of law production, government, while still producing different kinds of bills, will be induced to substitute conflictual for uncontroversial bills. Accordingly, the total mix of both types of bills will in the aggregate show altogether fewer, but more controversial bills.

For reasons of electoral utility, stirring up of controversy not for substantive policy reasons but for 'product differentiation' between government and opposition may be attractive for government if it can curb the resulting outcry of, and delaying attempts by, opposition parties through imposition of restrictive rules on bills.[3]

This simplified scheme of time constraint (end of legislative term), controversy and agenda control (part and parcel of which are restrictive rules) has been formalized by political scientist and economist Christian Henning, who proved that the intuition outlined in steps 1 to 5 above holds if subjected to rigorous formal modeling with the advanced apparatus of economics (Henning 1995). The theoretical rationale therefore becomes a matter for empirical operationalization and data analysis. A first step consists of answering the question of how many instruments for agenda control exist in each of the 18 Western European parliaments. A second step must then arrive at a comparative rank ordering of those instruments between countries according to 'more' or 'less' government control of the parliamentary agenda. On the basis of these two steps a cross-national rank order correlation between agenda control and average volume of legislation as well as average controversy in final voting on bills may provide an aggregate test of the first of the two Döring and Henning predictions.

3 The opposition, too, may try to play a similar game but is at a strong disadvantage if it wants to stir up contentious issues on matters where the government majority is divided. Huber reports from the French politics literature how opposition amendments to government bills are strategically used not to change policy but to embarrass the government trying to force it to take a stand on politically contentious issues (Huber 1996a: 73f). However, if the government possesses restrictive rules, it can curb such attempts.

Institutional Means of Government Agenda Control: Rank Ordering of Instruments across Western Europe

The notion of agenda control is crucial to empirically informed rational choice analyses of the working of modern parliaments. Shepsle and Weingast viewed 'legislative institutions as agenda-formation processes' that imply 'policy consequences' (1982: p.369). In spite of the importance of agenda control in legislative institutions, comparative research is surprisingly sparse. Moving towards closing this gap Döring (1995c) attempted an inventory of the institutional means of government agenda control in the procedure for deliberating bills in the plenary and committees in all of the first chambers of Western European parliaments including Switzerland. Identifying seven variables pertinent for government control of the agenda, Döring rank-ordered each of the seven variables according to whether they provided 'more' or 'less' government control (Döring 1995c; for a précis of these seven dimensions, see also Tsebelis 2002: pp.99-103). Masuyama (2000) has recently explored the utility of the Döring criteria for determining whether or not rules and procedures in the Japanese Diet are majoritarian or consensual.

When Döring calculated Spearman rank correlations between values for each of the seven variables, the variable *Authority to Determine the Plenary Agenda of Parliament* turned out to show stronger intercorrelations with more of the other six agenda-setting devices than any other of the seven variables (Döring 1995c: p.244, Table 7.8). Döring therefore suggested this intuitively plausible variable as an ordinal scale to proxy agenda control in comparative analysis. This qualitative measure for agenda control has seven modalities. At the two extremes, agendas can be determined by the Government or by the Parliament alone. The following list of possibilities may serve as an ordinal measure to establish the existence of 'more' or 'less' agenda control:

- I. The government sets the agenda alone (UK and Ireland).
- II. In a president's conference the government commands a majority larger than its share of seats in the chamber (France and Greece).
- III. Decision by majority rule at president's conference where party groups are proportionally represented (Luxembourg, Portugal, and Switzerland).
- IV. Consensus agreement of party groups sought in president's conference but the plenary majority can overturn the proposal (Austria, Belgium, Germany, Norway, and Spain).
- V. The president's decision after consultation of party groups cannot be challenged by the chamber (Denmark, Finland, Iceland, and Sweden).
- VI. Fragmentation of agenda setting centers if unanimous vote of party leaders cannot be reached (Italy).
- VII. The Chamber itself determines the agenda (Netherlands).

Tsebelis went a step further and ran a factor analysis of all of the seven Döring variables. He then took the factor scores assigned to each of the 18 countries as a quantitative proxy variable for the comparative strength of government agenda control across countries. The qualitative Döring index of *Authority to Determine the Plenary Agenda of Parliament* and these quantitative *Tsebelis Factor Scores of Countries* form the two best possible yet still less than perfect measures for a comparative cross-national measurement of the relative strength of government agenda control between the 18 countries of Western Europe.

Tsebelis justifiably criticized that, 'While the variable "agenda control" is the most advanced currently in the literature, country scores on that variable should not be considered final' (Tsebelis 2002: p.103). The seven variables rank ordered by Döring are a step towards 'compiling objective indicators about who can place items on the agenda and whether they can reduce discussion time on the floor or in the relevant committees, but further work is required' (Tsebelis 2002: p.104). For example, Tsebelis observes, the Heller (2001) and Weingast (1992) argument of 'fighting fire with fire,' that is introducing a last-minute amendment has not been included in Döring's list. Indeed, Döring almost exclusively focused on the timetable dimension of agenda control and only marginally paid attention to the amendment-control dimension of agenda control.

Table 6.1 juxtaposes the qualitative Döring index of *Authority to Determine the Plenary Agenda of Parliament* with the ability of governments to incur the last-amendment privilege on bills as registered by Heller (1999) for Western European democracies. From an inspection of Table 6.1 a trade-off between the two instruments emerges. Countries with little or no ability to control the order of the day of the plenary (high values signify little agenda control) to a large extent enjoy the privilege of being able to put the last amendment. Thus, they may save their policy against oppositional amendment activities even if they cannot easily control the timetable. A significant Spearman rank order correlation of -0.52 indicates this possible substitution effect to be no mere coincidence. This observation gives rise to the assumption that it is necessary to analytically distinguish between two dimensions of agenda control: timetable control and amendment control.

A first layer of restrictive rules is, indeed, formed by various devices for restricting initiatives and amendments (for a first comparative account covering Western Europe, see Mattson 1995). A second layer is, however, formed by restrictions safeguarding timetable control. Timetable restrictions grant to the agenda setter scheduling power for speeding up business of the House against delaying attempts up to outright obstruction from opposition parties. The amendment-control dimension of restrictive rules makes governmental policy stick by making a bill an up-or-down proposal and, thus, protecting it against hostile amendments from the floor. The timetable-control dimension of restrictive rules saves time for government and lowers decision-making costs.

Table 6.1 Authority to Determine the Plenary Agenda[1] and Last Amendment-Privilege of Government[2]

Agenda Control		Last Amendment: *Not available*	Last Amendment: *Does exist*
High	1	Ireland UK	
	2	Greece	France
	3	Luxembourg Portugal	
	4	Austria Belgium Germany Norway	Spain
	5	Finland	Denmark Sweden
	6		Italy
Low	7		Netherlands

Spearman's rank order correlation = - 0.52

Sources:
[1] Döring 1995b: p.227, Table 7.1
[2] Heller 2001, Tables 1-4

Why should agenda control be broken down into the two related but quite distinct components of amendment control and timetable control? An intuitively plausible answer is provided by comparing the 'parliamentary guillotines' French-style and British-style. They both carry the same name but mean different things – one amendment control and the other timetable control. The French guillotine according to the famous, and notorious, article 49.3, which is at the sole discretion of the Prime Minister, makes a contested bill an up-or-down proposal by linking it to a censure motion. Even without a vote the bill is declared passed if the Assemblée Nationale does not succeed in voting the government out of office.

This French-style parliamentary guillotine of the so-called confidence vote procedure has the side effect of restricting rights of Members of the Assemblée Nationale to discuss, amend, and vote specific aspects of a bill. The Assembly has no alternative but to vote the government out of office or accept the bill en bloc. However, the procedure does not permit the government 'to evade criticism during the debate on the censure motion' (Huber 1996a: p.136). Nor does the second of the two restrictive rules in France, the *vote bloqué*, by which only amendments originating from government are voted upon, save the government much parliamentary time on the floor. Members may continue proposing and defending amendments although these do not stand any chance of being voted upon: 'Contrary to the initial expectations of the framers of the Constitution (in Debré's working group), the use of the package vote does not preclude members of the legislature from using their full five minutes allotted for the oral defense of their amendments. Although the procedure does save time on actual voting, it cannot be used to break obstruction caused by a cascade of amendments' (Huber 1996a: p.101).

In stark contrast, the parliamentary guillotine in the Palace of Westminster, which aptly is also called an 'Allocation of Time Order', precisely intends to save precious government time in the Commons against delaying attempts by Her Majesty's Opposition (Barclay 1977: pp.44-56, Taylor 1979: pp.82f, 97, 145-148, 152). The British parliamentary guillotine stipulates that a vote shall be taken on a day fixed in advance, no matter how many clauses of the respective bill have been discussed up to the day the guillotine strikes. Only amendments accepted by discretion of the Speaker of the House shall be voted upon. Thus, the French guillotine saves policy but not time, whereas the British guillotine is designed to save both time and policy.

Restrictions referred to so far may be invoked or not be invoked by governments in a variety of ways. There are, however, a few more restrictions that apply to each and every bill within a country and show variation only across nations. For example, if standing orders in a given country prohibit any financial amendments of private members to government bills without prior approval of government, this rule applies to all bills without exception and is a 'constant' within, but a variable across countries (for the distribution of countries on this 'money bills' rule, see Döring 1995: p.232, Table 7.2). Researchers should, therefore, distinguish between constants and variables of agenda control.

Amendment control has, nevertheless, not just a policy-preserving but also a time-saving dimension. A battery of amendments may be brought forward, not with the serious intent of changing policy, but to use up valuable government time during the end of the legislative term. In most countries bills not voted upon lapse with the end of term (either a sessional term of one year, as in Britain, or the full legislative term of a few years). In only a few countries do 'bills never die' and may be carried over into the next legislative term. Therefore, a distinct dimension of barring further amendments is geared, not so much towards making policy stick, but rather to curbing delaying attempts by opposition parties who try to defeat a government bill by talking it out of business.

In spite of the above mentioned limitations of the qualitative Döring index and the quantitative Tsebelis factor scores, these two operationalizations for the cross-national variable 'agenda control' are 'the most advanced currently in the literature' (Tsebelis 2002: p.103). They may, thus, be used for a first tentative checking of hypotheses with aggregate cross-national data. In the previous book by the 'Parliaments and Majority Rule in Western Europe' research group Döring (1995d) correlated his qualitative index of *Authority to Determine the Plenary Agenda of Parliament* as a suitable proxy variable for overall agenda control with the average quantity of legislation per country. Aggregate data of the average number of bills per country were by members of the group provided from original sources written in different countries' languages. The theory was strongly supported by a Spearman coefficient of 0.73 (0.001). Controlling this positive bivariate result in partial correlations for spuriousness, Döring eliminated other plausible explanations including a country's population size, electoral barriers for party entry, number of parties in parliament, additional legislation at the subnational level, and the issuing of government decrees instead of acts of parliament (Döring 1995e).

The second prediction about high agenda control to be correlated with more controversy was also confirmed in aggregate analysis. In a preliminary analysis of the SPPL data set mean values for conflict in final voting on bills (323 valid cases out of 468 government bills) per country were cross-tabulated against the qualitative index of *Authority to Determine the Plenary Agenda of Parliament*. Results supported the theory. France, Greece, and the United Kingdom, which rank highest in government control of the agenda on average, pass more controversial bills (for operationalization, see Döring 2001: p.158f. with Table 4). Calculating Spearman correlations with non-grouped data of conflict in final voting yields a coefficient of 0.22 (0.000) for the qualitative Döring index and of 0.16 (0.011) for the quantitative Tsebelis index.

Aggregate analyses, thus, lend support to Döring and Henning's decision-making cost theory of government imposition of restrictive rules. However, because all analyses reported so far use countries as units of analysis, the danger of an ecological fallacy always looms large. From the mere existence of such rules in a given country it cannot be inferred that governments will always automatically use them. Indeed the Spearman correlation between the qualitative Döring index of agenda control and actual government imposition of restrictive rules on particular bills (for a description of this variable, see appendix to this chapter) is only 0.39 (0.000). Similarly its correlation with the quantitative Tsebelis index of agenda control is also no more than 0.39 (0.001). Restrictions on bills may be used for reasons other than those visible in cross-national aggregations. The exciting question, therefore, is whether aggregate results will prove sufficiently robust to be corroborated with individual bills as units of analysis.[4]

Controversy, Time Constraint and Restrictive Rules in Bivariate Individual Data Analysis

To examine the issue of agenda control, the SPPL data set includes specific questions geared to this question. The data set established, first of all, whether there were only one or several decisive readings regarding the policy content of a bill and whether further readings, if any, were only a formality. For one or several readings considered to be no mere formality, two further questions were then asked: 'Did government invoke restrictive procedures?' and, separately, 'Did government declare its intention to treat bill as a question of confidence?'. We may distinguish from the data set whether a confidence vote was invoked on a bill or whether any other restriction was imposed. It is not possible, however, to establish whether these 'other' restrictions belong to the amendment-control or timetable-control dimensions of agenda control.

Data were recoded into a variable labeled 'restrict' if some kind of restrictive rule was imposed in either of the decisive readings and into a variable labeled 'confid' if a bill was declared a matter of confidence.[5] Missing cases excluded, we have information for 512 bills across the 17 parliamentary systems of Western Europe. On the basis of these valid cases, only 8 bills were linked to a confidence vote and 74 to some other kind of restrictive rules. Half of the 8 cases of confidence vote took place in France, proving this procedure to be a French specialty in spite of theoretically being applicable to all parliamentary systems (Huber 1996b). Although restrictive rules, not least due to their explicit anchoring in the Constitution, are widespread in France, they are in the SPPL data set also to be found across all but three of the Western European parliamentary systems.[6] Given there were so few cases of the confidence vote procedure across Western Europe at large, confidence votes and other restrictive rules for the purpose of this

4 It goes without saying only the second part of Döring and Henning's prediction about controversy under time constraint can be examined here. The first part of the prediction about the reduced overall between-country volume of legislation in response to means for agenda control, cannot be examined with a random sample of bills taken from the total volume within each country.

5 The SPSS syntax is as follows: if (v91=1 and v98=1) restrict=1. if (v91=2 or v98=2) restrict=2. if (v91=1 and v98=9991) restrict=1. if (v91=1 and v98=9999) restrict=1. if (v92=2 and v99=2) confid=1. if (v92=1 or v99=1) confid=2. if (v92=2 and v99=9991) confid=1. if (v92=2 and v99=9999) confid=1.

6 No such restrictions were according to the data set imposed in Finland, Norway and Sweden.

analysis were combined into a single variable labeled 'impose', which indicates whether or not any kind of restriction (confidence or other) was invoked (1=no, 2=yes) during the decisive reading of a particular bill.[7]

This variable 'impose' forms the crucial dependent variable of this chapter. Let us now briefly describe which independent variables were used. How is controversy between government and opposition to be operationalized, given SPPL data? To make our analysis comparable with related studies in the field, the most suitable proxy variable for this issue appears to be 'efforts made by opposition to oppose bill's adoption'. Such a question had also been used by John D. Huber in his data set on the 'package vote' and the 'parliamentary guillotine' (art. 49, 3) of the French constitution. The SPPL data set, thus, established whether the opposition made none such efforts at all or demanded the verification of the quorum, demanded suspension of debate, moved the bill to be returned to committee or made 'any other' effort as described and reported by data collectors.[8] Given the unequal distribution of a variety of tactics employed, we constructed a dichotomous variable 'delay' (1=no, 2=yes) indicating whether any such efforts were made.[9]

Table 6.2 gives the basic descriptive results. The distribution of valid cases in a cross-tabulation of government imposition of restrictive rules ('impose') with delaying attempts of opposition parties ('delay') is supportive to the Döring and Henning theory. Where there had been no delaying attempts of opposition parties only 12.4 per cent of bills are subjected to restrictive rules and vice versa, whereas this figure rises to 27 per cent when there are delaying attempts.

---

7 The SPSS syntax for this dichotomous variable is as follows: if (restrict=1 and confid=1) impose=1. if (restrict=2 or confid=2) impose=2.

8 The frequency distribution of these categories of various delaying attempts prevents us from using this variable as an ordinal scale (Frequencies for v90 are none =410; demanding the verification of the quorum =3; demanding suspension of this debate =1; moving the bill to be returned to committee =14; other =74).

9 The SPSS syntax for this dichotomous variable is as follows: recode v90 (1=1) (2-5=2) into r90. recode v97 (1=1) (2-5=2)(9991=9991) (9999=9999) into r97. if (r90=2 or r97=2) delay=2. if (r90=1 and r97=1) delay=1. if (r90=1 and r97=9991) delay=1. if (r90=1 and r97=9999) delay=1.

Table 6.2 Controversy and Government Imposition of Restrictions

		Imposition of restrictions	
		No	*Yes*
Delaying attempts of opposition parties	*No*	332 (87.6%)	47 (12.4%)
	Yes	89 (73%)	33 (27%)
Total		421	80

Phi = 0.17 ($p<0.001$)

Note: For a description of variables, see appendix to this chapter.

The Phi coefficient is highly significant and, given the many possible other reasons for government imposition of restrictive rules (to be explained in the next section), reasonably large at a moderate 0.17. This result confirms and jibes with one of Huber's finding for France, i.e. the significant occurrence of delaying attempts with regard to both the French restrictive procedure, i.e. the confidence vote and the package vote (Huber 1996a: p.77-19 with Table 3.3, p102f. with Table 4.7 and 106f. with Table 4.8).

However, over and above controversy manifesting itself in delaying tactics, Huber emphasized a quite different dimension of conflict on substantial issues of policy. Distinguishing between 'controversy' and 'policy conflict', Huber studied amendments on bills as indicators for 'policy conflict'. Huber showed by formal modeling the very notion of policy conflict in relation to restrictive rules to be theoretically and logically impossible. He subsequently proved by careful analysis of French amendments on policy such a conflict, furthermore, not to have taken place at all in relation to imposition of restrictive rules (Huber 1996a: p.71-79).[10] This sophisticated distinction by Huber between 'policy conflict' and 'partisan conflict' opens up an avenue for further research. For the present analysis,

10 Such a meticulous documentation of amendments in final voting enabling Huber to conduct his analysis on amendments appears to be a particularity limited to France and two more countries, whereas in the majority of Western European countries similar statistics on amendments are unavailable. When the SPPL data set asked data collectors to establish whether or not there was a synopsis on amendments suggested, rejected and taken at various stages of a bill (v110) and, if there was one, to enclose this synopsis to the answered questionnaire, only in three of 17 countries (France, Greece and Italy) were such synopses regularly available. For France such synopses were added to all bills in the SPPL set.

however, it is irrelevant because the Döring and Henning theory focuses on 'partisan conflict' and not on 'policy conflict' in conjunction with imposition of restrictive rules.

Having confirmed Döring and Henning with regard to the first of their two crucial independent variables, i.e. increased controversy, we now turn to the second important independent variable, i.e. time constraint. There is a stark contradiction between findings of Huber for France and the cross-national evidence from the SPPL data set. In his data set for France of 346 government bills voted in first reading between 1978 and 1989 John D. Huber found no correlation whatever between time constraint and the French government's invocation of either of the two restrictive rules (Huber, 1996a: pp.78f, 104 and 107 with Tables 3.3, 4.7 and 4.8). This negative evidence may, however, be attributed to that French peculiarity mentioned in section 2 above, that restrictive rules save policy but not time. In contrast to Huber, Becker and Saalfeld (chapter 3 above) have already demonstrated with event-history techniques that the aggregate Döring index of the existence of possibilities for government to exercise restrictive rules, even if controlled for the actual imposition of such rules on bills, is correlated with a speedier passage of bills.[11]

Becker and Saalfeld had to exclude France from their analysis because many of the time variables needed were missing in the French questionnaires. With inclusion of France Table 3 gives once more, in addition to Becker and Saalfeld, bivariate correlations for time constraint and imposition restrictive rules.[12]

---

11 They tested the impact of 'invocation of restrictive rule' on the speed and success of the legislative process as an independent variable in the single-episode model and as a control variable in the multiple-episode model. As expected, the legislative process overall tends to be speedier and the success chances of bills tend to improve, if and when restrictive rules such as 'guillotine' or 'closure' motions are used at a decisive stage of the plenary deliberations (Table 3.7, Model 6a).

12 Inclusion of France becomes possible in this simplified design because the date of the final vote on the totality of a bill is contained in the SPPL data set for France even if many more variables on dates required for event-history analysis are missing.

Table 6.3 Time Constraint and Government Imposition of Restrictions

		Imposition of restrictions	
		No	*Yes*
Days until end of legislative term	*Up to a quarter of a year*	70 (66%)	36 (34%)
	Up to half a year	50 (82%)	11 (18%)
	More than half a year	117 (87.3%)	17 (12.7%)
Total		237 (78.7%)	64 (21.3%)
With non grouped-data, the correlation is Eta = 0.12			
Days until next election	*Up to a year*	95 (93.1%)	7 (6.9%)
	Up to two years	63 (84%)	12 (16%)
	More than two years	98 (89.1%)	12 (10.9%)
Total		256 (89.2%)	31 (10.8%)
With non grouped-data, the correlation is Eta = 0.02			

Note: For a description of variables, see appendix to this chapter.

The variable 'days until end of legislative term' significantly supports in Table 6.3 the Döring and Henning theory. However, it is neither supported nor rejected with 'days until next election'. For 'days until end of legislative term' the number of valid cases was divided into roughly three equal intervals, 34 per cent of bills witness a restrictive rule if only a quarter of a year is left until the end of term. This percentage decreases to 18 per cent if the time span is up to half a year and further decreases to only 12.7 per cent if more than half a year is left between the day of the final vote and the end of the legislative term. To exclude the distorting effect of grouped data, correlation coefficients are in Table 6.3 also given for the non-grouped originally coded days left until the end of the legislative term as well as to the next election. Looking for a bivariate correlation with non-grouped data, the Eta coefficient appears to be suitable for a correlation of a dichotomous variable such as imposition of restrictive rules with a continuous variable of number of days. The small Eta = 0.12 appears to be satisfactory if one takes into consideration that quite a few reasons for imposition of restrictive rules other than time constraint are possible (see next section). But it remains to be seen whether this small coefficient is sufficiently robust not to disappear in the concluding multivariate analysis in section 6.

From the second part of Table 3 it also becomes apparent that the Döring and Henning theory is neither supported nor rejected with respect to the 'days until next election'. Neither does the inspection of cases in the cells nor the Eta coefficient show any association whatever. This inconclusive finding should, however, be no reason for surprise. For if a pending bill is lost in Britain towards the end of the first session of parliament the House of Commons may still have four years to go until the next election. In some countries such as Denmark, Iceland and the United Kingdom bills die at the end of the session if not voted upon, whereas in other countries bills lapse only after a period of four to five years, when the legislature is dissolved before the next election. In only a few countries the carrying-over into the next legislature is possible, and in some countries 'bills never die' except when rejected by a vote (for 'maximum lifespan of a bill after which it lapses if not adopted' across 18 Western European countries, see Döring 1995c: p.242, Table 7.7). Given this highly variable discontinuity principle, the time span until the end of the respective legislative term, and not until the next election, appears to be the suitable proxy variable for time constraint.

In conclusion, with the suitable proxy variable for time constraint significantly positive and the second, less suitable proxy variable at least not negative but inconclusive, the Döring and Henning hypothesis about time constraint as a reason for governments to impose restrictive rules is confirmed with inclusion of France. This result is corroborated by the much more sophisticated event-history techniques used by Becker and Saalfeld (chapter 3) with exclusion of France. So Döring and Henning are warranted in bivariate analyses for both controversy and time constraint. It remains to be seen, however, whether the small yet significant correlations reported in this section will hold if controlled for other much more plausible reasons for government imposition of restrictive rules. In preparation of multivariate controls an inventory of empirically testable alternative rationales will in the next section be extracted from the rational choice literature on parliaments.

Towards Multivariate Controls: Alternative Rationales and Empirically Testable Hypotheses for Imposition of Restrictive Rules

Seven generalizations why governments are likely to resort to restrictive rules, including two hypotheses derived from Döring and Henning, may be singled out from a rational choice perspective on parliamentary behavior.[13] As references constantly are made to the literature where these hypotheses have been developed in a more rigorous way, including formal modelling in each case, it suffices to sketch out these hypotheses here just in a nutshell.

A grand debate is going on whether 'closed rules' in the United States Congress are imposed for 'informational' (Krehbiel) or 'distributional' (Shepsle) purposes.[14] Both Krehbiel's and Shepsle's analyses are geared to the committee system of the U.S. House of Representatives. John D. Huber has given a lead in translating these theoretical rationales into the institutional setting of Western European multi-party government. Attention was first drawn to the subject by his seminal article on 'Restrictive Legislative Procedures in France and the United States' (Huber 1992) to be followed by the major publication of 'Rationalizing Parliament. Legislative Institutions and Party Politics in France' (Huber 1996a). Here he transformed both rationales to become applicable not only to the US Congress, but also to parliamentary democracies.

Krehbiel's well-known 'informational' rationale about imposition of restrictive rules may be translated into the institutional setting of parliamentary democracies if one conjectures: a restriction on floor amendments will be invoked, not by a committee but by parliamentary government, if an unusually great deal of information has been collected on a bill long before it was introduced into parliament. From this argument follows:

Hypothesis 1 ('Information collection'): The probability of government imposition of restrictive procedures should increase with the amount of information collected on a particular bill.

Contrary to Krehbiel, however, Shepsle hypothesizes that granting of a restrictive rule serves not so much 'informational' as rather 'distributional' purposes.[15] In an ingenious and striking contribution to the controversy between the 'informational' and 'distributional' paradigms of rational choice institutionalism John D. Huber argued that it is not only difficult but also unnecessary to establish whether a policy measure be 'distributional' or 'informational'. What is important for the likelihood of restrictive rules being imposed is rather that the measure is 'jurisdictionally

---

13 An abridged version of sections 4 and 5 also appears in print in Döring 2004.

14 For the state of the debate, see the special issue of Legislative Studies Quarterly, Vol. 19 No. 2 (1994) edited by Shepsle and Weingast (1994).

15 See Mattson and Strøm (this volume) for a systematic consideration of distributive and informational perspectives.

complex' in the sense of putting multi-dimensional issues in a single package deal (Huber 1996a: p.88). From this argument follows:

Hypothesis 2 ('Jurisdictional complexity'): The probability of the government using the restrictive procedures should increase on bills that are 'jurisdictionally complex' rather than 'jurisdictionally simple' (Huber 1996a: p.83).

But there may be another dimension to complexity of bills. Government ministers from different parties might be trading favours between each other for the benefit of their diverse clienteles. Hence, the suspicion of 'gains from trade' always looms large if a bill is composed of more than one policy dimension. Huber is sceptical about the validity of the 'distributional' theory even for the US committee system.[16] Nevertheless, he gives the suspicion of distributional politics the benefit of the doubt for parliamentary systems and views the number of parties in government as a proxy indicator for logrolling. Others that make a distributional argument for many parties in government include Roubini and Sachs (1989a, 1989b) and Grilli, Masciandaro and Tabellini (1991). From their assumptions follows:

Hypothesis 3 ('Logrolls between government parties'): The probability of government using the restrictive procedures should decline when a single party controls a majority of seats in the legislature (Huber 1996a: p.83).

This hypothesis is, however, turned upside down by Tsebelis's veto players' theory providing us with a theoretical explanation why we should expect not less, but rather far more restrictive rules being imposed with fewer, or only one, party in government. Tsebelis shows by formal modelling in Euclidian geometry that the utility of agenda control should decrease with an increasing number of parties in parliamentary government and that, furthermore, it should also decrease with an increasing distance between the policy positions of parties in government (Tsebelis 2002: p.35f with figure 1.9). From the combined effect of number of and policy distance between parties in government, thus, follows:

16 'Even if we set aside the controversy about whether congressional committees are composed of individuals with extreme preferences, a major problem with the distributive interpretation of restrictive amendment rules is that only a small percentage of bills actually considered by Congress are "distributive" in the narrow sense of "pork barrel projects." Many of these are voted under open rules, and many issues that are not "distributive" are voted using closed or restrictive amendment rules' (Huber 1996a: p.86).

Hypothesis 4 ('Strategic position of veto players'): The probability of a government using restrictive procedures should decrease the more parties there are in government and the larger the policy distance between them is.

There is, however, in veto players' theory an important exception to and qualification of hypothesis 4. By the same formal modelling it was also shown by Tsebelis: If a veto player is centrally located in policy space, this player can make his own ideal point, provided the player commands agenda control, the basis of a take-it-or-leave-it proposal even if there are many veto players involved in a decision.

What real-world cases fit this rare condition of one among many veto players being centrally located in policy space and at the same time possessing the privilege of controlling the agenda by imposing a restrictive rule? It may be a prime minister entitled to impose a vote of confidence on a policy issue without consultation with his coalition partners (for a distribution of such rules in contemporary parliamentary democracies, see Huber 1996b: pp.270-272 with Table 1). It may also be a minority government of the single-party type if it is located in the center of the political space. Due to this policy position, it may be tolerated by parliamentary parties either to its left or right, or by both. Because these supporting parties do not formally form part of the government, no 'veto player party' may object in cabinet to the agenda being restricted in parliamentary voting on a bill. Hence a minority government may, if standing orders in a country (such as the last amendment privilege mentioned in section 2 above) allow for imposition of a restriction, make its own ideal policy point a take-it-or-leave-it proposal for the final outcome. (See for formal proof of this surprising but logically striking argument, Tsebelis 2002: pp.35f with Figure 1.9 and pp.97f with Figure 4.1.) From this reasoning follows:

Hypothesis 5 ('Single-party minority government'): There should be a high probability of restrictive rules being imposed by minority governments of the single-party format.

It may at first sight appear to be perplexing to assume that a minority government, which technically could easily be brought down any time by a vote of no confidence, is to be expected to frequently impose restrictive rules on the parliamentary majority. However, this is only true if the minority government's restricted proposal will be located within the 'winset' of the party coalition outside government voting for its proposal. Additional evidence for the importance of restrictive rules as a probable reason for the very existence of minority government has been found by Heller in his seminal article about the last amendment procedure. With aggregate data (percentages of minority governments over the last decades) he constructed a table showing that the percentage of minority governments between 1944 and 1989 is, indeed, high in countries where the last amendment procedure is possible (Heller 2001: pp.791f with Table 3). If one calculates for Heller's table a rank order correlation between last amendment privilege and the occurrence of minority governments Somer's d shows a symmetrical 0.41 which even turns to 0.59 if minority government is assumed to be the dependent variable.

Veto players' theory, as all other spatial theories of decision-making, focuses on the amendment-control component of restrictive rules. In this view, restrictive rules are imposed to make policies of an agenda setter stick by moving it closest to his ideal point within the game-theoretically defined feasible set ('winset') of obtainable policies. None of the theories referred to so far has paid any attention to the second, the timetable control dimension of the imposition of restrictive rules emphasised by Döring and Henning. From their decision-making-cost theory (already outlined in section 1 of this chapter) of agenda control, time constraint and controversy between government and opposition follows:

Hypothesis 6 ('Controversy'): The probability of a government using restrictive procedures should increase in the presence of delaying attempts from opposition parties.

The reduction of decision-making costs by imposition of timetable restrictions becomes more valuable towards the end of the legislative session because the marginal cost requirements for enacting controversial bills increases with fewer days left until the end of term. From this observation follows:

Hypothesis 7 ('Time constraint'): The likelihood of government imposition of restrictive rules should increase toward the end of the legislative term.

It remains to be seen whether hypotheses 6 and 7, which address the hitherto neglected timetable-control dimension of restrictive rules in addition to its much better known amendment-control dimension, will hold in subsequent empirical analyses with the SPPL data set.

Actually Observed Probabilities (Logistic Regression) for Invocation of Restrictive Rules in Final Decision over Bills

There may be many reasons why governments, depending on unique circumstances, resort to restrictive rules. What this last section is interested in, however, is not a compilation of particular cases but the discovery of general probabilities. To find out if the preceding seven hypotheses are true, a series of logistic regressions was run with the variable 'impose'. This variable combines, as will be recalled from notes 6 and 7, the two variables of (a) declarations of bills as a matter of confidence and (b) other restrictive rules into a single variable.[17] Listwise exclusion of missing cases, which appears to be the most appropriate way to rigorously check alternative theoretical explanations, reduced the number of valid cases from 512 to 353. Table 6.4 gives the results.

The columns of Table 6.4 are arranged according to the seven hypotheses outlined in the preceding section 4. *Column 1* includes into the regression four operationalizations indicative of the 'information collection' theory (Krehbiel) of the reason for imposition of restrictive rules. The theory is not supported by the data. It expects more restrictive rules to be imposed if the government had taken care to test its proposals in a consultation document preceding the introduction of a bill. In a similar way, appointment of a pre-parliamentary commission collecting information on the matter of the planned bill should show a positive sign but points into the wrong direction. Furthermore, an inconclusive neither/nor is revealed in respect of the bill being announced in a government declaration submitted to parliament at the beginning of the legislative term.

It is only with respect to the factual importance of the bill concerning a change of the legal status quo that the coefficient does point, but only weakly and insignificantly, into the expected direction. In summary, the only significant coefficient, appointment of a pre-parliamentary commission, has the wrong sign. The only other coefficient that is strong, the importance of a bill according to the assessment of independent experts, is not significant. The other two of the four variables may reasonably be neglected because their coefficients are small, highly insignificant, and wavering in the direction of their signs when variables from other theories are added in columns 2 to 7.

Column 2 adds two more variables to those already examined in column 1. These additional variables are indicative of the 'jurisdictional complexity of bill' theory. It leads us to expect that more restrictive rules will be imposed if there are more chapters/subheadings of a bill. Thus, multi-dimensional package deals within a single bill would be protected against being unravelled by floor amendments. This appears to be true for the 'number of chapters/sub-headings' indicator of complexity. Its significance even rises if tested against further hypotheses in subsequent regression models. However, multiple referral of bills to several committees, which would indicate its multi-dimensionality, does show an inconclusive neither/nor result. With the one indicator strongly positive and the other one not negative, complexity of a bill does, therefore, hold reasonably well as a predictor for government invoking a restrictive rule.

17 Separate regression analysis with 'restrictive rules' instead of 'impose' as the dependent variable yielded no substantially different results from those reported in Table 6.4. Separate regression analysis with 'confidence votes on bills' as the dependent variable showed only one significant reason for imposition, i.e. delaying attempts by opposition parties.

Table 6.4 Multiple Logistic Regression Models of Imposition of Restrictions

Standardized coefficients (significance levels in parentheses)

Independent Variables	Dependent variable: imposition of restrictions						
	(1)	*(2)*	*(3)*	*(4)*	*(5)*	*(6)*	*(7)*
INFORMATION COLLECTION							
Previous consultation document	-0.11 (0.54)	-0.09 (0.61)	-0.20 (0.29)	-0.19 (0.31)	0.11 (0.68)	0.07 (0.78)	0.09 (0.72)
Pre-parliamentary commission	-0.35 (0.05)	-0.38 (0.04)	-0.35 (0.08)	-0.38 (0.05)	-0.53 (0.02)	-0.57 (0.02)	-0.52 (0.03)
Bill announced in government declaration	-0.01 (0,95)	-0.06 (0.72)	-0.02 (0.91)	0.01 (0.97)	-0.28 (0.22)	-0.35 (0.14)	-0.29 (0.23)
Importance of bill due to expert assessment	0.18 (0.13)	0.16 (0.21)	0.13 (0.31)	0.12 (0.33)	0.19 (0.25)	0.16 (0.4)	0.15 (0.40)
JURISDICTIONAL COMPLEXITY							
Sub-chapters of bill		0.47 (0.06)	0.46 (0.09)	0.59 (0.05)	2.24 (0.01)	2.12 (0.02)	2.10 (0.02)
Number of committees to which bill was referred		0.04 (0.83)	0.27 (0.22)	0.26 (0.22)	-0.06 (0.79)	-0.08 (0.77)	0.06 (0.81)
LOGROLLS BETWEEN GOVERNMENT PARTIES							
Number of parties in government			-0.91 (0.00)	Alternative operationalizations for no. of parties below			
STRATEGIC POSITION OF VETO PLAYERS							
No. of govt parties * Policy distance of govt parties				-0.95 (0.00)			
Dummy single-party minority government					0.82 (0.05)	0.84 (0.05)	0.78 (0.07)
Dummy single-party majority government					0.60 (0.18)	0.64 (0.15)	0.66 (0.14)
Dummy coalition majority government					0.58 (0.29)	0.58 (0.29)	0.44 (0.42)
CONTROVERSY							
Delaying attempts of opposition parties						0.41 (0.03)	0.44 (0.02)
TIME CONSTRAINT							
Days until end of legislative term							1.00 (0.06)
Constant	-1.84 (0.00)	-1.80 (0.00)	-2.10 (0,00)	-2.10 (0,00)	-1.16 (0.00)	-1.23 (0.00)	-1.52 (0.00)
Log-likelihood	280.57	277.02	259.76	258.98	170.05	165.49	160.94
Nagelkerke's R^2	0.037	0.055	0.138	0.142	0.236	0.267	0.297
N	353	353	353	353	187	187	187

Note: For a description of variables, see appendix to this chapter.

Column 3, while retaining all previous variables, does add to the experiment a proxy variable for the 'distributional logrolls' theory. While we cannot directly establish whether a bill is 'distributional' or not, circumstantial reasoning leads us to expect more logrolling to have taken place if there had been more parties in government during the time of the parliamentary passage of the respective bill. This theory is quite conclusively rejected because the regression coefficient points strongly and highly significantly into the wrong direction.

But this negative finding is instantly turned into a first, and quite convincing, confirmation of Tsebelis's veto players' theory. It will be recalled from the previous section that veto players theory, in stark contrast to the logrolling theory, expects agenda control to be the less imposed the more parties there are in government. This is precisely the case if one re-interprets the 'wrong sign' for 'number of parties in government' column 3 in terms of Tsebelis's veto players' theory. This twist in re-interpreting the coefficient is another example of the fruitfulness of Lakatos's 'Methodology of Scientific Research Programmes' (Lakatos 1970, new edition 1995). The anomaly in, and defeat of, one theory may be accommodated by a powerful alternative explanation.

Number of parties in government is, however, only one of several dimensions of veto players' theory. According to this theory there are two other factors contributing to agenda-setting prerogatives of government being invoked during the passage of a bill. The first factor is the 'range' of the policy distance between the parties that form the extremes in a coalition. The second factor is the centrality of an agenda setter within the policy space. Both predictions are subsequently checked in columns 4 and 5.

Column 4 replaces 'number of parties in government' (as in column 3) with a variable measuring the effect of both 'number of parties in government' as well as the policy distance between them.[18] To capture a key feature of veto players' theory, this newly constructed multiplication variable makes use of the straightforward statistical device of measuring interaction by simply multiplying values for the 'number of parties in government' with values for 'range'. The result is another significant confirmation of veto players' theory. The coefficient carries the highest possible significance and points into the expected direction. If this multiplication variable of column 4 is replaced by 'range' only, the resulting regression coefficient for 'range', not shown in the table, yields an equally supportive -0.78 at a significance of 0.00.

Column 5 checks the 'minority government hypothesis' assuming that, contrary to intuition but logically derived from veto players' theory, it is minority government of the single-party format that will most frequently take recourse to restrictive rules. To check this hypothesis, for each bill information was coded into the data set about what type of government was in power during the time of the deliberation of the particular bill. This variable has 4 nominal categories: single-

18 Policy distance, or 'range', was calculated from Laver and Hunt (1992) for each particular bill in the data set as the distance between the two most extreme parties in government. For a single-party government this figure is set to 0, of course.

party majority, coalition majority, single-party minority, and coalition majority.[19] Results from column 5 strongly confirm the prediction. Even when all variables from all other preceding theories are included in the regression equation it is minority government of the single-party kind that carries, together with complexity of a bill, a significant sign in the expected direction.

Column 6 directs attention to the 'controversy' component of restrictive rules while also including all previous variables. Addition of the variable 'delaying attempts of opposition parties' allows an empirical assessment of the decision-making cost theory of agenda control developed by Döring and Henning. Does this theory stand any chance of being supported by the data if it is simultaneously analyzed together with other more prominent and already well-confirmed theories? Or will it be reduced to insignificance? Results from column 6 confirm Döring and Henning. In case of imposition we observe a higher degree of delaying attempts of opposition parties.

Column 7 finally adds the variable 'days until end of legislative term' in order to check the time constraint component of the Döring and Henning theory.[20] Time appears to be a scarce resource indeed strongly related with a reasonably significant positive coefficient to the probability of a restrictive rule being invoked by government. Increasing R^2s in columns 6 and 7 are an indication that the timetable-control dimension of agenda control in the decision making cost theory by Döring and Henning adds some predictive value to two other rational choice theories which stress jurisdictional complexity and amendment-control subject to the strategic position of veto players as reasons for government imposition of restrictive rules.

Somewhat paradoxically but well grounded in veto players' theory, it is single-party minority government that more frequently than any other type of government invokes restrictive rules. However, because minority governments are unable to command a majority in the Chamber they must for obvious reasons refrain from introducing conflictual bills. Therefore, it appears quite logical that with the inclusion of controversy in conjunction with time constraint over contentious bills in column 7 the single-party-minority dummy loses a little bit of its strength and becomes a little less significant. On the other hand, the single-party majority government, which should be in the best possible position to exploit restrictive rules as a means of distinguishing itself for reasons of electoral utility from the opposition by submitting contentious bills, slightly gains in strength.

---

19 In genuine dummy-coding, k-1 dummies are needed if the nominal variable has k categories. In column 5 'coalition minority' is set to this reference category.

20 A large number of missing cases for days between final voting on a bill and the end of legislative term reduced due to listwise exclusion of missing cases the number of cases from 353 to 187. To make comparisons between previous models and the time constraint hypothesis possible, the number of cases was in columns 5 and 6 equally set to 187. Separate analysis of column 5 with the full set of valid cases yielded no substantially different results.

Conclusion

This chapter explored general reasons for government imposition of restrictive rules on bills in final voting. From the angle of rational choice theories on parliamentary behavior, alternative rationales were singled out. Two central hypotheses were rejected by logistic regression analysis and another five confirmed. The (1) 'informational' as well as the (2) 'distributional' rationales for using restrictive rules were strongly and significantly rejected by suitable proxy variables. (3) Multidimensionality of a bill – no matter whether distributional or not – was one of the main reasons for protecting bills by restrictive rules from being rolled on the floor. This finding confirms for Western Europe at large what Huber (1996a) had already found for France.

Rejected, however, was his expectation that there would be more restrictive rules if a larger number of parties was in government. The empirical evidence points to the contrary. This negative correlation is a strong confirmation of (4) Tsebelis's veto players' theory, which predicts agenda control to be the less utilized the more parties participate in a government and the larger the policy distance between them is. Also confirmed was another prediction from veto players' theory: most restrictions were imposed by (5) minority governments of the single-party format. Strong and significant confirmation of this prediction by a genuine dummy coding of single-party minority government against three other types of government, one of which was set as reference category, not only confirms the theory but also gives rise to the conjecture that those single-party minority governments who did impose restrictions on parliament must have been located in or near the center of the political space.

Additional variance was explained by (6) delaying attempts of opposition parties (a proxy for controversy) as well as by (7) time constraint towards the end of the legislative term. These findings provide circumstantial evidence for the political decision making cost theory of agenda control by Döring and Henning. Even when all other rational choice theories are retained in the analysis, this theory is able to explain some further variance for government imposition of restrictive rules. Time constraint appears to be a significant reason for imposition of restrictive rules as predicted by Döring and Henning. Huber's findings to the contrary for France do not hold for Western Europe at large and may be attributed to a French particularity as explained in section 2 above.

There is no reason to worry about the relatively small amount of variance explained by the variables used in this chapter for the likelihood of restrictive rules being invoked by governments. There are many unknown contextual influences calling for the imposition of restrictive rules that may vary from case to case. These cannot be, and have not been, captured by cross-national pooled regression looking for a few general principles beyond time and space. If Alice were to enter, not Wonderland but Rational Choice Land, she might be surprised to learn how trenchantly simple the general concepts used in this realm really are. These rarefied and fairly abstract first principles are simple but not simplistic – according to the Latin saying 'simplex sigillum veri'. Given they cannot, and will not, describe the rich contexts of the passage of each bill, it is quite rewarding to see that they do explain such an amount of variance at all, with signs of the regression coefficients for five of the seven hypotheses in Table 6.4 significantly pointing into the theoretically expected directions.

Appendix: Variables used in this chapter (in alphabetical order)

Standardised variables were used in the multiple regression analysis.

Bill announced in government declaration	=	SPPL V8 – Was the policy problem addressed by the bill mentioned at all in a declaration submitted to parliament? Original coding: 1 = yes, 2 = no. Recoded into 1 = no, 2 = yes.
Days until end of legislative term	=	SPPL V62 (End of legislative term during deliberation of this bill) minus V101 (Date of final vote). Recoded into V101 minus V62 – fewer days until the end of the legislative term imply more time constraint.
Days until next election	=	SPPL follelec (Keesing's Contemporary Archives) minus V101 – distance between date of final vote and date of next election. Labeled scarce.
Delaying attempts of opposition parties	=	SPPL Combination of V90 and V97 – Efforts made by opposition to oppose bill's adoption in either of various readings of bill. Labeled delay. Coding: 1 = no, 2 = yes. For SPSS syntax, see footnote 9 in Chapter 6.
Dummy coalition majority government; Dummy single-party majority government; Dummy single-party minority government	=	Dummy variables for cabinet type (SPPL cabtype). Original categories: coalition majority, single-party majority, coalition minority, single-party minority. In genuine dummy coding of the four cabinet types, coalition minority serves as reference category, whereas the other three types were included as dummies into the regression analysis. Coding: 0 = no, 1 = yes.
Importance of bill due to expert assessment	=	SPPL V4 – Bill mentioned as important in Blanpain's Encyclopaedia. Original coding: 1 = yes, 2 = no. Recoded into 1 = no, 2 = yes.
Imposition of restrictive rules by government	=	SPPL V91, V92, V98, V99 – Restrictive rule invoked by government and/or bill declared as a question of confidence in either of various readings. Labeled impose. Coding: 1 = no, 2 = yes. For SPSS syntax, see footnote 7 in Chapter 6.
No. of government parties	=	Taken from Müller and Strøm (2000). Labeled n_gov_p.

No. of government parties * Policy distance of government parties	=	Multiplication of number of government parties and policy distance of government parties. Labeled vetopl.
Number of committees to which bill was referred	=	SPPL V37 – Number of committees to which bill was scheduled.
Policy distance of parties in government	=	Policy distance between extreme parties in government, taken from Laver and Hunt (1992). Labeled range.
Pre-parliamentary commission	=	SPPL: V7 – Was there a pre-parliamentary commission dealing with the content of the bill? Original coding: 1 = Yes, 2 = No. For the purpose of this analysis recoded into 1 = no, 2 = yes.
Previous consultation document	=	SPPL V6 Did Government first test proposals in an official discussion document? Original coding: 1 = yes, 2 = no. Recoded into 1 = no, 2 = yes.
Sub-chapters of bill	=	SPPL V18 – Number of chapters/sub-headings of bill.

Chapter 7

Veto Players and Law Production

George Tsebelis*

Party systems have traditionally been the fundamental variable of political analysis (Duverger [1954] 1969, Lijphart 1984, Sartori 1976). On the basis of the party system of a country (roughly speaking, the number of parties in parliament and the ideological distances between them), one expects to see systematic differences regarding the relationship between parliament and government (executive dominance) as well as differences in the nature of politics (for example, whether the system is polarized or moderate). Recently, an alternative middle-range theory was proposed. According to this theory, the fundamental political differences between countries are generated by the number of *veto players* (individual or collective actors whose agreement is necessary for a change of the status quo) (Tsebelis 1995a, 1995b).

The veto players' theory differs in two major dimensions from the middle-range theories in comparative politics mentioned above (in addition to having different independent variables).[1] First, it is policy consequential. That is, it takes policy outcomes as its primary concern, and works its way backwards to institutional and partisan characteristics that are responsible for the production of specific policy outcomes. Other theories result in classifications or typologies (Lange and Meadwell 1985). They make distinctions (two- and multi-party systems, presidential and parliamentary regimes, cadre and mass parties, et cetera) without relating them to policy differences. Second, the veto players' theory

---

* I would like to thank Herbert Döring for his brilliant idea to identify significant laws and for providing me with the actual legislative data, and Paul Warwick for offering me his government coalition dataset. I would like to thank Chiache Chang and Robyn Wornall for helping me with the transformation and merging of the datasets that made the rest of the calculations possible. I thank Kathy Bawn, Herbert Döring, Peter Lange, John Londregan, Philippe Van Parijs, Jonathan Rodden, Teddy Seidenfeld, Barbara Sinclair, Kaare Strøm, Michael Wallerstein, and Paul Warwick for many useful comments. A shorter version of this paper was published in *American Political Science Review* 93 (Sept. 1999): pp.591-608 and was the runner up for the Luebbert Award for best article in Comparative Politics in 1998 or 1999.

1 The independent variables are veto players, along with their congruence and cohesion. In a crude way, this translates to the number of *parties in government*, the ideological distance between those parties, and the cohesion of each one of them (instead of the *parties in parliament* used by the party system analyses).

applies the same framework of analysis to presidential and to parliamentary regimes, to two- and to multi-party systems, and to unicameral and to bicameral legislatures. In fact, in countries where veto powers are exercised by other players like the president (Portugal, presidential regimes) or the second chamber (Germany most of the times, the US, Switzerland), the number of veto players is increased and the framework applied accordingly.[2] Among other middle-range theories, only Lijphart's consociationalism has the same range of applicability. However, Lijphart reaches different conclusions. For example, he classifies the US along with the UK as majoritarian countries, falling at the opposite end of the spectrum from Italy,[3] which represents a consensus democracy. According to the veto players' theory, the US and Italy are categorized together as countries with multiple veto players, while the UK is distinct, as it has only one veto player.

The veto players' theory predicts that policy stability (defined as the impossibility of significant change of the status quo) will be the result of large coalition governments, particularly if the coalition partners have significant ideological differences among them. In turn, policy stability can be linked to a series of other political phenomena. As a result of this policy stability (that is, the inability to adapt to exogenous shocks), coalition governments will be short lived. A similar argument can be made about regime stability in presidential systems. Because the regime cannot adapt to sudden changes of the status quo, it may fall. In addition, if a government is unable to produce significant laws (policy stability), the judiciary will step in and play a more important role in countries with coalition governments than in countries with single-party governments. Furthermore, bureaucracies will be more independent during coalition rule than under single-party governments.

Let me situate the argument proposed and tested here with respect to three different streams of relevant arguments in the literature. The first stream is the 'divided government' literature in American politics. Some researchers (Fiorina 1992, Sundquist 1988) have argued that divided government will cause a reduction in significant legislation. The argument is very similar to the one proposed here, because divided government means that two of the veto players have significantly different preferences. However, empirical evidence collected by Mayhew (1991) on significant laws does not corroborate the divided government expectation.[4] Mayhew finds that there is no significant difference in legislation between periods of unified and divided government. Does this finding falsify the veto players'

---

2 For the counting rules see Tsebelis 1995b.

3 This is the classification in *Democracies* (1984); subsequently Lijphart introduced a second axis (federalism) to his analysis. The UK and the US differ along this axis. However even in this classification, Italy does not resemble the US (if anything, the difference increases because now they differ in two dimensions as opposed to one).

4 For a debate on the Mayhew dataset, see Kelly 1993 and Mayhew 1993. However, the major contribution to the debate was provided by Binder (1999) who identified the number of *potential* laws each year. Her analysis corroborates the veto players' expectations: the number of significant laws declines not only with divided government, but also with the distance of the two chambers of the US Congress.

theory presented here? The difference between Mayhew's findings and the findings I present below is that my analysis pertains to *majoritarian* institutions, while in the American political system one of the veto players (the Senate) is *supermajoritarian*. Let me clarify the difference that a supermajoritarian institution makes to the veto players' argument.[5] In the US Senate, individual senators can filibuster (talk nonstop in order to prevent a vote on a bill) and three-fifths of the votes are required to prevent an individual senator from filibustering (cloture). It follows that for every important bill, a minority of 40 senators can block the vote on the floor of the Senate. Consequently, in order for a significant bill to pass, the required support is 60 votes (qualified majority) not 50 (simple majority). It so happens, that historical cases of the minority party controlling less than 40 seats do not exist after 1979 (the three fifths rule was introduced in 1975), consequently all significant bills have to pass through the Senate with some level of bipartisan support. This means that divided government is built-in in US institutions not because of the requirement that all three veto players agree on a particular change of the status quo, but because of the filibuster rule which essentially prevents partisan legislation from passing the Senate. How about bipartisan legislation? Such legislation will pass the Senate (and the House) and is unlikely to be vetoed by the President of either party. In the unlikely occasion that a President vetoes such legislation, the two chambers are likely to have the two-thirds majority required to override the presidential veto. So the supermajoritarian nature of decision making in the Senate explains the peculiarity of US results and places them in comparative perspective.[6]

A second stream of argument present in the literature is the role of veto players on budget deficits or on inflation (Alt and Lowry 1994, McCubbins 1991, Roubini and Sachs 1989a). According to this argument, the more veto players, the more likely each one of them will ask for special favors for his constituency as a condition for supporting legislation, and the higher the deficit or inflation rate will be. This is a veto-players-as-collective-action problem argument, which neither reinforces nor contradicts the argument presented here. Let me give an example: According to the veto-players-as-collective-action argument, oversized coalitions will have higher deficits or inflation than minimum winning coalitions. According to my argument, oversized coalitions will be more locked in to the previously existing policy pattern (whatever that pattern happens to be).

Finally, there is a third stream of researchers that has identified or tested parts of the veto players' argument as presented in this article (as well as Tsebelis 1995a, 1995b). With regard to policy stability, Kathleen Bawn (1997), in an elegant article on government spending in Germany, categorizes issues as pro-SPD or pro-CDU/CSU, and demonstrates that participation by the SPD in the Grand Coalition in 1966 had as a consequence a significant increase in pro-SPD spending, but that

5 The reader can refer to Tsebelis (2000, and forthcoming) in order to see the development of a veto players' model which includes qualified majority decision making (filibuster and veto override).

6 For a detailed discussion along these lines see Jones (1998).

this spending remained constant in 1969, despite the fact that the SPD became the main party in a coalition government with the FDP. This finding is consistent with both Bawn's hypothesis that the FDP seeks to reduce spending and the veto players' theory. Similarly, Mark Hallerberg and Scott Basinger (1998), in an empirical article on one significant area of legislation – the reduction of business and highest-income personal taxation in advanced industrialized countries, 1986-1990 – discovered that tax reduction was more decisive in countries with single-party governments (whether of the right or the *left*). Amie Kreppel (1997) found legislative output in Italy negatively correlated with the number of parties in government. Robert Franzese (1996), in an analysis of budget deficits in advanced industrialized countries, concludes that countries with many veto players are locked into the same deficit pattern (for example, the ones with high debt have high deficits (like Italy), while the ones with low debt have low deficits (like Switzerland)). On the other side of the coin, countries with single-party governments (whether majority or minority) can move away from pre-existing patterns (for example, they have high or low deficits, regardless of the level of their debt). Franzese's study can be considered a crucial experiment between the veto players theory I proposed, and the veto-players-as-collective-action problem approach. Similarly, Daniel Treisman (1998) studying both advanced and developing countries, found that federal countries (for example countries with many veto players) are locked into patterns of high (developing) or low (advanced) inflation. Finally, most of the chapters and certainly the introduction and conclusions of *Do Institutions Matter?* (Weaver and Rockman 1993) claim that countries with multi-party parliamentary systems respond to exogenous shocks in a way similar to countries with presidential systems, a finding also consistent with the veto players' theory.

With respect to other variables, Paul Warwick (1994) has found that the ideological distance between government partners has negative effect on the *duration of government coalitions* in parliamentary democracies. The conventional wisdom on coalitions was that characteristics of the Parliament (number of parties in Parliament, ideological distances among them) affect the duration of government coalitions, because government partners look at the situation in Parliament to calculate their probabilities of participating in a new government (see Laver and Schofield (1990) for an overview). Warwick included both government and parliament variables in the same regression; it turns out that only the government characteristics (ideological distance between government partners) mattered, exactly as the veto players' theory predicts. Nicos Alivizatos (1995) studied the *importance of the judiciary* and found that the most active judges are in the countries with many veto players exactly as Tsebelis (1995a) expects. Similarly, Jenna Bednar, John Ferejohn, and Geoffrey Garrett (1996), examining the activism of the European Court of Justice, find that the introduction of qualified majority voting in the Council (which reduces the number of veto players in European institutions) led to a significant reduction of judicial activism. Examining one particular bureaucracy (the German Bundesbank), Susanne Lohmann (1998) found that *bureaucratic independence* increases during periods of opposing majorities in the Upper and Lower Houses (Bundestag and Bundesrat) of the German parliament. Her findings are also consistent with expectations generated by the veto players' theory.

This article aims at making a direct and cross-national test of the first and most important prediction generated by the veto players' theory: that the number of significant laws produced by coalition governments, particularly the ones with important ideological differences among government partners, is significantly lower than the number of significant laws produced by coalitions with partners that agree or by single-party government. This prediction has not been tested so far directly and cross-nationally because of the difficulty of identifying significant laws across different countries in a consistent way.[7] However, this obstacle has been overcome thanks to the work of Herbert Döring and his team (see Döring 1995a). I will revisit the articles in which the veto players' theory was introduced, extract their predictions, and then test these predictions using a new dataset of 'significant laws' on issues of 'working time and working conditions' provided by Döring.

The article is organized into four parts. The first provides a simple model designed to adapt the veto players' theory (which is designed for multidimensional spaces) to one dimension (the traditional left-right political spectrum). This model predicts that an increase in the ideological distance among coalition partners adversely affects the number of significant laws enacted in a country. The second presents the dataset, which combines information about significant laws in different West European countries with data about government coalitions (composition of governments and ideological positions of parties on a left-right scale). In this part, I explain how the different variables used in this study are generated. The third part presents the results and shows that the expectations of the model are corroborated. The last part compares the production of significant and overall legislation and comes to the conclusion that the two are inversely related as predicted by Tsebelis (1995b).

Veto Players, Ideology and Law Production in One Dimension

A veto player is an individual or collective actor whose agreement is necessary for a change of the status quo. On the basis of this definition, the argument underlying the veto players' theory is very simple: a significant policy change has to be approved by all veto players, and consequently it will be more difficult the larger the number of veto players and the greater the ideological distance among them. In

7 Hallerberg and Basinger (1998) as well as the articles in Weaver and Rockman (1993) use case studies. Bawn (forthcoming) and Kreppel (1997) study only one country each (Germany and Italy, respectively), and Franzese (1996) studies deficits which are the results of government policies as well as activities in the private sector and the overall performance of the economy.

a parliamentary system, veto players are the parties in government as well as other actors endowed with veto power. Let us analyze the different possibilities.

Veto players other than government parties include the upper house or the head of state. The upper house most frequently is either controlled by the same coalition as the government (Italy, Belgium, and Switzerland), or does not have the power to veto legislation (France, Spain, and UK).[8] The only country (in our sample of 15 West European countries) that has an upper house endowed with veto powers and that is not controlled by the same parties as the Lower House is Germany (for some of the period under examination). Consequently, in Germany for the periods that the upper house (Bundesrat) is controlled by a different party than the Lower House (Bundestag), I add one veto player to the parties in government. Indeed, during these periods, the parties in government are hostages to the opposition party and have to secure its approval for passing legislation.

The head of state has no veto powers in West European countries. This statement is true not only in the cases of royalty but also for elected heads of state that are considered strong, like the French or the Finnish President. There are two exceptions in my dataset. First, the Portuguese President is endowed with veto power over legislation (an attempt to modify the constitution in this respect in 1982 failed). Consequently, whenever the president has different preferences from the governing coalition, I include one additional veto player to the calculations for Portugal.[9] Second, the French President has veto power over government decrees. There was one case in the dataset when the President was supported by a different majority than the government in the dataset, and in this case I increased the number of veto players by one.

In all other cases, veto players are the government partners in a parliamentary system. This statement holds on the average in the case of oversized as well as minority governments. In the case of oversized government, the agreement of all government parties is formally not necessary for legislation to be approved. By the definition of 'oversized', some parties can be ignored, and legislation can be still accepted by a majority in parliament. However, what is formally possible may not be politically feasible. Trying to pass legislation against the will of minor government partners may lead to a government crisis, and the resignation of the government (Tsebelis 1995b). Consequently, if the passage of legislation is so important for some parties and so damaging for others, a different government can enact this legislation (after the dissident parties cause the government to fall).

---

8 Using Lijphart's (1984) terminology, bicameralism in the first set of countries is 'congruent' while in the second set is 'asymmetric'; in both cases it is 'weak.' Tsebelis and Money (1997) have demonstrated that, even in these cases, upper houses certainly influence and sometimes even abort legislation. But cases of abortion are the exception rather than the rule, so we will ignore it here.

9 Characterizing the political beliefs of the General Eanes who was in power in the first part of the period I examine was difficult. I ended up assimilating him with the Socialist party, which supported his election. The problem did not repeat itself with Soares, who was actually a Socialist.

The case of minority governments requires more explanation, because the predominant belief is that a minority government corresponds to some kind of divided government in a presidential system and that legislation requires the agreement of both government and parliament to be enacted (Laver and Shepsle 1996). My argument is that while the conventional wisdom is formally true, the dynamics of a parliamentary system work differently. Minority governments are equipped with significant positional and institutional weapons that enable them (most of the time) to impose their will on parliament, just as majority governments do. The positional advantage is the location of the government party. This party is usually at the center of the political system.[10] As a consequence, it can lean slightly one way or another and find allies ready to support different pieces of legislation. The institutional advantages of a government are the control it has over the parliamentary agenda (Döring 1995b). As Döring demonstrates, there are a variety of such advantages in each country. However, there is one advantage that is common to governments in all parliamentary systems: the question of confidence (Huber 1996b). This weapon enables the Prime Minister to transform a vote on a piece of legislation into a vote for or against the government under the threat of resignation and possible new elections. Consequently, it places the opponents of a particular law under significant pressure, enabling the government effectively to control the agenda.

The conclusion of this analysis is that, in parliamentary systems, veto players are (with the exceptions mentioned above) the partners in a government coalition. Consequently, the more partners in government, the more difficult it becomes to induce a significant change. In fact, if one defines the concept of the *winset of the status quo* as the set of points that are preferred over the status quo by the veto players, the following two propositions can be proven (see Tsebelis 1995a: pp.297-301).[11]

PROPOSITION 1: As the number of veto players increases, the winset of the status quo does not increase (for example, policy stability does not decrease).

PROPOSITION 2: As the distance between veto players increases along the same line, the winset of the status quo does not increase (for example, policy stability does not decrease).

In what follows, from propositions 1 and 2, I produce a corollary about the relationship between the number of veto players and the ideological distance between them in a single dimension. This adaptation is necessary because the

10 Laver and Schofield (1990) call this position the 'core' and argue that such a configuration is frequent with minority governments. A similar point is made by Strom (1990).

11 Tsebelis (1995a) proves three different propositions, one having to do with collective veto players. We will not use this proposition here, because its test would require data on the ideological cohesion of different parties in Europe.

dataset I analyze is in one dimension (the traditional left-right dimension of West European politics).

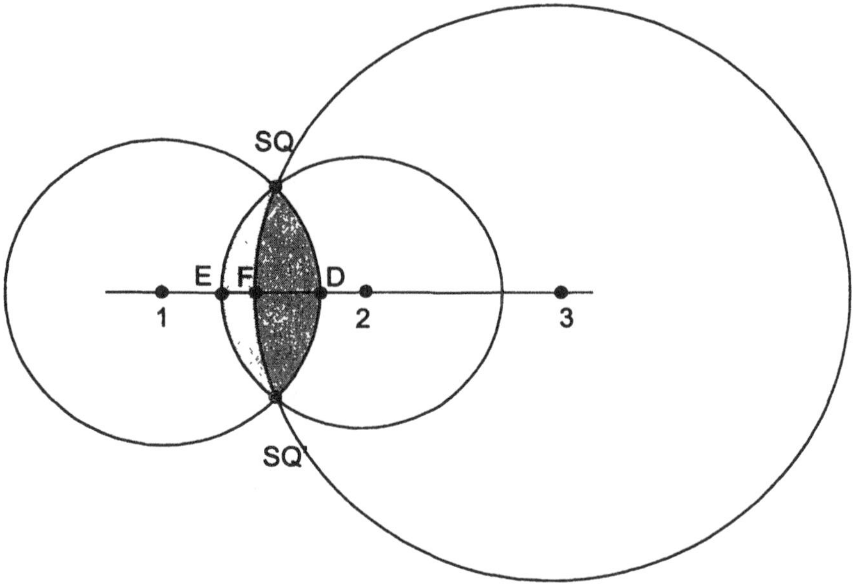

Figure 7.1 Winsets of VPs 1 and 3 is Contained within Winsets of VPs 1 and 2 (2 is Absorbed)

Figure 7.1 offers a graphic representation of a three-party government and the status quo (previous legislation in an area). Note that in Figure 7.1 the three parties in government are located on a straight line. This is a restriction that I impose in order to analyze the available (one-dimensional) data. From this restriction certain interesting modifications follow of the original multidimensional model. Note also that the status quo is not necessarily located on the same line, since in general a particular piece of legislation may address other issues as well as the subject matter of this study (labor legislation). In this sense, the 'in one dimension' in the title of this section refers only to the positions of the parties. Strictly speaking, the model is two dimensional, with the restriction that parties fall along one single dimension, while the status quo can be anywhere.

In Figure 7.1, I present three circles that indicate the areas that each party prefers over the status quo. What the coalition can do is presented inside the intersection of all three circles (the heavily shaded lens in the figure). Let us now walk through two possible coalition-building processes, step by step. Let us assume that parties 1 and 2 get together first, and they invite party 3 to join them later. What parties 1 and 2 could do in order to change the status quo together is represented inside the wide lens in the figure (lightly shaded). If the two parties want to add party 3 to their coalition, the consequence will be that they will restrict the area where they can move the status quo to the heavily shaded lens (intersection of the preferences of all three).

Now let's follow a different coalition-building path: let us assume that parties 1 and 3 get together first. They can select anything in the intersection of circles 1 and 3 (the heavily shaded area). If these two parties ask party 2 to join them in government, the addition of the new party will not restrict the ability of 1 and 3 to decide on an outcome. Indeed, nothing in the intersection of circles 1 and 3 is excluded by the addition of 2. In other words, adding one veto player in this case does not change the policy making ability of the initial coalition.

Why was policy making restricted in the first case but not in the second? The reason is that party 2 is located between parties 1 and 3, and consequently, it is impossible for the latter to have a joint preference over the status quo that party 2 will not share. In other words, the addition of a coalition partner with preferences between the extreme coalition partners does not affect policy making. Putting it differently still, and singling it out for subsequent testing:

COROLLARY (of PROPOSITIONS 1 and 2): in one dimension, policy stability depends on the maximum ideological distance between veto players, not on their number.

Proof: We can replicate the argument we made about the addition of party 2 to the coalition between 1 and 3 as many times as there are veto players (that is, parties in a coalition).

This corollary greatly simplifies our testing. Since our data are in one dimension, we have to test only the corollary instead of propositions 1 and 2. Note, however, that this corollary of the veto players' theory applies only when the ideal positions of parties are located in the same dimension (although there are ways to generalize it: Tsebelis (2002)).

One objection to the above argument is that it does not take into account the position of the status quo. One can use Figure 7.1 to draw the conclusion that the winset of the status quo increases when the status quo is further away from the party positions. In particular, if the status quo is constrained to be on the same straight line as the ideal points of the parties, then the argument can be made (and was made by one of the referees) that it is 'the location of the status quo that matters, rather than range'. However, the location of the status quo is not identifiable. That is, not only do data that locate *parties* not locate the status quo in the same space, but one cannot assume that the status quo was produced by the previous government and therefore use the location of that government as a proxy. In many cases, the 'status quo' for any particular law is produced by a compilation of different provisions of laws introduced by different governments, so the identification of the location of the status quo is impossible. However, one can make an estimate of the winset of the status quo over the whole range of possible status quo. This estimate is negatively related to the range of the coalition, because if the status quo is located within the range of the coalition, its winset is empty. To use an example: if the whole space is the [0, 1] interval and a coalition ranges from 0.5 to 1, then the winset of the status quo will be empty half of the time (whenever the status quo is located in the [0.5, 1] interval). If the range of the coalition shrinks to the [0.7, 1] interval, the winset of the status quo will be empty only 30 per cent of the time (assuming a uniform distribution of the status quo). The same argument can be made about the *significance* of the possible change. If one considers significant laws the ones that move the status quo by more than w, then one would have to add w or 2w to the range in order to find significant changes over the whole range of status quo. Consequently, even in this restricted case, the range of a coalition, on the average, will have a negative sign into the calculations of policy change.

Let us now focus on the implications of the corollary for our dataset. Tsebelis (1995b: p.103) has made the argument that: 'Since multiparty governments are incapable of producing significant laws (unless there is a dramatic shift in public opinion) while single-party governments are able to undertake such changes, over a long time period and in a wide set of countries one would expect to find more significant pieces of legislation in countries with fewer veto players ... The same argument should apply to government-enacted legislation (decrees).' The argument above is presented in terms of the number of veto players, but on the basis of the model I presented here, if the parties are located in the same single dimension, the argument has to be made on the basis of the ideological distances among the most extreme parties (the range of the necessary coalition). We should then expect lower numbers of significant pieces of legislation in countries where coalition governments have a large ideological range, and more pieces of significant legislation in countries with small ideological range (single-party majority or minority governments have range = 0).

Strictly speaking, in the absence of a generalized shift of public opinion,[12] a large coalition (large range) is a *sufficient condition*[13] for the absence of

12 In the case of a generalized shift of public opinion, even a universal coalition can enact legislation expressing this new consensus.

13 But not a necessary condition. The reader should note that the model I am testing is deterministic (hence the language of necessary and sufficient conditions). This may appear strange since we usually assume that 'the world is probabilistic.' But determinism is not an attribute of the world but of the model. In this sense, it falls in the same category with other arguments about necessary conditions (think of Barrington Moore's (1966: p.418) 'no bourgeois, no democracy') as well as with game theoretic models with a single equilibrium (like the median voter or the prisoners' dilemma to mention but a few). The fact that the model is deterministic does not mean that we can test it as such. There are measurement errors, omitted variables et cetera which will enable us to keep the model even if we had found a few falsifying instances (which will not be the case). In the remainder of this article when I speak about the theoretical model I will use the deterministic language, while when I speak about empirical tests I will use the probabilistic one.

significant legislation. We can visualize and expand the argument by referring to Figure 7.2.[14]

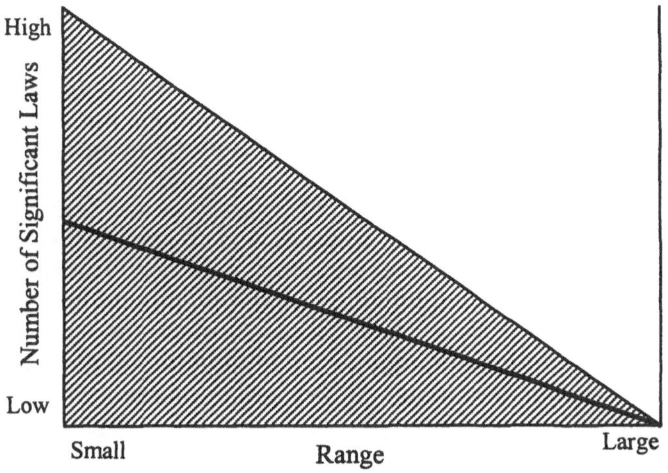

Figure 7.2 Expected Area of Significant Laws by Ideological Range of a Coalition

Since range is a sufficient condition for the absence of significant legislation, governments with large range cannot produce significant laws, but governments with a small range have the *possibility* of producing significant laws. The possible outcomes are presented in the shaded area. The heavy line represents the average number of significant laws. We can see that this line has a negative slope, or that the range of a government is negatively correlated with the number of significant laws. But Figure 7.2 leads to another expectation, one not identified by Tsebelis (1995a, 1995b). Since large range (in the absence of a generalized shift in public opinion) is a sufficient but not necessary condition for the absence of significant legislation, the *variance* (strictly speaking, the residuals) of significant laws will be negatively correlated with the range of a government. Indeed, the possible number of significant laws varies on the left side of the figure (among governments with small ideological range) but not on the right side (among governments with large ideological range).

In technical terms, the veto players' theory predicts that the range of a government will have a negative effect on the average number of laws, but also that the residuals will be heteroskedastically distributed as a function of the

14 The reader can refer to Tsebelis (1995b: Table 3.1) for another version of this argument.

(same) range of government. I single out these expectations and call them *R* for *results*:[15]

R1: The range of a government coalition negatively affects the number of significant laws.

R2: The range of a coalition negatively affects the variance of the number of significant laws. (More accurately, the residuals of the previous regression will be heteroskedastically distributed and inversely related to the range).

Another argument made by Tsebelis (1995b: p.105) was: 'There are two other factors that I would expect to affect the production of significant laws. The first is the length of time that a given government stays in office. One would expect that governments take some time before they present significant laws in parliament, consequently, short-lived governments would produce less legislative work. A second factor is alternation of parties in government. A consequence of the argument presented in this section is that a government with a new coalition partner would be expected to make more changes the bigger the ideological distance of the parties that succeed each other in government.' In other words:

R3: Government duration and alternation of parties have a positive effect on the number of significant laws.

R3 essentially introduces two control variables into R1. It is possible that while the duration of a government is positively associated with production of significant laws, the rate of production *declines* over time. This means that a government will produce more significant laws in the beginning of its term than towards the end. In the third part of this article, I will operationalize and test these predictions.

The Data

In order to test the above propositions, I created a dataset by merging data on significant legislation (laws and decrees) on 'working time and working conditions' in fifteen countries of Western Europe for the period 1981-1991 with data on coalition governments for the same countries and the same period. I received the data on significant legislation from Herbert Döring, and the data on government coalitions from Paul Warwick. In this section, I will explain what was included in the original datasets as well as the additional manipulations for the construction of specific variables.

15 I use the term 'results' instead for the more usual 'hypotheses' because the propositions above have been logically derived instead of posited a priori.

Significant legislation

Döring and his team identified the number of significant laws for all Western European countries in the area of labor legislation (legislation on 'working time and working conditions') for the period 1981-1991. For that purpose they used the computerized database NATLEX that had been compiled by the International Labor Organization (ILO), located in Geneva. While this database started being collected at the beginning of the 1970s, the dataset became complete only since the beginning of the 1980s. Consequently, the beginning of the dataset that I analyze is January 1, 1981. This dataset has been indexed by subject matter, so that one can identify all laws put to a vote and all decrees issued on any specific topic in all European countries. While this database is of excellent use in identifying any subject in labor legislation and has been used by Döring and his team to generate reliable numbers of pieces of legislation in different areas, it provides no indication of 'significant' legislation, the dependent variable for a test of the veto players' theory.

The next step would have been to identify some proxy for importance. Such a proxy should not be size or length of legislation because a law can be written to enumerate areas of applicability (in which case length is correlated with significance) or areas of exception (in which case length is negatively correlated with significance). The alternative proxies that come to mind are: the size of the budget needed for implementation, or the number of people affected by its enactment. Both criteria would indicate that a bill on euthanasia or on same-sex marriage would not be significant. This short discussion indicates that criteria for selection of 'significant' laws have an important ingredient of subjectivity which can undermine the results of any analysis for a reader who does not share the same criteria for selection.

In the face of this problem, Döring had the brilliant idea of using the *Encyclopaedia of Labor Law* in order to generate the variable 'significant laws'. The encyclopaedia is edited by Roger Blanpain and was written for labor lawyers originating in one European country who wanted to practice law in another. According to the introduction, '*National Legislation* intends to make available to the subscribers and users of the Encyclopaedia pertinent provisions of the *most important acts* of Parliament, governmental *decrees*, national, and interindustry wide major *collective agreements*, or other legal sources, where they cover a country as a whole ...' (Blanpain Suppl. 194 (July 1997): subsection 5; emphasis in the original). Each country is covered by a 150- to 250-page monograph authored by a law professor or a judge and explaining to readers the significant legislation in the area. The monographs have a common pattern, which facilitates subject matter identification. Norway and Iceland are not covered by the Encyclopaedia. Laws that were in the intersection of both sources are considered 'significant', while laws existing only in the NATLEX database were considered not to be significant.

Blanpain's *Encyclopaedia* provided a validation test for the NATLEX database, since for the 1981-1991 period, all the laws mentioned in Blanpain were included in NATLEX. This was not true for the period before 1981, which, in turn, validates the cutoff point for the study.[16] The dates of promulgation of the significant laws of each country were compared with the dates that governments were in power, so that laws were attributed to the governments that sponsored them.

Governments

The dataset on governments included the dates of beginning and end of governments in the 15 countries of the study (Austria, Belgium, Denmark, Finland, France, Germany, Greece, Ireland, Italy, Luxembourg, Netherlands, Portugal, Spain, Sweden, and UK). The dates of beginning and end of the study (January 1, 1981, and December 31, 1991) were considered the dates of beginning or end of the government in office at that date.[17] On the basis of these dates of beginning and end of different governments, I calculated the duration in years of each one of them.

The dataset on governments used conventional methods to account for beginning and end of governments. Warwick (1994: p.27) is very explicit about what constitutes beginning: 'A government typically begins when it is appointed by a head of state.' As for ending, he adopts the criteria proposed by Browne, Gleiber, and Mashoba (1984: p.7).[18] However, the variable that matters for the veto players' theory is the partisan composition of government. Therefore, two successive governments with identical composition should be counted as a single government, even if they are separated by an election, which changes the size of the different parties in parliament.[19] The reason is that the variable that enters into a veto players' analysis in not the relative strength of different parties in government

16 These choices are described in more detail, along with legal questions that arise when a law is inadequately or insufficiently described in Blanpain, in an essay co-authored by Georgios Trantas, the lawyer who following Döring's idea actually identified the intersection of Blanpain and NATLEX (Scholz and Trantas 1995).

17 As a result the governments of each country at the beginning and ending of the period have been truncated (they lasted longer than indicated, and may have produced legislation outside the period of this study).

18 According to Browne et al. 'A government is considered terminated whenever: (1) parliamentary elections are held, (2) the head of government changes, (3) the party composition of the government changes, or (4) the government tenders its resignation, which is accepted by the head of state' (Warwick 1994: p.28). On this fourth point Warwick presents a variation and counts as termination even resignations that are not subsequently accepted by the head of state.

19 For a similar argument concerning Italian governments which succeed each other while the party (and sometimes the person) composition is the same, see Di Palma (1977: p.31).

or parliament, but the fact that each one of them needs to agree in order for legislation to pass.[20]

In order to operationalize the above argument, I created a dataset of 'merged' governments, in which successive governments with the same composition were considered a single government regardless of whether they were separated by a resignation and/or an election. Obviously, merging affects the values of duration and the number of laws produced by a government. To account for this change, I added the number of laws produced by different governments to be merged and credited the resulting government with this total number of laws. Duration was recalculated as the sum of the duration of consecutive governments (this excludes possible caretaker governments and periods when a resigned government waits to be replaced that would have been included if I recalculated on the basis of the new beginning and ending dates). As a result of merging, the number of cases in the dataset decreased from 105[21] to 58.[22]

The difference between the merged government dataset used in this study and the traditional method of counting governments, becomes clear in the following two cases. First, in Greece, the Socialist government (PASOK) came into power in 1981 and, according to the dataset, it produced four significant laws in the area of 'working time and working conditions'. In 1985, the Socialists were reelected in government, and the new government produced two additional significant laws. According to the merged government dataset, the two PASOK governments are counted as one, which did not complete its legislative program in the first period, and continued changing the legislative framework of the right wing governments of 1974-1981 during its second term.

The second example is drawn from France. After Francois Mitterrand was elected President of the Republic in 1981, he appointed Pierre Maurois as the Prime Minister of a coalition government, which included the Socialists and the Communists. That government produced four significant laws in the area under study. In 1983, a second Maurois government with the same party composition replaced the existing Maurois government. This second government stayed in

---

20 It is interesting that Franzese (1996) considered two different specifications in his empirical analysis: one on the basis of veto players (counting only parties which were members of a government), and another 'bargaining' approach, in which government participants were weighted by their size. The veto players' specification was significantly more accurate in predicting deficits than the bargaining one.

21 There were 106 political governments, but two of them although formally political had a caretaker character (were formed to take the country to elections): 1. In France, the Maurois government that Mitterrand appointed immediately after his election and the dissolution of Parliament in May of 1981 (lasted 30 days); 2. In Italy, the Fanfani government formed in April of 1987 and was voted down by Parliament even before it could proclaim elections (lasted eight days).

22 It would have been 57, but I double count the French government during the cohabitation period of 1986-88: I consider only the two participating parties as veto players with respect to legislation, but I add the President when I consider a government decree that they issued.

power for one year, until the Communists dropped out of the coalition because of the austerity policies that Mitterrand was about to impose in order to remain in the European monetary system. The second Maurois government did not produce any new laws on 'working time and working conditions'. In my dataset, the two governments count as one: in a three-year period the Socialist-Communist coalition produced four significant laws. Implicit in my account is that the second Maurois government did not produce any laws because the first had completed its work in this area.[23]

Ideology

The government dataset included also the composition of different governments (the parties participating in government coalitions to which I added the positions of the President of Portugal and France and the Bundesrat in Germany in the cases indicated in the first part of this article) and their 'ideological scores' on the basis of three indices. The first was from Paul Warwick's (1994) *Government Survival in Western European Parliamentary Democracies* (Warwick expanded the dataset collected by Browne et al. 1984, who had expanded the dataset collected by Dodd 1976). This index was generated from 40 different measures that were developed from experts, party manifestos, and survey sources. Of the governments included in this dataset, the index ranged from a low of -6 (left) to a high of 5 (right).

The second index was provided by Castles and Mair (1984) in 'Left-Right Political Scales: Some "Expert" Judgments'. These ideological scores were generated from a questionnaire survey of more than 115 political scientists from Western Europe and the United States (Castles and Mair 1984: p.75). The questionnaire asked each respondent to place all of the parties holding seats in his/her national legislature on the left-right political spectrum ranging from zero (ultra-left) to 10 (ultra-right), with 2.5 representing the moderate left, 5 the center, and 7.5 the moderate right. Castles and Mair present the results from those countries that had at least three respondents. The ideological score reported for each party was the average of available responses. Given the ten-point scale, the potential range of responses was (0.10). Of the parties analyzed here, however, the low score was 1.4, received by the Communist Party of France, and the high was 8.2, received by the Gaullist party.

The third index was drawn from Laver and Hunt's (1992) first dimension variable, 'increase services vs. cut taxes'. Respondents were professional political scientists (Laver and Hunt 1992: pp.38-41, p.122). Each respondent was asked to locate the policy positions of both the party leaders and voters for each party in his/her country on the left-right spectrum. In addition to the parties that won seats in the most recent election, respondents were asked to evaluate every party that won at least 1 per cent of the national vote, as well as any significant regional parties. The scale adopted by Laver and Hunt was a 20-point scale (to

---

23 All the calculations in this article were replicated with the traditional way of counting governments, and led to the same qualitative results.

accommodate for the fact that the countries included in their study contained up to 14 parties to be placed on the scale). For the first dimension – taxes vs. public services – respondents assigned each party a score ranging from 1 ('promote raising taxes to increase public services') to 20 ('promote cutting public services to cut taxes'). Among the cases included in the dataset, the Laver Hunt (first dimension) variable ranged from a low of 2.1 to a high of 17.4.

Only Laver and Hunt included all 15 countries in their study. Warwick did not code the parties of France V, and Greece. In addition, some government parties in Ireland, Italy, Spain, and Sweden were not scored. Castles and Mair did not include Luxembourg, Portugal, and Greece.

On the basis of each one of these measures of ideology, I was able to construct new variables representing the 'range' of each government according to the index, as well as the 'alternation' from one government to the next. The range variable was created by taking the absolute value of the distance between the most extreme parties of a coalition. These two parties were usually (but not always) the same for different indices. However, the correlations among the range variables calculated on the basis of the cases covered by all three indices were quite high.[24]

The alternation variable was calculated by finding the mid-range position of each government, and taking the difference between two successive governments.[25] Because this measure was calculated using the previous government, I needed information on the government preceding the one that was in power in 1981. Again, the three different indices produced highly correlated values of alternation for the cases covered by all three indices.[26]

The New 'Range' and 'Alternation' Variables

These three range and alternation variables covered different countries, and were calculated on the basis of different questions all of which were relevant to the left-right division. In order to preserve the size of my dataset, as well as use all the available information, I constructed new measures of range and alternation, based on the values of *all* available indices. To accomplish this, I standardized each one of the indices and then took the average of the standardized scores that were available for each case government. For standardization, I used only the values of the variables for the countries covered by all three indices. This procedure was run separately on all three range and alternation variables, resulting in three standardized range and three standardized alternation variables. The average range and alternation variables used all the available information in the following way: In

24 The correlations between any two of these indexes were above 0.80.

25 The formula I used was the following: (maxgovt1+mingovt1) - (maxgovt2+mingovt2), where max- and min-govt1 are the ideological scores of the preceding government, and max- and min-govt2 are the ideological scores of the 'current' government. For instance, if a government succeeded (or 'replaced') a government with the same party structure, then all of the alternation variables would equal zero.

26 The correlations between any two of these indexes were also above 0.80.

the case that all three indices existed, the average was calculated on the basis of all three; for countries with two indices only the average was calculated on the basis of the two standardized indices; in the cases covered by one single analyst (Greece), I used that one standardized score. In the regressions I used the absolute value of alternation as calculated above, because it makes no difference whether a left wing government is replaced by a right wing government, or vice versa.

In the Appendix I present all the variables discussed above, along with others generated in order to control for other possible effects (government ideology, government control of the legislative agenda, and corporatism (see below)).

Testing the Implications of the Veto Players' Theory

In this section, I will test all the predictions made in section I. I test result R1 by regressing the variable *LAWS* (that is, the number of significant laws and decrees), on the variable *RANGE* (average normalized ideological distance of extreme partners of a government coalition, corrected for institutional rules like the President of Portugal). I test result R2 by analyzing the residuals of the previous regression, more specifically, by testing the squared residuals for heteroskedasticity. I test result R3 by introducing a series of additional variables: *ALTERNATION* (absolute value of the average normalized difference between two successive governments), *DURATION* (years of a government in office), as well as others that turn out not to be significant (as predicted).

Table 7.1 Bivariate Models of Significant Legislation (Tests of R1 and R2)

Variables	Model 1		Model 2		Model 3	
Constant	1.17***	(0.22)	2.46***	(0.57)	1.14***	(0.20)
Range	-0.59**	(0.23)	-1.66**	(0.59)	-.058**	(0.22)
N	58		58		56	
R^2	0.106		0.124		NR	
Adjusted R^2	0.090		0.109		NR	
White test	NR		7.192		NR	

standard errors in ( )

* significant at the 0.05 level

** significant at the 0.01 level

*** significant at the 0.001 level

NR: Non Relevant

All tests are one tailed.

Testing R1 and R2

Table 7.1 presents three different models. The first tests the bivariate hypothesized negative relationship between *RANGE* and *LAWS*. The second regresses the squared residuals of the first regression on *RANGE*. According to R2 this relationship should be negative and significant. Model 3 uses the results of the first two models to correct for the heteroskedasticity present in Model 1.

There are two reasons behind the simultaneous testing of R1 and R2. First, since the theory presented in this paper expects heteroskedasticity in Model 1, the OLS estimate is inefficient, so Model 3 corrects for that. The second and most important point is a general methodological one: when a theory states that high X (in our case, range) is a sufficient but not necessary condition to discourage Y (in our case, low Y is a small number of significant laws), it not only makes a simple prediction about the mean value of Y (number of significant laws) as a function of X (range), but *also* a statement about the variance of Y. It claims that the combination of high X and high Y (large range and large number of significant laws) is unlikely. Consequently, the residuals in the low X area of the figure (low range side) will be large, while the residuals in high X area of the figure (large range) will be small. Translated into statistical terms, this predicts heteroskedasticity and, as a result, low significance of the test of means (the traditional regression) is possible. But the appropriate test for such a theory predicting a sufficient but not necessary condition is a combination of a test of means (regression) with low statistical significance *and* a test of the variance (residuals) for heteroskedasticity. Similarly, the appropriate test for a theory identifying necessary (but not sufficient) conditions is a test of means (regression) *and* a test of the residuals for heteroskedasticity. If both predictions turn out to be corroborated (as they are), then the confidence to the theory that predicted both relationships ought to be significantly higher than the p-value of any one coefficient.

Model 1 provides the bivariate OLS test of R1: the relationship between *RANGE* and *LAWS* is negative and significant at the 0.01 level. However, I have predicted that this relationship will be heteroskedastic, and if I am correct, the estimation of the variance in Model 1 is inefficient. In order to correct for this inefficiency I use Model 2. In model 2 I take the squared residuals form Model 1 and regress them on *RANGE*. Confirming expectations, the coefficient is negative.

However Model 2 is not an ordinary regression model. In fact, in a non-finite sample its error term has a nonzero mean, is heteroskedastic, and correlated across observations. The first and third of these problems disappear in large samples, so we can expect the coefficients estimated by this regression to be consistent (Greene 1997: p.559). This is all that is required in order to correct the inefficient estimation of Model 1. Model 3 uses the estimated coefficients from Model 2 to correct the variance-covariance matrix in Model 1, and produces efficient estimates (in practice I used the inverse of the square root of the predicted values from

Model 2 as weights for a GLS estimation). Model 3 indicates that the negative relationship between *RANGE* and *LAWS* is significant at the 0.01 level.[27]

What remains to be shown is that the heteroskedasticity predicted by the theory is present in the data. For reasons explained in the previous paragraph we cannot use the variance estimated in Model 2 because 'the finite sample properties of this estimator remain uncertain' (Green 1997: p.559). However there are a series of homoskedasticity tests that can be performed on the residuals. I will use the weakest one of them introduced for the first time by White (1980). My reasoning is the following: if even the weakest test soundly rejects homoskedasticity, then there is little doubt that the error terms of Model 1 are heteroskedastic. According to the White test the statistic nR^2 from Model 2 (where n is the number of observations) is asymptotically distributed as chi-squared with 1 degree of freedom (Pindyck and Rubinfeld 1998: p.158). From Model 2 in Table 7.1 we see that the value of the nR^2 statistic is 7.192. From the chi-squared tables with one degree of freedom we obtain a one tailed value of 0.00732, which permits the confident rejection of the null hypothesis of homoskedasticity (at the 0.01 level).

In conclusion, from the combination of Models 1, 2, and 3 in Table 7.1 we find that both results R1 and R2 indicating a negative and heteroskedastic relationship between *RANGE* and *LAWS* are corroborated at the 0.01 confidence level. More direct evidence is provided by Figures 7.3 and 7.4.

Figure 7.3 presents the relationship between *LAWS* and *RANGE*. In this Figure (for reasons I will explain below) I have separated minimum winning coalition governments (indicated by x in the Figure) from the rest (indicated by o). The data are fitted by three bivariate regression lines. The top line summarizes the relationship between laws and range occurring in minimum winning coalitions. The bottom line summarizes the relationship between the same variables in other governments. The middle line is the regression line for the whole dataset. Comparison of Figure 7.3 with Figure 7.2 (which I used to introduce the theory) indicates the high degree of fit between theory and data (which also appeared in the regressions of Table 7.1).

Figure 7.4 gives a graphic representation of the absolute value of the residuals from Model 1 in Table 7.1. I selected the absolute value for this Figure because the graphic of squared residuals is visually misleading (it eliminates small residuals and exacerbates large ones). Again, I divided governments into minimum winning coalitions and all the rest, but this time there is no difference between the regression lines representing the whole dataset and each one of the two parts. We can see that the slope is negative and very significant, exactly as result R2 leads us to believe.

---

27 The estimated variance for two governments is negative, so Model 3 excludes these observations. The result is not different if one uses a non-linear function so that all estimated values for the variance are positive.

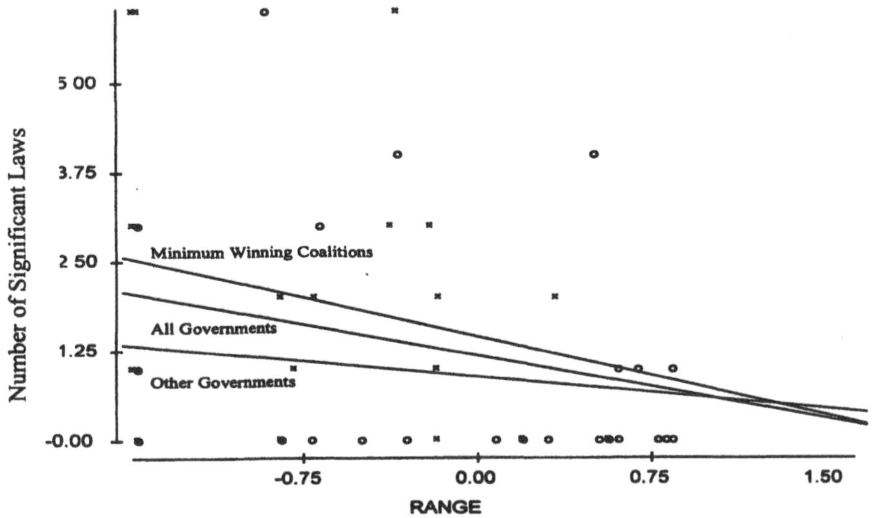

x minimum winning coalitions
o other governments

Figure 7.3 Number of Significant Laws by Ideological Range of Coalition

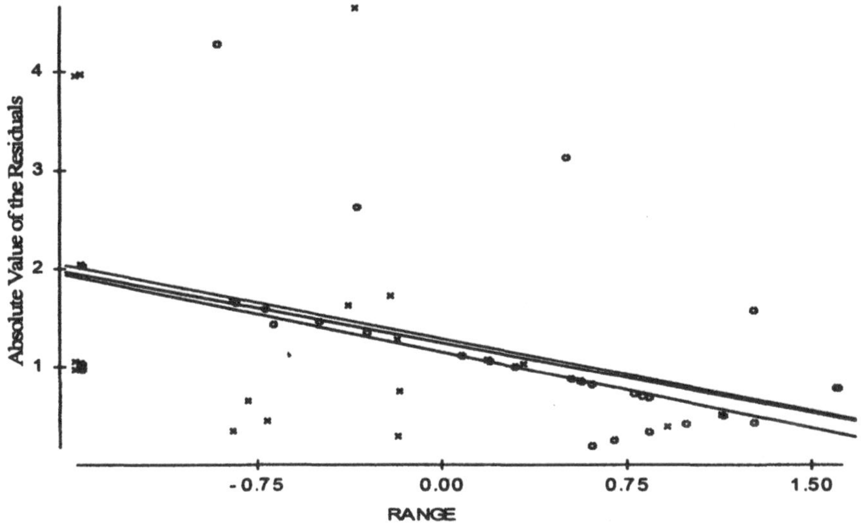

x minimum winning coalitions
o other governments

Figure 7.4 Residuals (Absolute Value) of Significant Laws by Ideological Range of Coalition

Test of R3

The models in this section are multivariate and introduce a series of control variables. According to result R3 two additional control variables (*DURATION* and *ALTERNATION*) are expected to have positive signs. *ALTERNATION* (the difference between the midpoints of the current from the previous government) is one way to introduce a proxy for the status quo in case legislation was introduced by the previous government. Of course, there is no guarantee that this was actually the case (see above). In all multivariate models heteroskedasticity is significantly reduced. In fact, the White test (see above) does not permit to reject the homoskedasticity assumption at conventional levels of significance. This is why I will correct for heteroskedasticity only the most important of the models from Table 7.2.

Table 7.2 Multivariate Models of Significant Legislation (Tests of R3)

Variable	Model 1	Model 2	Model 2A MWC	Model 2B Other	Model 3	Model 4
Constant	-0.20	0 21	-0.26	0 42	0.22	0.36
	(0.27)	(0 24)	(0 47)	(0.33)	(0 26)	(0 24)
Range	-0.27	-0.35*	-0 62*	-0 25	-0.37*	-0.39*
	(0.18)	(0.18)	(0 33)	(0 23)	(0 19)	(0.17)
Alternation	0 54*	0 70**	0.86*	0.41	0 68**	0 53*
	(0.25)	(0.24)	(0.34)	(0 39)	(0 25)	(0 23)
Duration	0.36***	–	–	–	–	–
	(0 07)					
Ln(Duration)		1 85***	2 07**	1 68**	1 89***	1.76***
		(0 38)	(0 63)	(0 53)	(0.42)	(0 37)
Agenda					0.0004	
					(0 002)	
Corporatism					0 034	
					(0.25)	
Left					0 025	
					(0 15)	
N	58	58	23	35	58	56
R^2	0 518	0 501	0 630	0 303	0 503	NR
Adjusted R^2	0 491	0 473	0.571	0.236	0 445	NR

standard errors in ( )
* significant at the 0.05 level
** significant at the 0.01 level
*** significant at the 0.001 level
MWC: minimum winning coalition
NR: Non Relevant
All tests are one tailed.

Model 1 in Table 7.2 introduces both control variables in their linear form. Model 2 introduces the idea of a declining rate of production of significant laws by using the natural logarithm of duration as an independent variable. This model corroborates all the expectations generated by the veto players' theory. This is why I subject it to two additional tests. The first test is to examine whether the findings hold for different subsets of the data. Models 2A and 2B separate the different governments into minimum winning coalitions (23 cases), and 'others' (minority, and oversized coalitions) (35 cases) and re-test the model for each one of these categories. The second test is to introduce a series of control variables in order to test for spuriousness of the results. Model 3 introduces three plausible control variables (*AGENDA CONTROL*, *CORPORATISM*, and *LEFT IDEOLOGY* of the government) which existing literatures suggest as alternative explanations for the findings.

As Table 7.2 shows all the hypothesized relationships come out with the correct sign (negative for range, and positive for alternation and duration). On the basis of model 2, one can say that the production of significant laws is affected negatively by the range of government, positively by the difference between current and previous government (alternation), and that duration increases the number of laws but at a declining rate.

Models 2A and 2B replicate the analysis for minimum winning coalitions, and other governments respectively. All the signs of the coefficients are as hypothesized, but conventional levels of statistical significance are lost, except for the case of minimum winning coalitions.[28]

Let me now discuss model 3, which introduces three different control variables. The first of them is *AGENDA CONTROL*. Döring (1995c, 1995d, 1995e) has identified the importance of government agenda setting for both the quantity and quality of legislation produced in a country. In a nutshell, his argument is that government control of the agenda increases the number of important bills and reduces legislative inflation (few small bills). Döring defined agenda control in two different ways: qualitatively, and quantitatively.[29] He hypothesized a positive

28 I thank an anonymous referee for the suggestion of subdividing the dataset. The division applied the standard criteria in most countries. However, in Germany I had to take into account the Bundesrat if controlled by the opposition, in Portugal the President if his party was not included in the government, and in one case of a government decree in France I took into account the President of the Republic. In all these cases the standard status of the government was altered to take into account the veto players' theory: for example, in Germany a minimum winning coalition government was coded as oversized if the support of an opposition controlled Bundesrat was required.

29 The qualitative measure of agenda control scores countries the following way: 1. the government alone controls the plenary agenda of parliament; 2. the government controls a bigger majority in the President's conference than it controls in parliament; 3. the President's conference is proportionally controlled by parties; 4. consensus agreement is sought in the President's Conference, subject to approval by a majority in the chamber; 5. The President's decision after consultation of party groups cannot be challenged by the chamber; 6. agenda setting is fragmented, in the absence of unanimity; 7. the chamber itself determines the agenda (Döring 1995b: p.225). The quantitative measure uses five additional indicators (like who controls the timetable of a bill, whether parliamentary committees can rewrite it et cetera (for detailed analysis see Döring 1995b)); Döring applies factor analysis to all six indicators, and takes the country loadings on the first factor (Döring (1995c: p.684)). In my analyses I used both measures with similar results.

relationship between significant laws and agenda control. However, Döring was discussing countries as units of analysis, and his measures (which I use) refer to countries. Consequently, the variance of significant legislation within each country cannot possibly be captured by Döring's variables.

CORPORATISM was the second variable introduced for control purposes. I introduced *CORPORATISM* both as a trichotomous variable (with Belgium, Germany, Luxembourg and Switzerland as ambiguous cases), and as a dichotomous one (with the above countries considered corporatist). Like *AGENDA CONTROL*, it is considered constant by country. In this respect, I follow most of the literature on corporatism, despite the fact that contemporary research finds significant fluctuations in the variables that comprise the concept over time (Golden, Wallerstein, and Lange 1999).

In corporatist countries, the argument goes, peak associations of employers and unions negotiate the subjects covered by this article, and only if they do not agree does parliament step in and legislate or does the Government Issue decrees. Because of this, corporatist countries (where government ranges are in general high) presumably produce less significant labor legislation. There are two problems with this argument. First, in corporatist countries legislation is produced whether the social partners agree or not. If they agree, the parliament or the government issues legislation or decrees confirming the agreement. If they disagree, the legislative institutions of the country decide on the disagreement. For example, at the end of the 1980s the problem in both Norway and Sweden was the need to cut wages to prevent unemployment from rising. In Norway, the social partners (unions and employers) agreed to a wage freeze and asked the social democratic minority government to put it into legislation so that it would be universally binding. The legislation was passed by parliament, while the independent unions (that is, those not affiliated with the main confederation) complained that they were being victimized, wages declined and unemployment did not grow very much. In Sweden, at the same time, the social partners failed to agree to control wages, so the social democratic minority government introduced legislation to freeze wages. In the Swedish case, all of the unions protested, the proposal was defeated, the government fell, wages continued to rise rapidly and unemployment went much higher than in Norway. Second, if the argument were correct, one would expect less *overall* labor legislation in corporatist countries, not just less *significant* legislation. However, corporatist countries have more overall legislation in the area of working time and working conditions.

The third variable was the *ideology* of each government. Since the dependent variable is labor legislation, one may assume that left-wing governments produce more of it. In my view, this interpretation ignores the possibility of right-wing governments repealing labor laws, or undoing what left-wing governments have done. *LEFT IDEOLOGY* was measured exactly the same way as *RANGE* and *ALTERNATION*, so it varies by government and the empirical results will be conclusive.

As model 3 indicates, none of the three control variables above has any impact on the results of model 2. The additional three variables come out very close to zero and completely insignificant. In addition, there is no increase in the R^2 of the model, and the adjusted R^2 shrinks. It is safe to say that statistically these variables do not explain anything (although conceptually one has to refer back to the discussion in the previous paragraphs to understand why it is so).

Finally, in order to make sure that these results are not generated because of peculiarities in any one country, I examined the points of highest leverage (the four cases (three points, but one of them is double) in the upper left quarter of Figure 7.3) in order to make sure that they do not reflect unusual situations. These four points represent governments of Belgium, Sweden, Greece and the UK. In the case of the first two countries, the governments produced an extraordinary amount of laws because their range was unusually small. In the case of the second two countries, the rule was single party governments, and two of them (both comprised of two or more actual governments) produced a high number of significant laws. Even without these cases, the negative relationship between range and significant laws is preserved, although statistical significance is lost.

Since some of the numbers in the table do not lend themselves to an immediate political interpretation, I will provide such an interpretation. I also caution the reader that the numbers will appear 'small' because I am dealing with a single area of legislation. One would have to aggregate across different areas to find the overall effect.[30]

Model 2 corroborates all the predictions of the theory, and additional variables suggested by the literature do not improve upon it. Model 4 replicates Model 2 by using GLS (I used the same technique for weighing observations as in Table 7.1). My numerical analysis will be based on Model 4, which is both theoretically supported, and empirically corroborating. Given that the coefficient of the natural logarithm of duration is positive we can say that the effect of duration on government legislation is twofold. On the one hand, duration has a positive effect on legislation; on the other, the rate of law production declines with duration.

For the range variable, the coefficient is -0.39. The highest normalized value of range is approximately 1.6, while the lowest (any single-party government), is approximately -1.5. The difference between these two governments in their capacity for producing laws is that the single party government on average produces 1.2 laws more than the largest coalition.

Finally, with respect to alternation, the coefficient (0.53) should be interpreted the following way: The highest value of alternation in our dataset represents the shift from Mr. Callaghan's Labour (remember the wave of strikes in Britain's

---

30 In this aggregation, one would have to replicate the logic of this analysis, not extrapolate mechanically the results. For example, the positions of government parties on environmental issues should be considered in order to predict environmental legislation, not the left-right scale used here. So, it is perfectly reasonable to expect that a government composed of parties close to each other on the left-right scale and produces many significant laws on labor may produce few significant environmental laws if the veto players are far away from each other in the environmental policy dimension.

'winter of discontent') to Mrs. Thatcher's Conservative party in 1979 with a value of 3.0 (we remind the reader that although 1979 is not in the dataset, when a government is in place in 1981, we find the previous government in order to calculate the value of alternation). The lowest possible alternation (that is, keeping the range of government intact from one government to the next) receives a score of 0.13. The difference between these two extreme governments in terms of law production is approximately 1.5 significant laws in the area under examination. This is the substantive interpretation of the coefficients.

Let us examine the policy significance of these findings. Results R1, R2, and R3 taken together indicate that large range coalitions are unlikely to produce significant legislation, while small range coalitions and single party governments may or may not produce such laws and decrees. In other words, policy stability is the characteristic of the first, while the *possibility* of significant policy change is the characteristic of the second.

Policy stability is another way of saying that the composition of the government or the political institutions of a country enable political actors credibly to commit that there will be no significant policy changes. This, in turn, reduces the uncertainty of actors in the civil society in making their own decisions. In particular, actors in the economy may make decisions to invest without fear that the legislative environment is going to change.

At the other extreme, the possibility of single-party or small range government to change the status quo significantly may enable a country to adapt more easily to exogenous policy shocks. Hallerberg and Basinger (1998) offer an example of this in their analysis of tax laws. Once the United States under Reagan reduced taxes for companies along with citizens in the highest personal income bracket, other industrialized countries followed. Among these countries, some adjusted their rates by large amounts, and some by small. Among the countries that performed large adjustments were the single-party labor governments of New Zealand and Australia. These governments were left wing (although moderate), and therefore, in principle they were not advocating tax reductions for the rich. However, once they decided to decrease taxes, their partisanship was immaterial: they reduced taxes at a level comparable to Mrs. Thatcher's Conservative government in the UK.

It is not the goal of this article to argue in favor of either policy stability or instability. Similarly, I do not want to argue in favor of government flexibility or in favor of credible commitments. Nor is it the goal of the article to deny the possibility that governments that take decisive steps can overshoot and then correct their actions, and that governments that take small steps can make several such steps one at a time, arriving at the same outcome in the long run. The argument is that, depending on government composition (or on institutional structures that consistently produce single or multiple veto players), one can get either policy stability or the potential for policy change, but not both.[31]

Veto Players and Incremental Legislation

Having established the relation between vps, range, and significant legislation (lack of policy stability), we now turn to the incremental (non-significant) legislation and the total number of laws. In volume I I had argued: 'Ceteris paribus, significant and non-significant laws should vary inversely, because of time constraints. The ceteris paribus clause assumes that the Parliament has limited time and uses it to pass legislation (either significant or trivial). If there are other uses of time like questions to ministers, general debates, et cetera, or if the time of meetings is itself variable, controls must be introduced for these factors' (Tsebelis 1995b: p.104). In this section, I will test whether the above expectation is corroborated. The unit of analysis becomes the country instead of the government, because data at the government level are not available.

Döring (1995b, 1995d, 1995e) has established the importance of government agenda setting for both the quantity and quality of legislation produced in a country. In a nutshell, his argument is that government control of the agenda increases the number of important bills and reduces legislative inflation (few small bills). Döring (1995d, 1995e) used actual legislative data to test his insights. The tests not only corroborated the intuition that government agenda control reduces legislative inflation, but they also eliminated other plausible explanations (including a country's population size, electoral barriers for party entry, number of parties in parliament, additional legislation at the subnational level, et cetera) along the way. So, from a different perspective, Döring has come to the same conclusions as the vps theory: as the number of significant laws increases, legislative inflation goes down; but for him, it is government control of the legislative agenda that connects the two.

In order to revisit Döring's findings I will use Döring's first indicator of government agenda control, or his quantitative index.

Table 7.3 introduces a series of variables for each country: the number of significant laws and decrees (the sum of such legislative instruments for the whole period under examination), the average number of laws per country (from Table 18.1 of the Döring (1995d) book), an average number of vps per country, as well as government agenda control calculated on the basis of Döring's first indicator.

Some explanations of these data are necessary. For the number of laws per country variable, Sweden has two numbers: one taken from Table 18.1 of Döring

31 Unless a single-party government finds a technology to commit credibly: by appointing an independent agency and assigning jurisdiction, or by claiming that the status quo is its own ideal point, et cetera. I am not going to enter into the discussion of commitment technologies, but the bottom line is that multi-party governments have difficulty changing the status quo, while single-party governments do not (see discussion on taxation above).

and the other, the average number of new laws provided by Ingvar Mattson of the Department of Political Science of Lund University. Apparently in Sweden they count each amendment as a separate law. So the number in Döring, although technically correct, is inflated by comparative standards. In terms of vps, countries with single-party governments receive a score of 1, countries with a mixture of single and up to two parties in government receive a score of 2, and countries with more than two parties in government receive a score of 3. These scores reflect the situation prevailing in these countries for a substantially longer period than the 10 years we have been studying so far. The only country requiring additional explanation is Germany. The number 3 reflects the fact that, while the government coalitions since the beginning of the 1950s involve only two parties, the Bundesrat has been controlled by an opposing majority for significant periods of time.

Table 7.3 Number of Laws, Important Laws, Veto Players, and Government Control of Legislative Agenda

Country	import. laws (work. time)	laws/year	veto players (qual)	veto players (numer)	agenda control (qual)
Austria	3	121	2	1.79	4
Belgium	7	49	3	4.29	4
Denmark	5	165	3	3.57	5
Finland	4	343	3	3.89	5
France	8	94	2	1.57	2
GB	6	62	1	1	1
Germany	2	83	3	2.19	4
Greece	10	88	1	1	2
Ireland	2	35	2	1.78	1
Italy	1	264	3	4.70	6
Luxembourg	6	66	2	2	3
Netherlands	1	134	3	2.13	7
Portugal	5	69	2	2.34	3
Spain	3	56	2	1	4
Sweden	9	375 (56 new)	2	1.82	5

numbers of important laws from this study;
numbers of laws, qualitative agenda control and agenda control from Döring (1995c,d,e)
veto players average

Table 7.4 presents the correlation coefficients of the variables included in Table 7.3. The three versions depend on whether Sweden is included with 375 annual laws (Table 7.4a), with 56 such laws (Table 7.4b), or excluded from the data set altogether (Table 7.4c). The reader can verify that the correlation between all laws and significant laws is negative in the version of the table that excludes

Sweden. So, in the most reliable of the three versions, the expectation of negative correlation between significant and overall legislation is corroborated.

More interesting, however, are the relationships between vps and the number of laws, as well as the relationship between vps and agenda control by the government. Vps correlated positively with the number of all laws, and negatively with the number of significant laws in all three versions of Table 7.4. Similarly, as Döring has convincingly demonstrated, agenda control by the government is negatively correlated with legislative inflation (the number is positive in Table 7.4 because higher numbers indicate *less* control by the government). Finally, the most interesting finding is that the number of vps is highly correlated with (the lack of) agenda control (again, in all versions of Table 7.4).

Table 7.4a Correlations among Veto Players, Agenda Setting, and Legislation

	Important Laws	Laws/year	Vps qualitative	Vps average	Ag. contr. qualitative
Important laws	1.000				
Laws/year	0.048	1.000			
Vps qualitative	-0.540	0.332	1.000		
Vps average	-0.272	0.420	0.793	1.000	
Agenda control qualitative	-0.411	0.588	0.757	0.562	1.000

Sweden included with 375 bills/year

Table 7.4b Correlations among Veto Players, Agenda Setting, and Legislation

	Important Laws	Laws/ year	Vps qualitative	Vps average	Ag. contr. qualitative
Important laws	1.000				
Laws/year	0.048	1.000			
Vps qualitative	-0.540	0.516	1.000		
Vps average	-0.272	0.639	0.793	1.000	
Agenda control qualitative	-0.411	0.545	0.757	0.562	1.000

Sweden included with 56 bills/year

Table 7.4c Correlations among Veto Players, Agenda Setting, and Legislation

	Important Laws	Laws/year	Vps qualitative	Vps average	Ag. contr. qualitative
Important laws	1.000				
Laws/year	-0.284	1.000			
Vps qualitative	-0.547	0.508	1.000		
Vps average	-0.246	0.632	0.791	1.000	
Agenda control qualitative	-0.550	0.603	0.799	0.602	1.000

Sweden excluded

How can we interpret these findings? I think the positive correlation of vps and (lack of) agenda control with the total number of laws and the negative correlation of the same variables with the number of significant laws (when Sweden is excluded) point toward a difference in the very concept of 'law' among countries. 'Laws' in countries with many vps and low government agenda control produce incremental changes of the status quo, while in countries with few vps and significant government agenda control, they produce sweeping changes.

But why is (lack of) agenda setting by the government correlated with the number of vps? Is it a coincidental relation or a causal one? Several arguments can be made that it is not a mere correlation. While a causal argument attributing the existence of vps to the lack of agenda control is difficult, a strategic argument going from agenda control to vps is possible. In countries with strong government agenda control, party negotiations for coalition governments will end up in a minority government or a government with few vps. Conversely, in countries without government agenda control, parties will form oversized government coalitions in order to control the legislature. On the other hand, a causal argument going from vps to agenda control is straightforward: the existence of many vps makes them incapable of passing through parliament the many and significant pieces of legislation required for agenda control. This argument considers agenda control to be a collection of significant pieces of legislation. Consequently, we expect *not to see it* in countries with many vps. Finally, a third argument can be made: that vps and agenda control have common origins. The same sociological and historical factors that fragment a country into many competing parties (none of which has a majority) make these parties sufficiently suspicious of each other, so that they reject the idea of allowing whoever is in government to have significant control over legislation.

Which one of the three explanations is closer to the truth? This is a major question for further investigation. In order to address this question, one would have to collect data on the adoption (and possible repeal) of the different agenda-control mechanisms and analyze them in relation to the governments that produced them. In other words, one would have to replicate this study with agenda control as the subject matter.

Conclusions

I have presented the implications of the veto players' theory when parties are located in a one-dimensional space and analyzed data on significant pieces of legislation in 15 West European countries. All of the expectations of the theory were corroborated by the data. The number of significant laws varies inversely with the range of governments that produce them (R1). In addition, the relation is heteroskedastic with respect to the range of the coalition (R2). Each one of these relations is significant at the .01 level, increasing further the confidence to a theory that made both predictions. The explanation for both these relationships is that a wide range is a sufficient (but not necessary) condition for the absence of significant legislation. Finally the number of significant laws increases in proportion to the natural logarithm of government duration (indicating a declining rate of production of significant laws) and in proportion to the difference between ideological positions of the current and previous government (R3).

With this analysis, the missing empirical link between veto players and a series of important features of parliamentary systems has been established. Many veto players with large ideological distances between them mean that legislation can only be incremental. If an exogenous shock occurs, a government with many veto players with big ideological distances among them cannot handle the situation and cannot agree on the necessary policies (unless public opinion is unanimous on the subject). This is the reason that Franzese (1996) finds that countries with many veto players have a locked pattern of debt and deficit: countries with high (low) debt (accumulated deficits) have high (low) deficits. If an exogenous shock creates a pressing problem, the multiparty government unable to handle it will resign and be replaced by another government with fewer veto players or smaller ideological distances among them (that is, a government that can handle the crisis). This is the reason for low longevity of multiparty governments established by Warwick (1994). Similarly, in the absence of political leadership, a series of non-political actors like bureaucracies and judges may step in to fill the void. This is the reason that the judiciary (Alivizatos 1995) or bureaucracies (Lohmann 1998) become more important and independent in countries or in periods with multiparty governments.

Finally, the number of vps is positively correlated with the number of overall pieces of legislation in a country. This generates the expectation that the very concept of 'law' differs from one country to the next, with countries with a large number of vps implementing more incremental legislation. The positive relation between vps and total pieces of legislation and the negative relationship between vps and significant pieces imply an overall negative relationship between total number of laws and significant pieces of legislation (when Sweden is excluded).

The conclusion from this analysis is that now the missing empirical link between vps and a series of important features of parliamentary systems has been established. Many vps with big ideological distances between them means that legislation can only be incremental. If an exogenous shock occurs, a government with many vps with big ideological distances among them cannot handle the situation and cannot agree on the necessary policies (except if the public opinion is unanimous on the subject). Finally, the relationship between vps and agenda control that we identified here leads to the conclusion that many vps affect the relationship between government and parliament in West European countries. Many vps are correlated with lack of agenda control by the government and lack of agenda control means weaker governments and stronger parliaments. I provided three arguments linking veto players with the lack of agenda control by the government. However, this relationship has to be more thoroughly investigated in the future.

Conclusion

Herbert Döring and Mark Hallerberg

Which patterns of parliamentary behavior emerge if we draw together the principle variables used in the book to explain some of the constraints and possibilities for passing legislation in the parliamentary systems of Western Europe? This conclusion confines itself to summarizing linkages, not only between the various chapters of this book, but also between current individual-level data analyses using bills as units for analysis and previous aggregate data findings of the 'Parliaments and Majority Rule in Western Europe' research group. We highlight fourteen basic findings mentioned in more than one chapter and we explain the connections between chapters.

Connecting Findings across Chapters

1. Imposition of restrictive rules is used – but by single-party governments only – to contain possible 'pork barrel' behavior resulting from features of the electoral system and from a 'common pool resource problem'.

Government imposition of restrictive rules is fact of life not only in France but in most parliamentary democracies of Western Europe. In the SPPL data set for the study of the parliamentary passage of legislation no less than 80 of 512 bills were enacted by some kind of restrictive rule across 17 parliamentary systems. The logic linking features of the electoral system to deputies' behavior starts out from Olson's (1965) logic of collective action. As outlined by Hallerberg (chapter 1) a small district magnitude 'M' of the number of deputies elected per constituency (Lancaster 1986; Lancaster and Patterson 1990) and the possibility for a 'personal vote' (Shugart and Carey 1992: pp. 175f.; Carey and Shugart 1998) may induce pork barrel behavior of MPs. To cope with undesirable behavioral consequences of both 'pork barrel politics' and the 'common pool resource problem' (i.e. cabinet ministers handing out particular benefits out of general tax receipts), rules are invented as solutions to collective action dilemmas (Cox and McCubbins 1993: chapters 4 and 5; Hallerberg 2000; Hallerberg and von Hagen 1999).

Hallerberg found that restrictive procedures on bills (also studied in chapters 3 and 6) are three times as often imposed in one of the three types of cabinet organization than in the other two. In keeping with his theoretical expectations on institutional solutions to the 'common pool resource problem' it is those single-party governments that delegate monitoring authority over ministerial spending to a string finance minister acting as 'legislative leviathan' (in the sense of Cox and McCubbins 1993) that use restrictive rules most. These findings are consistent with the theory: parliament represents a last opportunity for spending ministers to try to add back in spending that the minister of finance cut at the cabinet level. In order for *delegation* to a strong finance minister to be effective in practice, a decision made in cabinet should not be easily overturned in parliament.

Hallerberg found his expectations about the use of restrictive rules on bills were not equally supported for the other two government types defined by him. What he calls 'commitment states', i.e. multi-party cabinets relying on binding agreements, possibly enshrined in a coalition contract, rarely invoked restrictive procedures. This finding appears to suggest confidence that parliamentarians will not try to sabotage the existing contracts. Indeed, it would be plausible that the potential damage from any defections on the part of ministers voting as parliamentarians on the floor would be high, including a possible end of the coalition with this punishment serving as an effective deterrent. Restrictive procedures in parliament would then be superfluous. This tentative reasoning is in subsequent chapters confirmed from a principal agent perspective by De Winter (chapter 2). It is also supported by Tsebelis's veto players' theory used in various chapters throughout the book (chapters 3, 6 and 7). Both observations will now be explained in turn in sections 2 and 3.

2. In multi-party governments restrictive rules on bills may be replaced by binding commitments in coalition contracts forming a substitute for government control of the legislative agenda.

In a previous publication De Winter had already demonstrated with aggregate data a significant trade-off that exists between the constant availability of instruments for government control of the legislative agenda in a given country and the average amount of time invested in working out elaborate coalition contracts across countries (De Winter 1995: 142-146, with figure 4.1). De Winter used one of the two Döring indices of existing instrumental possibilities for government to control the legislative agenda (constructed by Döring 1995c and 1995e and also used here in chapters 3, 5, 6, and 7). A significant trade-off between agenda control and coalition contracts became visible in De Winter's scatterplot between the aggregate index of agenda control and the proxy variable of average time needed for negotiating such coalition contracts, yielding (with two outliers excluded) a Pearson correlation of -0.82 (De Winter 1995: p.146).

From this finding it follows that coalition contracts may form a substitute for government control of the legislative agenda. Hallerberg calls such coalition contracts from a budgetary perspective 'commitments' to fiscal contracts. From his expectation that such negotiated agreements are particularly frequent under multi-party governments, it furthermore follows that one would expect few actual impositions of restrictive rules on particular bills in 'commitment states' because they might have replaced restrictive rules by commitments. Hallerberg's empirical evidence confirms this expectation, but the failure of restrictive rules to show up in 'commitment states' (in Hallerberg's terminology) may also be explained by veto players' theory.

3. Restrictive rules, which form part and parcel of parliamentary agenda control, become less important with the increasing number of, and policy distance between, parties in government.

From veto players theory we should expect restrictive rules, which are part of the overall dimension of agenda control, to be utilized less often the more parties there are in government and the larger, furthermore, the policy distances between them are (see for formal proof, Tsebelis 2002: pp.33-37 with Figure 1.9). This is precisely what Döring finds in chapter 6 with logistic regression analysis of the reasons for government imposition of restrictive rules on individual bills. And more parties in government are the very rationale for Hallerberg's 'commitment' solution to the CRC problem.

Using the aggregate Döring index of agenda control instead of restrictions on individual bills, Tsebelis finds in chapter 7 that the 'constant' availability of government agenda control within a country is closely related to his prediction from veto players theory: there are fewer such rules in a given country where the number of veto players normally tends to be high. Another prediction derived from veto players theory is, however, rejected by Becker and Saalfeld in chapter 3.

4. Existence of few or many veto players shows in event-history statistics no impact at all on the speed of the legislative process.

On a variable that interests most in operationalization of Tsebelis's veto players' theory, i.e., the number of partisan veto players and the maximal ideological range between them, Becker and Saalfeld's results challenge a veto players' prediction. Whether a bill is introduced under a one-party government with an ideological range of zero or a multi-party coalition cabinet with a considerable ideological range does not have any significant impact on the likelihood of a bill's successful passage, or indeed on the speed of passage, if one looks at the entire legislative process (one episode). They only find that veto players' theory has explanatory power for single episodes during the life of a bill, but limited empirical support for the entire life cycle of a bill.

5. The stronger a government's control over the agenda the speedier the process and the higher the general success chances of bills are.

Using the aggregate Döring index of agenda control, Becker and Saalfeld found both for the single-episode and the multiple-episode design government control of the floor agenda to speed up the legislative process and to improve the survival chances of a bill. To be sure, the mere existence of such rules, as measured by the aggregate Döring index, may have an impact in itself, influencing the strategic options available to governments and oppositional minorities, but the actual use of such procedures remains a factor that needs to be controlled for. For this purpose, the SPPL questionnaire asks whether a government declared its intention to treat a bill as a matter of confidence or whether the government imposed any restrictive rule on a particular bill in the data set, a variable included by Becker and Saalfeld as control.

6. Public hearings in committees do not serve so much the purpose of collecting information as they are used as forums to announce dissent.

As mentioned by Hallerberg in chapter 1, Krehbiel (1991) would expect public hearings to signal to other legislators the general quality of a bill. But findings from Hallerberg's chapter show that the way public hearings were used in the SPPL data set were not indicative of information collection. These hearings were almost always public, but, as a general rule, they did not include anyone of substance who would know something about policy – only rarely was either a government minister or civil servant invited. This suggests that the hearings themselves are not important. If, however, government ministers were heard at all, more often than not (64.5 per cent against only 31.1 per cent) the policy problem of the bill at issue had been mentioned in the government declaration (chapter 2). This finding indicates hearings could be a convenient opportunity for parliamentarians to display in a public forum any disagreements they have with the government. In a similar vein, it emerges from Damgaard and Mattson in chapter 5 that conflict in committees was more probable if hearings were held, from which they concluded, that hearings may often be used (especially by the minority) to 'announce' disagreements since hearings have a potential to attract the interest of the media.

7. Committees do not function as an arena where conflict is resolved through compromise: this finding represents a rejection of predictions from Sartori's (1987) decision-making theory of democracy.

Conflict between government and opposition can be expressed in several ways and there is, as observed by many authors in the book, a difficulty to operationalize the degree of conflict in the procedure for passing legislation (see chapters 2, 4, 5, 6). Focusing on conflict in committees, Damgaard and Mattson in chapter 5 settle for a straightforward and convincing measurement of conflict, according to which conflict exists in a committee if a nay vote has been registered during the committee stage, or if a minority report has been attached to the committee report, or if another committee dissent was recorded. When none of these three conditions apply, they classify the case as consensual.

If a bill was so important as to change the status quo according to expert assessment in the encyclopaedia of labor law by Blanpain (v4 in the SPPL data set), more conflict was visible in committees than for bills not judged to be that important. This variable has also been employed in table 6.1 and forms – together with the number of government decrees obviously not contained in the SPPL dataset covering the passage of bills in parliaments – the crucial dependent variable in chapter 7. The fact that this significant Blanpain variable becomes insignificant in multivariate logistic regression may be attributable to the inclusion of only bills in our data set, whereas some of the most important changes of the status quo were achieved, as shown by Tsebelis in chapter 7, not by laws enacted by parliament, but by government regulation by force of decrees.

The most important finding from chapter 5 is, however, that little is left of a famous hypothesis. Based on assumptions drawn from economics and psychology, Sartori (1987: chapter 8) predicted parliamentary committees (provided they were small, permanent and in possession of jurisdiction for a policy field) would function as an arena where conflict is resolved through compromise. But as meticulously documented in bivariate tables and confirmed by multivariate logistic regression, little is left of this Sartori hypothesis. Seasoned researchers know from the history of sciences that, no matter how strongly a prominent theory appears to be refuted by experimental facts, it is not the correctness of the theory that is normally doubted but the validity of data used for its refutation (Kuhn 1996; Lakatos 1970). Knowing about this psychology was one of the reasons we decided to make the SPPL data set available to everybody with publication of this book to scrutinize results and try to find any pitfalls.

8. The 'informational' rationale for committee work (Krehbiel 1991) appears not to be applicable to Western European parliamentary systems.

Mattson and Strom find little evidence for Krehbiel's hypothesis that the organization and activity of committees is inspired by the purpose of collecting better information. The overall fate of bills is hardly correlated with the role of committees. Among successful bills in their sample, 25 per cent are subject to hearings or subcommittee. The corresponding figure for unsuccessful bills is 27. This result is contrary to their expectations, since it suggests that in aggregate they could not reject the 'null hypothesis' that parliamentary committees are mainly arenas for grand-standing which enjoy little or no deference from the floor.

An important part of the disagreement between the 'distributional' theory by Shepsle and the 'informational' theory by Krehbiel concerns the reasons for granting a bill a restrictive rule in the plenary. Döring's logistic regressions of the likely reasons for government imposition of restrictive rules on 80 of the 512 bills across 17 parliamentary democracies of Western Europe, indicate that proxy variables for previous information collection have no impact at all. Another finding emerging from the chapters by Mattson and Strøm and by Döring is that the multiple referral of bills so prominent in the US Congress appears to be infrequently and unsystematically used in Western European parliamentary systems (Figure 4.1 and Table 6.4).

9. Restrictive rules are imposed to protect complexity of multi-dimensional bills against being rolled on the floor.

John D. Huber argues that it is not only difficult but also unnecessary to establish whether a policy measure be 'distributional' or 'informational'. What is important for the likelihood of restrictive rules other than the confidence vote being imposed is rather that the measure is 'jurisdictionally complex' in the sense of putting multi-dimensional issues into a single package deal (Huber 1996a: p.88). Huber for France proved this to be the case for the package vote but not for the confidence vote procedure (Huber 1996a: p.106 with Table 4.8). Döring's logistic regressions in this volume confirm this major finding by Huber for France to carry universal significance for Western Europe at large: restrictive rules are, indeed, likely to be imposed by governments to protect multi-dimensional bills against being disentangled by amendments on the floor. More restrictive rules are imposed if there are more chapters/subheadings of a bill.

10. Even if bills enacted under restrictive rules are multi-dimensional, they do not appear to result from distributional logrolls among many parties in government.

Government ministers from different parties might be trading favors with each other for the 'distributional' benefit of their diverse clienteles at the expense of the public interest. Hence, the suspicion of 'gains from trade' always looms large if there are many parties in government and a bill is at the same time composed of more than one policy dimension. (We may recall here, though, from chapter 1 this vicious circle of distributional overspending out of the 'common pool' of tax receipts may be broken by coalition contracts committing the actors to fiscal discipline.) Huber was skeptical about the validity of the 'distributional' theory even for the U.S. committee system: 'Even if we set aside the controversy about whether congressional committees are composed of individuals with extreme preferences, a major problem with the distributive interpretation of restrictive amendment rules is that only a small percentage of bills actually considered by Congress are "distributive" in the narrow sense of "pork barrel projects". Many of these are voted under open rules, and many issues that are not 'distributive' are voted using closed or restrictive amendment rules. These observations have led some scholars to criticize the "distributive theory"' (Huber 1996a: p.86).

Nevertheless, he gave the 'distributional logrolls by many parties' argument the benefit of the doubt and suggested as a proxy indicator no more and no less than the number of parties in government because some political-economy theories assume there will be more particular benefits the more parties there are in a coalition (Roubini and Sachs 1989a, 1989b; Grilli, et al. 1991). Using this proxy variable for distributional logrolls as a key indicator for government imposition of a restrictive rule on a bill, it was significantly and strikingly rejected. One must, however, be cautious in drawing inferences because Döring measures only the number of coalition parties, not the actual distributional content of bills. Still, the finding is another corroboration of Tsebelis's veto players' theory, which anticipates that strong agenda control is negatively related to number of parties in government.

11. Instruments for agenda control tend to work as a behavioral inducement for governments to submit altogether fewer, yet more controversial, bills for enactment by parliament.

In the previous book by the 'Parliaments and Majority Rule in Western Europe' research group, Döring (1995b) and Henning (1995) suggested a new theoretical rationale about the electoral utility of contentious bills submitted by government under time constraint towards the end of the legislative term. Based on a decision-making cost argument of neoclassical economics, they argued that the mere existence of instruments for agenda control would induce governments to submit for electoral purposes, and not for reasons of substantive policy, altogether fewer, but substantially more controversial bills.

With aggregate data for the average number of bills per country, Döring (1995d) correlated his indices for agenda control with the quantity of legislation produced in a country. Controlling the theoretically expected negative bivariate result (fewer legislative inflation with stronger agenda control) in partial correlations for spuriousness, he eliminated other plausible explanations including a country's population size, electoral barriers for party entry, number of parties in parliament, additional legislation at the sub-national level (Döring 1995e). The second part of the Döring and Henning prediction that bills in countries with strong agenda control would on average be more conflictual was also borne out by another aggregate analysis (Döring 2001).

In the current volume, Döring checks in chapter 6 the robustness of his previous aggregate results against evidence from individual bills in the SPPL data set concerning the actual imposition of restrictive rules and/or the declaration of a bill as a matter of confidence. Both time constraint towards the end of the legislative term (also used in chapter 3) and controversy between government and opposition hold up well in multivariate logistic regression as reasons for imposition of restrictive rules even when rigorously checked against other received theories of agenda control.

12. Restrictive rules are most frequently utilized by minority governments of the single-party type.

A prediction derived by formal proof from veto players' theory is that agenda control is most likely to be exercised by minority government if it is of the single-party format centrally located in policy space (Tsebelis 2002: 33-37). Hallerberg finds in Table 1.6 no correlation between minority government and imposition of restrictive rules, whereas Döring finds in Table 6.4 a strong correlation between single-party minority government and imposition of restrictive rules. A possible contradiction between the two findings would, however, be only apparent and not real. For what counts in veto players' theory is not so much minority government as single-party minority government and Hallerberg, too, documents in his table a strong negative correlation between coalition government and imposition of restrictive rules.

13. More parties in government tend to submit on average more, yet altogether less important, pieces of legislation to parliament.

Chapter 7 brings Tsebelis's veto players' theory to bear on the amount and type of legislation. In the first volume of the multinational research group, Tsebelis applied veto players' theory to derive specific predictions about law production (Tsebelis 1995b). In a subsequent article published by the *American Political Science Review* (Tsebelis 1999) he showed predictions to be borne out by data: the larger the range of policy preferences between veto players, i.e. parties in government, the less likely it was that significant laws changing the status quo were passed. In this volume Tsebelis extends his analysis from 'substantive' laws to the average amount of total legislation per country. He shows with aggregate data across countries that a higher number of parties in government is correlated with altogether more pieces of legislation. These tend to be, however, less 'substantial' as measured by expert assessements than in countries with on average fewer parties in government.

14. Agenda control contributes to a reduction of legislative inflation but is in multivariate analysis not correlated with an increase of important legislation.

There are less instruments for agenda control with more parties in government, as shown in chapters 6 and 7. (Readers who are inclined to inspect Tables 7.4A to 7.4C should note that higher numbers for agenda control indicate *less* government control so that correlations must be given a reverse interpretation.) On the one hand, Tsebelis confirms in chapter 7 a previous finding by Döring (1995d): strong agenda control by government is correlated with less legislative inflation (fewer pieces of insignificant laws). On the other hand, a bivariate correlation between higher agenda control and more 'substantive' laws vanishes in multivariate analysis. If controlled for the impact of veto players, it is a small 'range' of policy preferences between parties in government and not agenda control that explains an increase of more important legislation.

What Has Been Left out and what Can be Done next?

Any account of rational choice theories used to explain parliamentary behavior would be incomplete without mentioning last, but by no means least, a hypothesis first suggested in the seminal book by John Huber about the French National Assembly: Linking an up-or-down proposal on policy to a vote of confidence serves as a strategy for creating 'party discipline by default' in the presence of incohesive parties (Huber 1996a; Huber 1996b; Döring 2004). This hypothesis is, however, not testable by quantitative data such as provided by the SPPL data set. Even John Huber did not prove it with statistical analysis but by case studies in spite of having created an original data set for 356 government bills between 1978 and 1989. He assessed his hypothesis about the sophisticated strategic use of linking policy to the confidence vote procedure for strategic, and sometimes twisted, electoral purposes with illuminating case studies and not with statistical analyses (Huber 1996a: chapters 6 and 7). Not everything is suitable for and liable to quantitative statistical analyses.

Let us finish our summary by asking to what extent this book lived up to a golden rule of comparative research succinctly phrased by Guy Peters: 'maximise experimental variance, minimise error variance, and control extraneous variance' (Peters 1998: p.30). Fashioning a behavioral research tool for comparative analysis, as the authors of this book did in a multinational effort using 650 bills from 18 countries as units for analysis is like knitting a fishing net for a research expedition into fairly uncharted waters. However, Karl Deutsch, himself one of the foremost scholars of empirical behavioral research, once tellingly remarked that to rely exclusively on empirical evidence from nothing else but such a fishing net was tantamount to believing there were no fish below 3.5 inches in that part of the ocean because the 3.5 inches net did not catch any. In other words, even if the catch of our net is big, there surely must be a large amount of unexplored, or extraneous, variance in this book that escaped the SPPL data set.

Using this metaphor of the fishing net, the question now is, what possibly slipped through the holes of our tightly knit net? A few open questions necessitating further research that cannot be done with the SPPL data set already come to mind. One question concerns De Winter's finding, mentioned in section 2, of a trade-off between agenda control and coalition contracts. In fact, with individual data there is no correlation whatever between a bill having been mentioned in a government declaration and government's imposition of restrictive rules on bills (Pearson's r between the two variables is essentially Zero). In future research we should, therefore, control to what extent most bills whose policy problem had been mentioned in a government declaration at the beginning of the legislative term had also been included (the single-party governments in our sample notwithstanding) beforehand in a coalition contract. If there really is a trade-off in behavioral terms of conventions and customs between agenda control and detailed coalition contracts, such controls might resolve the as-yet unresolved puzzle of this surprisingly non-existent correlation between bills mentioned in government declarations and the conspicuous absence of restrictions imposed on such bills.

Thought provoking, too, is the observation that contrary to what may be attributed to Tsebelis's veto players' theory it is not more but rather much less time that is required for the total passage of legislation the more extreme the 'range' between parties in government (and hence the presumed retarding effect of veto players) is. Perhaps Döring's suggestion to divide the concept of agenda control into a timetable-control and an amendment-control dimension may contribute to solving this contradiction. It appears to be worthwhile, if largely overlooked by the rational choice literature on agenda control, to distinguish between the two amendment-control and timetable-control dimensions of agenda control (Döring 2004 and chapter 6 in this volume). Becker and Saalfeld's rejections of veto players' theory exclusively focuses on timetable control. If Tsebelis's theory only applies to amendment control, it would be no reason for surprise that Becker and Saalfeld do not find an impact of veto players when they look for timetable control. However, our key variable used in the SPPL data set to analyze imposition of restrictive rules does not record the difference between amendment control and timetable control. If one were empirically to take up the argument about the differential impact of timetable restrictions and amendment restrictions, one would have to go back to the archives and libraries of parliaments to establish, and additionally to code into the data set, the type of restrictions for 80 out of 512 bills.

There are other puzzles concerning the speed of the legislative procedure that cannot be solved with existing data from SPPL alone. Quite contrary to expectations, De Winter (chapter 2) finds government bills considered so important to be mentioned in a declaration submitted to parliament at the beginning of the legislative term to be treated slower in terms of time passed between the moment of the first formal introduction of the bill until final promulgation. Based on their theoretical reasoning, Becker and Saalfeld, too, expect a high level of committee independence to be related to a slower passage of bills and *vice versa*. The opposite is the case: In the single-episode design, higher levels of committee independence in setting their own agendas tend to lead to speedier passage of a bill overall. These findings are largely confirmed when they applied a multiple-episode design with the exception of the committee deliberations themselves. Addressing this puzzle, Becker and Saalfeld formulate an intriguing research question worth consideration in the future. Although committees may enjoy a high degree of independence according to the parliamentary rules of procedure, they may in fact be tightly controlled by the parliamentary parties, which delegate and instruct their members on the committee.

Other pertinent questions for future research have already been formulated by various authors. Hallerberg extrapolates from his discussion of the common pool resource problem in parliaments the request to study Italy but also to go beyond Western Europe and study expected changes in parliamentary organization in New Zealand and Japan. All of these countries changed their electoral systems in ways possibly leading to results predicted by his theory.

Tsebelis delineates two further research questions transgressing observable behavioral results reported in this book. From a first observation that the number of veto players is positively correlated with the number of overall pieces of legislation in a country, but negatively with important legislative changes of the status quo, a topic for further research arises. Tsebelis conjectures that the very concept of 'law' may differ from one country to the next because countries with a consistently large number of veto players over decades, or even over a century, may have become accustomed to developing and implementing an incremental style legislation.

Another conjecture that might be taken up concerns the lack of a correlation between agenda control by the government and the number of veto players. Several arguments can be made that the finding is not a coincidence. In order to address these various scenarios outlined by Tsebelis, one would have to collect, he concludes, data on the adoption (and possible repeal) of the different agenda-control mechanisms over time and analyze them in relation to the governments that produced them.

To end with a note of caution, readers are invited to check and chase our results for spuriousness. The best avenue for so doing is perhaps to code systems variables representing country properties as additional variables into the SPPL data set. (Authors of this volume already did so by using variables taken from sources outside the SPPL data set such as, for example, the degree of consociationalizm or corporatism according to widely accepted cross-national measures.) Re-analyzing our findings for individual data on the 650 bills across 18 countries within the context of other such systems variables for industrial relations (see for example Crouch 1996) can show whether some individual-level findings would partly, or completely, vanish if controlled for country properties we have hitherto treated as extraneous variance. We are confident this rarely happens, but it remains to be seen.

Bibliography

Aghion, Philippe and Tirole, Jean (1997), 'Formal and Real Authority in Organisations', *Journal of Political Economy*, Vol. 105, pp. 1-19.

Alivizatos, Nicos (1995), 'Judges as Veto Players', in Döring, Herbert (ed.), *Parliaments and Majority Rule in Western Europe*, Campus/St. Martin's, Frankfurt/New York, pp. 566-589.

Alt, James E. (2000), *Credibility, Transparency, Accountability, Institutions: An Exploration and Some Examples. Paper Presented at the 2000 American Political Science Association Meeting*, Washington, D.C.

Alt, James E. and Lowry, Robert C. (1994), 'Divided Government, Fiscal Institutions, and Budget Deficits: Evidence from the States', *American Political Science Review*, Vol. 88, pp. 811-828.

Anderson, Gary M. and Tollison, Robert D. (1988), 'Legislative Monopoly and the Size of Government', *Southern Economic Journal*, Vol. 54, pp. 529-545.

Andeweg, Rudy (2000), 'Ministers as Double Agents? The Delegation Process between Cabinet and Ministers', *European Journal of Political Research*, Vol. 37, pp. 377-395.

Andeweg, Rudy and Timmermans, Arco (2004), 'Conflict Resolution in Coalition Governments', in Strøm, Kaare, Müller, Wolfgang C. and Bergman, Torbjörn (eds), *Coalition Governance in Western Europe*, Oxford University Press, Oxford.

Armingeon, Klaus (1983), *Neo-korporatistische Einkommenspolitik. Eine vergleichende Untersuchung von Einkommenspolitiken in westeuropäischen Ländern in den 70er Jahren*, Haag und Herchen, Frankfurt.

Arter, David (1984), *The Nordic Parliaments. A Comparative Analysis*, Hurst, London.

Axelrodt, Robert (1984), *The Evolution of Cooperation*, Basic Books, New York.

Bach, Stanley (1990), 'Suspension of the Rules, the Order of Business, and the Development of Congressional Procedure', *Legislative Studies Quarterly*, Vol. 15, pp. 49-63.

Barclay, H.M. (1977), '"Guillotine Motions" in the House of Commons', *Constitutional and Parliamentary Information*, Vol. 109, pp. 44-56.

Baron, David P. (1991), 'Majoritarian Incentives, Pork Barrel Programs, and Procedural Control', *American Journal of Political Science*, Vol. 35, pp. 57-90.

Baron, David P. and Ferejohn, John A. (1989), 'Bargaining in Legislatures', *American Political Science Review*, Vol. 83, pp. 1181-1206.

Bawn, Kathleen (1997), 'Money and Majorities in the Federal Republic of Germany: Evidence for a Veto Players Model of Government Spending', UCLA, Mimeo.

Bawn, Kathleen (1999), 'Money and Majorities in the Federal Republic of Germany: Evidence for a Veto Players Model of Government Spending', *American Journal of Political Science*, Vol. 43, pp. 707-736.

Becker, Lawrence C. (1986), *Reciprocity*, Routledge & Kegan Paul, London.

Bednar, Jenna, Ferejohn, John P. and Garrett, Geoffrey (1996), 'The Politics of European Federalism', *International Review of Law and Economics*, Vol. 16, pp. 279-294.

Bergman, Torbjörn (1993), 'Formation Rules and Minority Governments', *European Journal of Political Research*, Vol. 23, pp. 55-66.

Beyme, Klaus von (1998), *The Legislator. German Parliament as a Centre of Political Decision-Making*, Ashgate, Aldershot.

Binder, Sarah (ed.) (1997), *Minority Rights, Majority Rule*, Cambridge University Press, Cambridge and New York.

Binder, Sarah (1999), 'The Dynamics of Legislative Gridlock, 1947-96', *American Political Science Review*, Vol. 93, pp. 519-533.

Binder, Sarah and Smith, Steven S. (1997), *Politics or Principle? Filibustering in the United States Senate*, Brookings Institution Press, Washington, D.C.

Birk, Rolf (1987), 'Flexibilisierung des Arbeitsrechts – eine europäische Herausforderung (Einführung)', *Zeitschrift für ausländisches und internationales Arbeits- und Sozialrecht (ZIAG)*, Vol. 1, pp. 222-228.

Blanpain, Roger (since 1977, continuously updated), *International Encyclopaedia for Labour Law and Industrial Relations, Loose-leaf, 21 volumes, March 1993*, Kluwer, Amsterdam.

Blossfeld, Hans-Peter and Rohwer, Götz (eds) (1995), *Techniques of Event History Modeling: New Approaches to Causal Analysis*, Earlbaum, Mawah, N.J.

Blossfeld, Hans-Peter and Rohwer, Götz (1997), 'Causal Inference, Time and Observation Plans in the Social Sciences', *Quality & Quantity*, Vol. 31, pp. 361-384.

Brennan, Geoffrey and Hamlin, Alan (eds) (2000), *Democratic Devices and Desires: Theories of Institutional Design*, Cambridge University Press, Cambridge.

Brown, B.R. (1977), 'Face-Saving and Face-Restoration in Negotiation', in Druckman, Daniel (ed.), *Negotiations. Social-Psychological Perspectives*, Sage, London.

Browne, Eric C., Frendreis, John P. and Gleiber, Dennis W. (1984), 'An "Events" Approach to the Problem of Cabinet Stability', *Comparative Political Studies*, Vol. 17, pp. 167-197.

Browne, Eric C., Gleiber, Dennis W. and Mashoba, Carolyn (1984), 'Evaluating Conflict of Interest Theory: Western European Cabinet Coalitions, 1945-80', *British Journal of Political Science*, Vol. 14, pp. 1-32.

Buchanan, James M. and Tullock, Gordon (1962, reprint 1987), *The Calculus of Consent. Logical Foundations of Constitutional Democracy*, University of Michigan Press, Ann Arbor.

Budge, Ian and Laver, Michael J. (1992), 'The Relationship Between Party and Coalition Policy in Europe: An Empirical Synthesis', in Laver, Michael J. and

Budge, Ian (eds), *Party Policy and Government Coalitions*, St. Martin's Press, New York, pp. 409-430.

Burch, Martin (1993), 'Organising the Flow of Business in Western European Cabinets', in Blondel, Jean and Müller-Rommel, Ferdinand (eds), *Governing Together. The Extent and Limits of Joint Decision-Making in Western European Cabinets*, Macmillan, London, pp. 99-130.

Butt, Ronald (1967), *The Power of Parliament*, Constable, London.

Calmfors, Lars and Driffill, John (1988), 'Bargaining Structure, Corporatism, and Macroeconomic Performance', *Economic Policy*, Vol. 6, pp. 13-62.

Carey, John M. and Shugart, Matthew Soberg (1995), 'Incentives to Cultivate a Personal Vote: A Rank Ordering of Electoral Formulas', *Electoral Studies*, Vol. 14, pp. 417-439.

Carey, John M. and Shugart, Matthew Soberg (eds) (1998), *Executive Decree Authority*, Cambridge University Press, Cambridge.

Castles, Francis G. and Mair, Peter (1984), 'Left-Right Political Scales: Some "Expert" Judgments', *European Journal of Political Research*, Vol. 12, pp. 73-88.

Clark, William Roberts and Hallerberg, Mark (2000), 'Strategic Interaction Between Monetary and Fiscal Actors Under Full Capital Mobility', *American Political Science Review*, Vol. 94, pp. 323-346.

Coleman, James S. (1981), *Longitudinal Data Analysis*, Basic Books, New York.

Cowhey, Peter F. and McCubbins, Mathew D. (1995), 'Introduction', in Cowhey, Peter F. and McCubbins, Mathew D. (eds), *Structures and Policy in Japan and the United States*, Cambridge University Press, Cambridge, pp. 1-16.

Cox, Gary W. and McCubbins, Mathew D. (1993), *Legislative Leviathan: Party Government in the House*, University of California Press, Berkeley and Los Angeles.

Cox, Gary W. (1997), *Making Votes Count. Strategic Coordination in the World's Electoral Systems*, Cambridge University Press, Cambridge.

Crain, W. Mark (1979), 'Cost and Output in the Legislative Firm', *Journal of Legal Studies*, Vol. 8, pp. 607-621.

Crain, W. Mark, Holcombe, Randall, and Tollison, Robert (1979), 'Monopoly Aspects of Political Parties', *Atlantic Economic Journal*, Vol. 7, pp. 54-58.

Crain, W. Mark and Tollison, Robert D. (1979), 'Constitutional Change in an Interest-Group Perspective', *Journal of Legal Studies*, Vol. 8, pp. 165-175.

Crouch, Colin (1996), *Industrial Relations and European State Traditions*, Clarendon Press, Oxford.

Dahl, Robert A. (1971), *Polyarchy. Participation and Opposition*, Yale University Press, New Haven.

Dahl, Robert A. and Tufte, Edward R. (eds) (1973), *Size and Democracy*, Stanford University Press, Stanford.

Dahrendorf, Ralf, Aubry, Martine, Fraser, Douglas, Isaac, Joseph and others (1986), *Labour Market Flexibility: Report by the High-Level Group of Experts to the Secretary-General of the OECD*, OECD, Paris.

Damgaard, Erik (1992), *Parliamentary Change in the Nordic Countries*, Scandinavian University Press, Oslo.

Damgaard, Erik (1995), 'How Parties Control Committee Members', in Döring, Herbert (ed.), *Parliaments and Majority Rule in Western Europe*, Campus/St. Martin's, Frankfurt/New York, pp. 308-325.

De Winter, Lieven (1995), 'The Role of Parliament in Government Formation and Resignation', in Döring, Herbert (ed.), *Parliaments and Majority Rule in Western Europe*, Campus/St. Martin's, Frankfurt/New York, pp. 115-151.

De Winter, Lieven (2002), 'Parties and Government Formation, Portfolio Allocation and Policy Definition', in Luther, K. Richard and Müller-Rommel, Ferdinand (eds), *Political Parties in the New Western Europe. Political and Analytical Challenges*, Oxford University Press, Oxford, pp. 171-206.

De Winter, Lieven and Dumont, Patrick (2004), 'The Complexity of the Coalition Bargaining Process: Formation Duration and Bargaining Rounds', in Strøm, Kaare, Müller, Wolfgang C. and Bergman, Torbjörn (eds), *Coalition Governance in Western Europe*, Oxford University Press, Oxford.

De Winter, Lieven, Timmermans, Arco, and Dumont, Patrick (2000), 'Coalition Formation and Governance in Belgium: of Government Gospels, Evangelist, Followers and Traitors', in Müller, Wolfgang C. and Strøm, Kaare (eds), *Coalition Governments in Western Europe*, Oxford University Press, Oxford, pp. 300-355.

Di Palma, Guiseppe (1976), 'Institutional Rules and Legislative Outcomes in the Italian Parliament', *Legislative Studies Quarterly*, Vol. 1, pp. 147-179.

Di Palma, Giuseppe (1977), *Surviving without Governing. The Italian Parties in Parliament*, University of California Press, Berkeley and Los Angeles.

Diermeier, Daniel and Feddersen, Timothy J. (1998), 'Cohesion in Legislatures and the Vote of Confidence Procedure', *American Political Science Review*, Vol. 92, pp. 611-621.

Diermeier, Daniel and Stevenson, Randy T. (1999), 'Cabinet Survival and Competing Risks', *American Journal of Political Science*, Vol. 43, pp. 1051-1098.

Dion, Douglas (1998), *Turning the Legislative Thumbscrew. Minority Rights and Procedural Change in Legislative Politics*, The University of Michigan Press, Ann Arbor.

Dixit, Avinash K. (1996), *The Making of Economic Policy: A Transaction Cost Politics Perspective*, MIT Press, Cambridge.

Dodd, Lawrence C. (1976), *Coalitions in Parliamentary Government*, Princeton University Press, Princeton.

Döring, Herbert (1994), 'Parlament und Regierung', in Gabriel, Oscar W. (ed), *Die EU-Staaten im Vergleich. Strukturen, Prozesse, Politikinhalte*, Westdeutscher Verlag, Opladen, pp. 336-358.

Döring, Herbert (ed.) (1995a), *Parliaments and Majority Rule in Western Europe*, Campus/St. Martin's, Frankfurt/New York.

Döring, Herbert (1995b), 'Institutions and Policies: Why We Need Cross-National Analysis', in Döring, Herbert (ed.), *Parliaments and Majority Rule in Western Europe*, Campus/St. Martin's, Frankfurt/New York, pp. 27-50.

Döring, Herbert (1995c), 'Time as a Scarce Resource: Government Control of the Agenda', in Döring, Herbert (ed.), *Parliaments and Majority Rule in Western Europe*, Campus/St. Martin's, Frankfurt/New York, pp. 223-247.

Döring, Herbert (1995d), 'Fewer Though Presumably more Conflictual Bills: Parliamentary Government Acting as a Monopolist', in Döring, Herbert (ed.), *Parliaments and Majority Rule in Western Europe*, Campus/St. Martin's, Frankfurt/New York, pp. 593-600.

Döring, Herbert (1995e), 'Is Government Control of the Agenda Likely to Keep "Legislative Inflation" at Bay?', in Döring, Herbert (ed.), *Parliaments and Majority Rule in Western Europe*, Campus/St. Martin's, Frankfurt/New York, pp. 654-687.

Döring, Herbert (2001), 'Parliamentary Agenda Control and Legislative Outcomes in Western Europe', *Legislative Studies Quarterly*, Vol. 26, pp. 145-165.

Döring, Herbert (2004), 'Party Discipline and Government Imposition of Restrictive Rules', *Journal of Legislative Studies*, forthcoming.

Doron, Gideon and Sened, Itai (2001), *Political Bargaining: Theory, Practice and Process*, Sage, London.

Downs, Anthony (1957), *An Economic Theory of Democracy*, Harper & Row, New York.

Downs, William M. (1998), *Coalition Government, Subnational Style*, Ohio State University Press, Columbus.

Duverger, Maurice (1954, reprint 1969), *Political Parties: Their Organization and Activity in the Modern State*, Wiley, New York.

Easton, David (1965), *A Framework for Political Analysis*, Prentice-Hall, Englewood-Cliffs.

Elster, Jon (1989), *The Cement of Society: A Study of Social Order*, Cambridge University, Cambridge.

Epstein, David and O'Halloran, Sharyn (1999), *Delegating Powers: A Transaction Cost Politics Approach to Policy Making under Separate Powers*, Cambridge University Press, Cambridge.

Fenno, Richard (1973), *Congressmen in Committees*, Little, Brown & Co., Boston.

Fiorina, Morris (1992), *Divided Government*, Macmillan, New York.

Franzese, Robert John (1996), *The Political Economy of Over-Commitment: A Comparative Study of Democratic Management of the Keynesian Welfare State, Chapter 3, Ph.D. Dissertation*, Harvard University.

Gallagher, Michael, Laver, Michael J. and Mair, Peter (eds) (1995), *Representative Government in Modern Europe*, McGraw-Hill, New York et al.

Gilligan, Thomas W. and Krehbiel, Keith (1989), 'Asymmetric Information and Legislative Rules with a Heterogeneous Committee', *American Journal of Political Science*, Vol. 33, pp. 459-490.

Gilligan, Thomas W. and Krehbiel, Keith (1994), 'The Gains from Exchange Hypothesis of Legislative Organization', *Legislative Studies Quarterly*, Vol. 19, pp. 181-214.

Golden, Miriam, Wallerstein, Michael, and Lange, Peter (1999), 'Postwar Trade Union Organization and Industrial Relations in Twelve Countries', in Kitschelt, Herbert, Lange, Peter, Marks, Gary and Stephens, John D. (eds), *Continuity and Change in Contemporary Capitalism*, Cambridge University Press, Cambridge, pp. 194-230.

Greene, William H. (1997), *Econometric Analysis*, Prentice-Hall, New Jersey.

Grey, J.E. (1982), 'Procedure for Passing Legislation', *Constitutional and Parliamentary Information*, Vol. 131, pp. 75-176.

Griffith, J.A.G. and Ryle, Michael (1989), *Parliament: Functions, Practice and Procedures*, Sweet & Maxwell, London.

Grilli, Vittorio, Masciandaro, Donato, and Tabellini, Guido (1991), 'Institutions and Policies', *Economic Policy*, Vol. 6, pp. 341-391.

Hagen, Jürgen von (1992), *Budgeting Procedures and Fiscal Performance in the European Communities. Commission of the European Communities. Directorate-General for Economic and Financial Affairs. Economic Papers, 96, II/453/92-EN/REV*, Commission of the European Communities, Brussels.

Haggard, Stephan and McCubbins, Mathew D. (eds) (2001), *Presidents, Parliaments and Policy*, Cambridge University Press, Cambridge.

Hallerberg, Mark (2000), 'The Role of Parliamentary Committees in the Budgetary Process within Europe', in Strauch, Rolf and Hagen, Jürgen von (eds), *Institutions, Politics and Fiscal Policy*, Kluwer, Amsterdam, pp. 87-106.

Hallerberg, Mark (2003), *The Treaty of Maastricht and the Making of Budgets in Europe 1973-2002. Book Manuscript*, University of Pittsburgh.

Hallerberg, Mark and Basinger, Scott (1998), 'Internationalization and Changes in Tax Policy in OECD Countries: The Importance of Domestic Veto Players', *Comparative Political Studies*, Vol. 31, pp. 321-353.

Hallerberg, Mark and Hagen, Jürgen von (1999), 'Electoral Institutions, Cabinet Negotiations, and Budget Deficits within the European Union', in Poterba, James and Hagen, Jürgen von (eds), *Fiscal Institutions and Fiscal Performance*, University of Chicago Press, Chicago, pp. 209-232.

Hallerberg, Mark and Marier, Patrik (2003), *Endogenous Budget Institutions, Common Pool Resource Problems, and Budget Discipline in Latin American and Caribbean Countries, Manuscript*, University of Pittsburgh.

Hannan, Michael T. and Freeman, John (1989), *Organizational Ecology*, Harvard University Press, Cambridge.

Hansard Society (1992), *Making the Law: The Report of The Hansard Society Commission on the Legislative Process*, The Hansard Society for Parliamentary Government, London.

Heller, William B. (1994), *Holding the Line on Policy: Amendments and Government Legislation in Italy. Paper Public Choice Society*, Mimeo, Austin, Texas.

Heller, William B. (2001), 'Making Policy Stick: Why the Government Gets What it Wants in Multiparty Parliaments', *American Journal of Political Science*, Vol. 45, pp. 780-798.

Henning, Christian (1995), 'A Formal Model of Law Production by Government as a "Natural Monopoly"', in Döring, Herbert (ed.), *Parliaments and Majority Rule in Western Europe*, Campus/St. Martin's, Frankfurt/New York, pp. 601-614.

Hogwood, Brian W. and Gunn, Lewis A. (1984), *Policy Analysis for the Real World*, Oxford University Press, London.

Horn, Murray J. (1995), *The Political Economy of Public Administration: Institutional Choice in the Public Sector*, Cambridge University Press, Cambridge.

Huber, John D. (1992), 'Restrictive Legislative Procedures in France and the United States', *American Political Science Review*, Vol. 86, pp. 675-687.

Huber, John D. (1996a), *Rationalizing Parliament. Legislative Institutions and Party Politics in France*, University Press, Cambridge.

Huber, John D. (1996b), 'The Vote of Confidence in Parliamentary Democracies', *American Political Science Review*, Vol. 90, pp. 269-282.

ILO (ed.) *Natlex. The Labour and Social Security Legislation Database (Permission to be obtained from International Labour Office. Ch-1211 Geneva 22 Switzerland. ILO Homepage www.ilo.org)*.

Immergut, Ellen M. (1992), *Health Politics: Interests and Institutions in Western Europe*, Cambridge University Press, Cambridge.

Jones, David (1998), *Parties and Gridlock, Ph.D. Dissertation*, UCLA.

Jönsson, Christer (1990), *Communication in International Bargaining*, Pinter, London.

Katz, Richard S. (1980), *A Theory of Parties and Electoral Systems*, John Hopkins University Press, Baltimore.

Katzenstein, Peter J. (1987), *Policy and Politics in West Germany: The Growth of a Semisovereign State*, Temple University Press, Philadelphia.

Kelly, Sean Q. (1993), 'Divided We Govern? A Reassessment', *Polity*, Vol. 25, pp. 475-484.

Keman, Hans (2002), 'Parties and Government Output: Policy-Making Capacities of Liberal Democracies', in Luther, K. Richard and Müller-Rommel, Ferdinand (eds), *Political Parties and Democracy in Western Europe*, Oxford University Press, Oxford, pp. 207-245.

Kiewiet, D. Roderick and McCubbins, Mathew D. (1991), *The Logic of Delegation. Congressional Parties and the Appropriations Process*, University of Chicago Press, Chicago.

Kimmel, Adolf (1983), *Die Nationalversammlung in der V. französischen Republik*, Carl Heymanns, Köln.

King, Gary, Alt, James E., Burns, Nancy Elizabeth and Laver, Michael J. (1990), 'A Unified Model of Cabinet Dissolution in Parliamentary Democracies', *American Journal of Political Science*, Vol. 34, pp. 846-871.

Klingemann, Hans-Dieter, Hofferbert, Richard I., and Budge, Ian (1994), *Parties, Policies, and Democracy*, Westview, Boulder.

Krehbiel, Keith (1991, reprint 1992), *Information and Legislative Organization*, University of Michigan Press, Ann Arbor.

Kreppel, Amie (1997), 'The Impact of Parties in Government on Legislative Output in Italy', *European Journal of Political Research*, Vol. 31, pp. 327-350.

Kuhn, Thomas S. (1996), *Structure of Scientific Revolutions*, University of Chicago Press, Chicago.

Lakatos, Imre (1970, reprint 1995), 'Falsification and the Methodology of Scientific Research Programmes', in Lakatos, Imre and Musgrave, Alan (eds), *Criticism and the Growth of Knowledge*, Cambridge University Press, London, pp. 91-195.

Lancaster, Thomas D. (1986), 'Electoral Structures and Pork Barrel Politics', *International Political Science Review*, Vol. 7, pp. 67-81.

Lancaster, Thomas D. and Patterson, William D. (1990), 'Comparative Pork Barrel Politics. Perceptions from the German Bundestag', *Comparative Political Studies*, Vol. 22, pp. 458-477.

Lane, Jan-Erik and Ersson, Svante O. (1995), *Politics and Society in Western Europe*, Sage, London/Beverly Hills.

Lange, Peter and Meadwell, Hudson (1985), 'Typologies of Democratic Systems: From Political Inputs to Political Economy', in Wiarda, Howard (ed.), *New Directions in Comparative Politics*, Westview Press, Boulder, pp. 80-112.

Laundy, Philip (1989), *Parliaments in the Modern World*, Dartmouth/Gower, Aldershot.

Laver, Michael J. and Hunt, W. Ben (1992), *Policy and Party Competition*, Routledge, New York.

Laver, Michael J. and Schofield, Norman (1990), *Multiparty Government. The Politics of Coalition in Europe*, Oxford University Press, Oxford.

Laver, Michael J. and Shepsle, Kenneth A. (eds) (1994), *Cabinet Ministers and Parliamentary Government*, Cambridge University Press, Cambridge.

Laver, Michael J. and Shepsle, Kenneth A. (1996), *Making and Breaking Governments. Cabinets and Legislatures in Parliamentary Democracies*, Cambridge University Press, Cambridge.

Lees, John D. and Shaw, Malcolm (1979), 'Introduction', in Lees, John D. and Shaw, Malcolm (eds), *Committees in Legislatures: A Comparative Analysis*, Martin Robertson, Oxford.

Lightfood, Simon and Luckin, David (2000), 'The 1999 Ecological Tax Reform Law', *German Politics*, Vol. 9, pp. 136-140.

Lijphart, Arend (1984), *Democracies. Patterns of Majoritarian and Consensus Government in Twenty-One Countries*, Yale University Press, New Haven/London.

Lijphart, Arend (ed.) (1992), *Parliamentary Versus Presidential Government*, Oxford University Press, Oxford.

Lijphart, Arend (1994), *Electoral Systems and Party Systems. A Study of Twenty-Seven Democracies, 1945-1990*, Oxford University Press, Oxford.

Lijphart, Arend (1999), *Patterns of Democracy. Government Forms and Performance in Thirty-Six Countries*, Yale University Press, New Haven/London.

Lohmann, Susanne (1998), 'Federalism and Central Bank Independence: The Politics of German Monetary Policy, 1957-1992', *World Politics*, Vol. 50, pp. 401-446.

Luebbert, Gregory M. (1986), *Comparative Democracy: Policymaking and Governing Coalitions in Europe and Israel*, Columbia University Press, New York.

Lupia, Arthur and McCubbins, Mathew D. (1994), 'Who Controls? Information and the Structure of Legislative Decision Making', *Legislative Studies Quarterly*, Vol. 19, pp. 361-384.

Lupia, Arthur and McCubbins, Mathew D. (2000), 'Representation or Abdication? How Citizens Use Institutions to Help Delegation Succeed', *European Journal of Political Research*, Vol. 37, pp. 291-307.

Lupia, Arthur and Strøm, Kaare (1995), 'Coalition Termination and the Strategic Timing of Parliamentary Elections', *American Political Science Review*, Vol. 89, pp. 648-665.

Lupia, Arthur and Strøm, Kaare (2004), 'A Theory of Coalition Governance: Bargaining Models, Walk-Away Values and the Electoral Connection', in Strøm, Kaare, Müller, Wolfgang C. and Bergman, Torbjörn (eds), *Coalition Governance in Western Europe*, Oxford University Press, Oxford.

Mantl, Wolfgang (1995), 'Aufriß der Problemlage', in Mantl, Wolfgang, *Effizienz der Gesetzesproduktion: Abbau der Regelungsdichte im internationalen Vergleich*, Signum, Wien, pp. 17-58.

March, James G. and Olsen, Johan P. (1995), *Democratic Governance*, Free Press, New York.

Marshall, Bryan W. (2002), 'Explaining the Role of Restrictive Rules in the Postreform House', *Legislative Studies Quarterly*, Vol. 27, pp. 61-86.

Masuyama, Mikitaka (2000), 'Is the Japanese Diet Consensual?', *The Journal of Legislative Studies*, Vol. 6, pp. 9-28.

Mattson, Ingvar (1995), 'Private Members' Initiatives and Amendments', in Döring, Herbert (ed.), *Parliaments and Majority Rule in Western Europe*, Campus/St. Martin's, Frankfurt/New York, pp. 448-487.

Mattson, Ingvar (1996), 'Negotiations in Parliamentary Committees', in Stenelo, Lars-Göran and Jerneck, Magnus (eds), *The Bargaining Democracy*, Lund University Press, Lund, pp. 61-144.

Mattson, Ingvar and Strøm, Kaare (1995), 'Parliamentary Committees', in Döring, Herbert (ed), *Parliaments and Majority Rule in Western Europe*, Campus/St. Martin's, Frankfurt/New York, pp. 249-307.

Mayhew, David R. (1974), *Congress: The Electoral Connection*, Yale University, New Haven.

Mayhew, David R. (1991), *Divided We Govern. Party Control, Lawmaking, and Investigations, 1946-1990*, Yale University Press, New Haven.

Mayhew, David R. (1993), 'Reply: Let's Stick With the Longer List', *Polity*, Vol. 25 (Spring), pp. 485-488.

McCubbins, Mathew D. (1991), 'Government on Lay-Away: Federal Spending and Deficits under Divided Party Control', in Cox, Gary W. and Kernell, Samuel (eds), *The Politics of Divided Government*, Westview, Boulder, pp. 113-153.

McCubbins, Mathew D. and Schwartz, Thomas (1984), 'Congressional Oversight Overloooked: Police Patrols versus Fire Alarms', *American Journal of Political Science*, Vol. 28, pp. 165-79.

McKelvey, Richard D. (1976), 'Intransitivities in Multidimensional Voting Models and Some Implications for Agenda Control', *Journal of Economic Theory*, Vol. 12, pp. 472-482.

Moe, Terry and Caldwell, Michael (1994), 'The Institutional Foundations of Democratic Government: A Comparison of Presidential and Parliamentary Systems', *Journal of Institutional and Theoretical Economics*, Vol. 150, pp. 171-195.

Moore, Barrington (1966), *Social Origins of Dictatorship and Democracy*, Beacon, Boston.

Mueller, Dennis C. (1989), *Public Choice II. A Revised Edition*, Cambridge University Press, Cambridge.

Müller, Wolfgang C. and Strøm, Kaare (eds) (1997), *Koalitionsregierungen in Westeuropa. Bildung, Arbeitsweise und Beendigung*, Signum, Wien.

Müller, Wolfgang C. and Strøm, Kaare (eds) (1999), *Policy, Office, or Votes? How Political Parties in Western Europe Make Hard Choices*, Cambridge University Press, Cambridge.

Müller, Wolfgang C. and Strøm, Kaare (eds) (2000), *Coalition Governments in Western Europe*, Oxford University Press, Oxford.

Narud, Hanne Marthe and Strøm, Kaare (2000), 'Norway: A Fragile Coalitional Order', in Müller, Wolfgang C. and Strøm, Kaare (eds), *Coalition Governments in Western Europe*, Oxford University Press, Oxford, pp. 158-191.

Neto, Octavio Amorim and Cox, Gary W. (1997), 'Electoral Institutions, Cleavage Structures, and the Number of Parties', *American Journal of Political Science*, Vol. 41, pp. 149-174.

Norton, Philip (1999), 'Parliamentary Procedure: The Hidden Power?', in Butler, David, Bogdanor, Vernon and Summers, Robert (eds), *The Law, Politics, and the Constitution: Essays in Honour of Geoffrey Marshall*, Oxford University Press, Oxford, pp. 153-171.

Nurmi, Hannu (1991), 'Att jämföra röstningsförfaranden', in Nurmi, Hannu (ed.), *Gruppbeslut och rangordning – om demokratiska röstningsmetoder*, Forskningsrådsnämnden, Stockholm.

OECD (ed.) (1995), *Flexible Working Time. Collective Bargaining and Government Intervention*, OECD, Paris.

Olson, David M. (1980), *The Legislative Process: A Comparative Approach*, Harper & Row, New York.

Olson, David M. and Mezey, Michael M. (eds) (1991), *Legislatures in the Policy Process. The Dilemmas of Economic Policy*, Cambridge University Press, Cambridge.

Olson, Mancur (1965), *The Logic of Collective Action: Public Goods and the Theory of Groups*, Harvard University Press, Cambridge, Mass.

Ostrom, Elinor (1990), *Governing the Commons. The Evolution of Institutions for Collective Action*, Cambridge University Press, Cambridge.

Patzelt, Werner J. (1993), *Abgeordnete und Repräsentation: Amtsverständnis und Wahlkreisarbeit*, Wissenschaftsverlag Richard Rothe, Passau.

Peters, Guy B. (1998), *Comparative Politics: Theory and Methods*, Macmillan, Houndsmills.

Peterson, Robert L. and De Ridder, Martine M. (1986), 'Government Formation as a Policy-Making Arena', *Legislative Studies Quarterly*, Vol. 11, pp. 565-581.

Peterson, Robert L., De Ridder, Martine M., Hobbs, J.D. and McClellan, E.F. (1983), 'Government Formation and Policy Formulation. Patterns in Belgium and the Netherlands', *Res Publica*, Vol. 25, pp. 49-82.

Pindyck, Robert S. and Rubinfeld, Daniel L. (1998), *Econometric Models and Economic Forecasts*, McGraw-Hill, New York.

Rasch, Bjørn Erik (1995), 'Parliamentary Voting Procedures', in Döring, Herbert (ed.), *Parliaments and Majority Rule in Western Europe*, Campus, Frankfurt, a.M., pp. 488-527.

Rasch, Bjørn Erik (2000), 'Parliamentary Floor Voting Procedures and Agenda Setting in Europe', *Legislative Studies Quaterly*, Vol. 25, pp. 3-23.

Rasmusen, Eric (1989), *Games and Information: An Introduction to Game Theory*, Blackwell, Oxford.

Riescher, Gisela (1994), *Zeit und Politik. Zur institutionellen Bedeutung von Zeitstrukturen in parlamentarischen und präsidentiellen Regierungssystemen*, Nomos, Baden-Baden.

Riescher, Gisela (1997), 'Parlamentarische Zeitstrukturen zwischen geschichtlichen Traditionslinien und moderner Funktionalität', *Zeitschrift für Politik*, Vol. 44, pp. 101-115.

Rohwer, Götz (1994), *Kontingente Lebensläufe. Soziologische und statistische Aspekte ihrer Beschreibung und Erklärung, Habilitationsschrift*, Universität Bremen.

Rommetvedt, Hilmar (1984), *Borgerlig samarbeid: sprikende staur eller laftet tømmer?*, Universitetforlaget, Stavanger.

Rommetvedt, Hilmar (1998), 'Norwegian Parliamentary Committees: Performance, Structural Change and External Relations', *Journal of Legislative Studies*, Vol. 1, pp. 60-84.

Rose, Richard (1973), 'Comparing Public Policy: An Overview', *European Journal of Political Research*, Vol. 1, pp. 67-94.

Rose, Richard (1980), *Do Parties Make a Difference?*, Macmillan, London.

Ross, Alf (1967), *Hvorfor demokrati?*, Nyt nordisk Forlag, Arnold Busck, Copenhagen.

Roubini, Nouriel and Sachs, Jeffrey D. (1989a), 'Government Spending and Budget Deficits in the Industrialized Countries', *Economic Policy*, Vol. 8, pp. 99-132.

Roubini, Nouriel and Sachs, Jeffrey D. (1989b), 'Political and Economic Determinants of Budget Deficits in the Industrial Democracies', *European Economic Review*, Vol. 33, pp. 903-938.

Saalfeld, Thomas (2000), 'Members of Parliament and Governments in Western Europe: Agency Relations and Problems of Oversight', *European Journal of Political Research*, Vol. 37, pp. 353-376.

Saalfeld, Thomas (2004), 'Cabinet Survival in the Parliamentary and Semi-Presidential Democracies of Western Europe (1945-1998)', in Strøm, Kaare, Müller, Wolfgang C., and Bergman, Torbjörn (eds), *Coalition Governance in Parliamentary Democracies*, Oxford University Press, Oxford.

Saalfeld, Thomas and Becker, Rolf (2003), *Veto-Players, Agency Relationships and the Dynamics of the Legislative Process in 17 West European Parliaments, 1981-1991, Unpublished Manuscript*, mimeographed.

Sannerstedt, Anders (1992), *Förhandlingar i riksdagen*, Lund University Press, Lund.

Sartori, Giovanni (1976), *Parties and Party Systems. A Framework for Analysis*, Cambridge University Press, Cambridge.

Sartori, Giovanni (1987), *The Theory of Democracy Revisited*, Chatham House, Chatham, New Jersey.

Sawyer, Jack and Guetzkow, Harold (1965), 'Bargaining and Negotiation in International Relations', in Kelman, Herbert C. (ed.), *International Behavior*, Holt, Rinehart & Winston, New York, pp. 464-520.

Scharpf, Fritz W. (1988), 'The Joint-Decision Trap: Lessons from German Federalism and European Integration', *Public Administration*, Vol. 66, pp. 239-278.

Scharpf, Fritz W. (1993), 'Games Real Actors Could Play: Positive and Negative Coordination in Embedded Negotiations', *Journal of Theoretical Politics*, Vol. 6, pp. 27-53.

Scharpf, Fritz W. (1997a), *Games Real Actors Play. Actor-Centered Institutionalism in Policy Research*, Westview, Boulder, Colorado.

Scharpf, Fritz W. (1997b), 'A Game-Theoretical Interpretation of Inflation and Unemployment in Western Europe', in Scharpf, Fritz W., *Games Real Actors Play. Actor-Centered Institutionalism in Policy Research*, Westview, Boulder, Colorado, pp. 217-244.

Schelling, Thomas C. (1960), *The Strategy of Conflict*, Oxford University Press, Oxford.

Schellknecht, H. (1984), 'The System of Parliamentary Committees', *Constitutional and Parliamentary Information*, Vol. 139-140, pp. 86-158.

Schindler, Peter (1994), *Datenhandbuch zur Geschichte des Deutschen Bundestages 1983 bis 1991*, Nomos, Baden-Baden.

Schmidt, Manfred G. (1996), 'Germany. The Grand Coalition State', in Colomer, Josep Maria (ed.), *Political Institutions in Europe*, Routledge, London/New York, pp. 62-98.

Schmidt, Manfred G. (1997, 3rd enlarged ed. 2000), *Demokratietheorien*, Leske + Budrich, Opladen.

Scholz, Evi and Trantas, Georgios (1995), 'Legislation on "Benefits" and on Regulatory Matters: Social Security and Labour Market', in Döring, Herbert (ed.), *Parliaments and Majority Rule in Western Europe*, Campus/St. Martin's, Frankfurt/New York, pp. 628-653.

Schüttemeyer, Suzanne S. (1994), 'Hierarchy and Efficiency in the Bundestag: The German Answer for Institutionalizing Parliament', in Copeland, Gary W. and Patterson, Samuel C. (eds), *Parliaments in the Modern World: Changing Institutions*, University of Michigan Press, Ann Arbor, pp. 29-58.

Sen, Amartya (1988), *Kollektiva beslut och social välfärd*, Thales, Stockholm.

Shaw, Malcolm (1979), 'Conclusions', in Lees, John D. and Shaw, Malcom (eds), *Committees in Legislatures: A Comparative Analysis*, Martin Robertson, Oxford, pp. 361-434.

Shaw, Malcolm (1998), 'Parliamentary Committees: A Global Perspective', *Journal of Legislative Studies*, Vol. 4, pp. 225-251.

Shepsle, Kenneth A. (1978), *The Giant Jigsaw Puzzle: Democratic Committee Assignments in the Modern House*, Chicago University Press, Chicago.

Shepsle, Kenneth A. (1986), 'Institutional Equilibrium and Equilibrium Institutions', in Weisenberg, Herbert F. (ed.), *Political Science: The Science of Politics*, Agathon, New York, pp. 51-81.

Shepsle, Kenneth A. (1996), 'Political Deals in Institutional Settings', in Goodin, Robert (ed.), *The Theory of Institutional Design*, Cambridge University Press, Cambridge, pp. 227-239.

Shepsle, Kenneth A. and Bonchek, Mark S. (1997), *Analyzing Politics. Rationality, Behavior, and Institutions*, Norton, New York/London.

Shepsle, Kenneth A. and Weingast, Barry R. (1981), 'Structure Induced Equilibrium and Legislative Choice', *Public Choice*, Vol. 37, pp. 503-519.

Shepsle, Kenneth A. and Weingast, Barry R. (1982), 'Institutionalizing Majority Rule: A Social Choice Theory with Policy Implications', *American Economic Review*, Vol. 72, pp. 367-371.

Shepsle, Kenneth A. and Weingast, Barry R. (1994), 'Positive Theories of Congressional Institutions', *Legislative Studies Quarterly*, Vol. 19, pp. 149-179.

Shugart, Matthew Soberg and Carey, John M. (1992), *Presidents and Assemblies. Constitutional Design and Electoral Dynamics*, Cambridge University Press, Cambridge.

Shugart, Matthew Soberg and Haggard, Stephan (2001), 'Institutions and Public Policy in Presidential Systems', in Haggard, Stephan and McCubbins, Mathew D. (eds), *Presidents, Parliaments and Policy*, Cambridge University Press, Cambridge.

Sjöblin, Mats (1993), *Coalition Politics and Parliamentary Power*, Lund University Press, Lund.

Stenelo, Lars Göran (1972), *Mediation in International Negotiations*, Studentlitteratur, Lund.

Strøm, Kaare (1990), *Minority Government and Majority Rule*, Cambridge University Press, Cambridge.

Strøm, Kaare (1995), 'Parliamentary Government and Legislative Organisation', in Döring, Herbert (ed.), *Parliaments and Majority Rule in Western Europe*, Campus/St. Martin's, Frankfurt/New York, pp. 51-82.

Strøm, Kaare (1998), 'Institutions and Strategy in Parliamentary Democracy: A Review Article', *Legislative Studies Quarterly*, Vol. 28, pp. 127-143.

Strøm, Kaare (2000), 'Delegation and Accountability in Parliamentary Democracies', *European Journal of Political Research*, Vol. 37, pp. 261-289.

Strøm, Kaare and Müller, Wolfgang C. (1999), 'The Keys to Togetherness: Coalition Agreements in Parliamentary Democracies', *Journal of Legislative Studies*, Vol. 3-4, pp. 255-282.

Strøm, Kaare and Müller, Wolfgang C. (2004), 'Coalition Governance Institutions in Parliamentary Democracies', in Strøm, Kaare, Müller, Wolfgang C. and Bergman, Torbjörn (eds), *Coalition Governance in Parliamentary Democracies*, Oxford University Press, Oxford.

Sundquist, James L. (1988), 'Needed: A Political Theory for the New Era of Coalition Government in the United States', *Political Science Quarterly*, Vol. 103 (Winter), pp. 613-635.

Taagepera, Rein and Shugart, Matthew Soberg (1989), *Seats and Votes. The Effects and Determinants of Electoral Systems*, Yale University Press, New Haven/London.

Taylor, Eric (1979), *The House of Commons at Work*, Penguin, London.

Thomson, Robert (1999), 'Election Pledges and Coalition Agreements in the Netherlands, 1986-1994', *Acta Politica*, pp. 302-330.

Tingsten, Herbert (1971), *Demokratiens problem*, Bonniers, Stockholm.

Treisman, Daniel (1998), *Decentralization and Inflation in Developed and Developing Countries*, mimeo UCLA.

Tsebelis, George (1990), *Nested Games. Rational Choice in Comparative Politics*, University of California Press, Berkeley and Los Angeles.

Tsebelis, George (1995a), 'Decision-Making in Political Systems: Veto Players in Presidentialism, Parliamentarism, Multicameralism, and Multipartyism', *British Journal of Political Science*, Vol. 25, pp. 289-326.

Tsebelis, George (1995b), 'Veto Players and Law Production in Parliamentary Democracies', in Döring, Herbert (ed.), *Parliaments and Majority Rule in Western Europe*, Campus/St. Martin's, Frankfurt/New York, pp. 83-111.

Tsebelis, George (1999), 'Veto Players and Law Production in Parliamentary Democracies: An Empirical Analysis', *American Political Science Review*, Vol. 93, pp. 591-608.

Tsebelis, George (2000), 'Veto Players and Institutional Analysis', *Governance*, Vol. 13, pp. 441-474.

Tsebelis, George (2002), *Veto Players: How Political Institutions Work*, Princeton University Press, New York.

Tsebelis, George and Money, Jeannettè (1997), *Bicameralism*, Cambridge University Press, Cambridge.

Tsebelis, George and Rasch, Bjørn Erik (1995), 'Patterns of Bicameralism', in Döring, Herbert (ed.), *Parliaments and Majority Rule in Western Europe*, Campus/St. Martin's, Frankfurt/New York, pp. 365-390.

Tuma, Nancy B. and Hannan, Michael T. (1984), *Social Dynamics*, Academic Press, Orlando.

Van Schagen, Jan (1997), 'The Principle of Discontinuity and the Efficiency of the Legislative Process', *Journal of Legislative Studies*, Vol. 3, pp. 115-125.

Velasco, Andrés (1999), 'A Model of Endogenous Fiscal Deficits and Delayed Fiscal Reforms', in Poterba, James and Hagen, Jürgen von (eds), *Fiscal Institutions and Fiscal Performance*, University of Chicago Press, Chicago, pp. 37-58.

Warwick, Paul (1994), *Government Survival in Parliamentary Democracies*, Cambridge University Press, Cambridge.

Weaver, Kent R. and Rockman, Bert A. (eds) (1993), *Do Institutions Matter? Government Capabilities in the U.S. and Abroad*, Brookings Institution, Washington, D.C.

Weingast, Barry R. (1992), 'Fighting Fire with Fire: Amending Activity and Institutional Change in the Postreform Congress', in Davidson, Roger H. (ed.), *The Postreform Congress*, St. Martin's Press, New York, pp. 143-168.

Weingast, Barry R. and Marshall, William J. (1988), 'The Industrial Organization of Congress; or, Why Legislatures, Like Firms, Are not Organized as Markets', *Journal of Political Economy*, Vol. 96, pp. 132-163.

Weingast, Barry R. and Moran, Mark J. (1983), 'Bureaucratic Discretion or Congressional Control? Regulatory Policymaking by the Federal Trade Commission', *Journal of Political Economy*, Vol. 91, pp. 765-800.

Weingast, Barry R., Shepsle, Kenneth A. and Johnsen, Christopher (1981), 'The Political Economy of Benefits and Costs: A Neoclassical Approach to Distributive Politics', *Journal of Political Economy*, Vol. 89, pp. 642-664.

White, Halbert (1980), 'A Heteroskedasticity-Consistent Covariance Matrix Estimator and a Direct Test for Heteroskedasticity', *Econometrica*, Vol. 48, pp. 817-838.

Wiberg, Matti (1991), 'Nice Timing! – Electoral Cycles of Parliamentary Questioning in the Finnish Parliament 1945-1987', in Wiberg, Matti (ed.), *The Political Life of Institutions: Scripta in honorem professoris Jaakko Nousiainen sexagesimum annum complentis*, Finni Political Science Association, Helsinki, pp. 189-203.

Wilson, Rick K. (1999), 'Transitional Governance in the United States: Lessons from the First Federal Congress', *Legislative Studies Quarterly*, Vol. 4, pp. 543-568.

Wilson, Woodrow (1885), *Congressional Government*, Houghton Mifflin, Boston.

Zartman, Ira William (ed.) (1983), *The 50% Solution: How to Bargain Successfully with Hijackers, Strikers, Bosses, Oil Magnates, Arabs, Russians and Other Worthy Opponents in this Modern World*, Yale University Press, New Haven.

Index